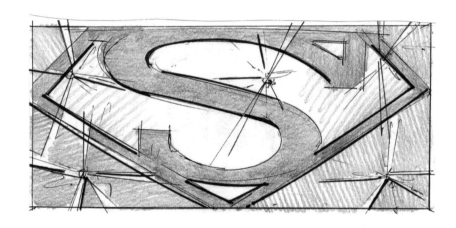

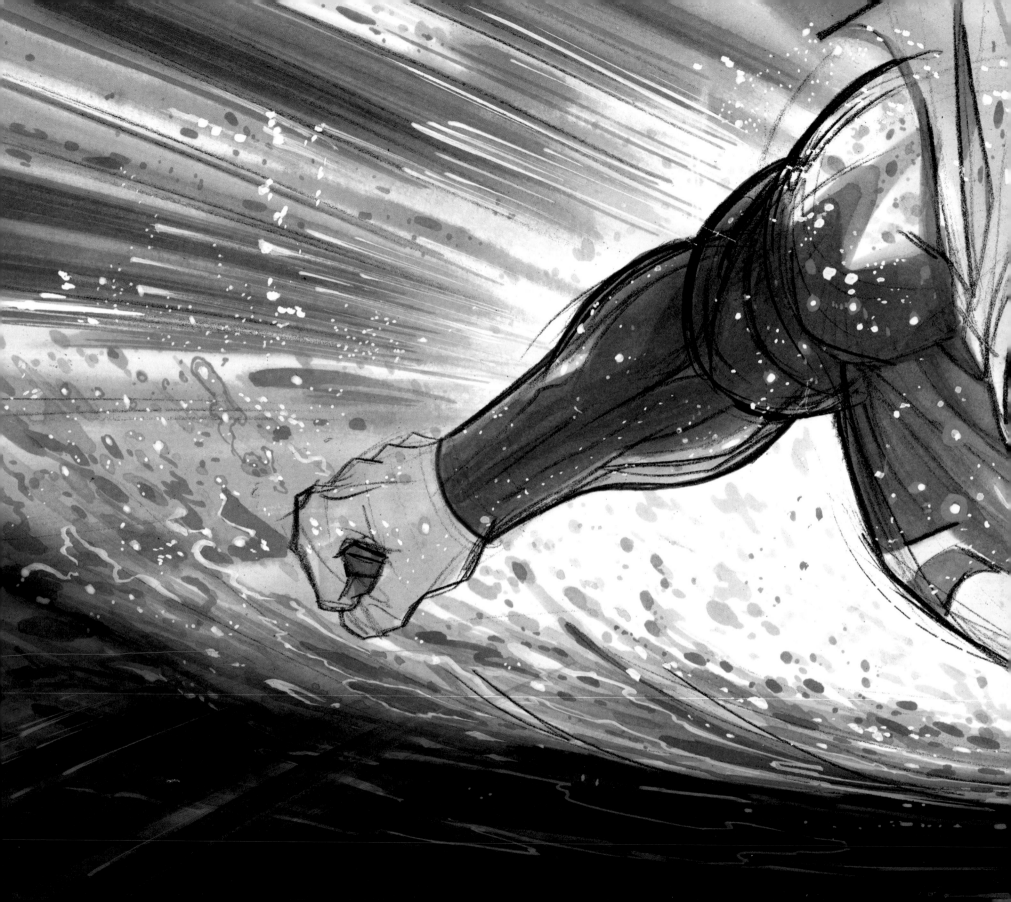

THE ART OF
SUPERMAN RETURNS

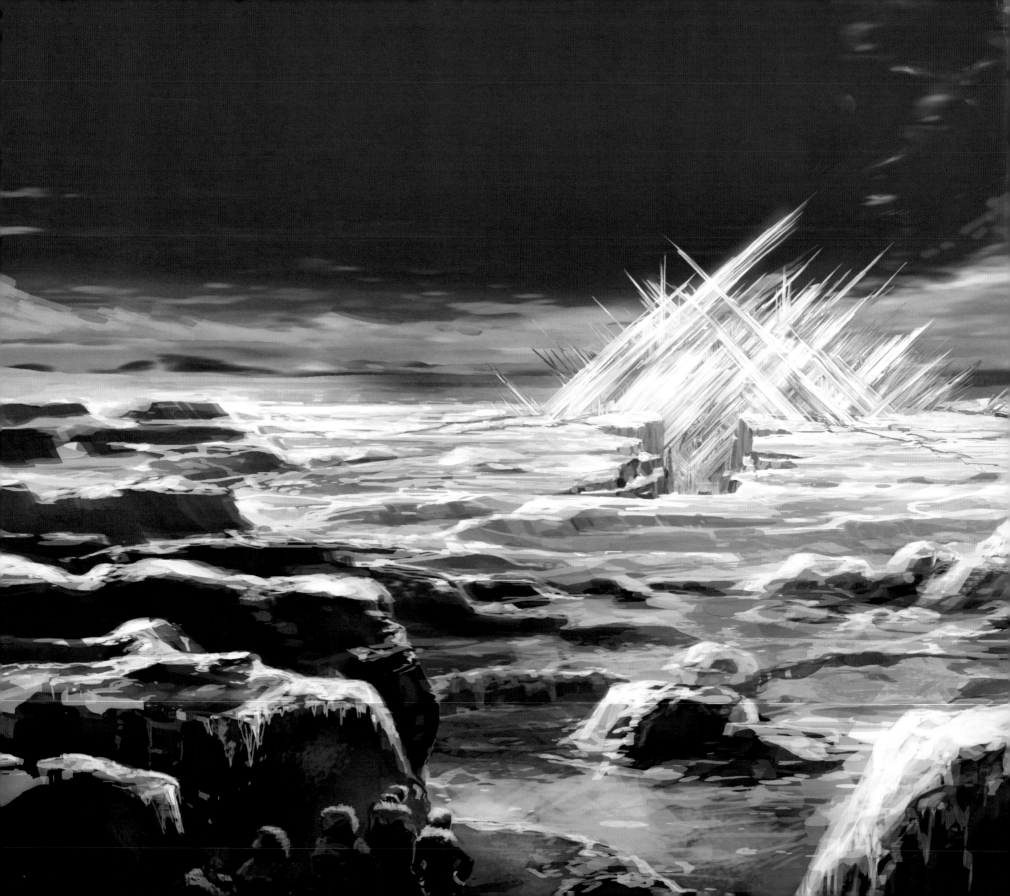

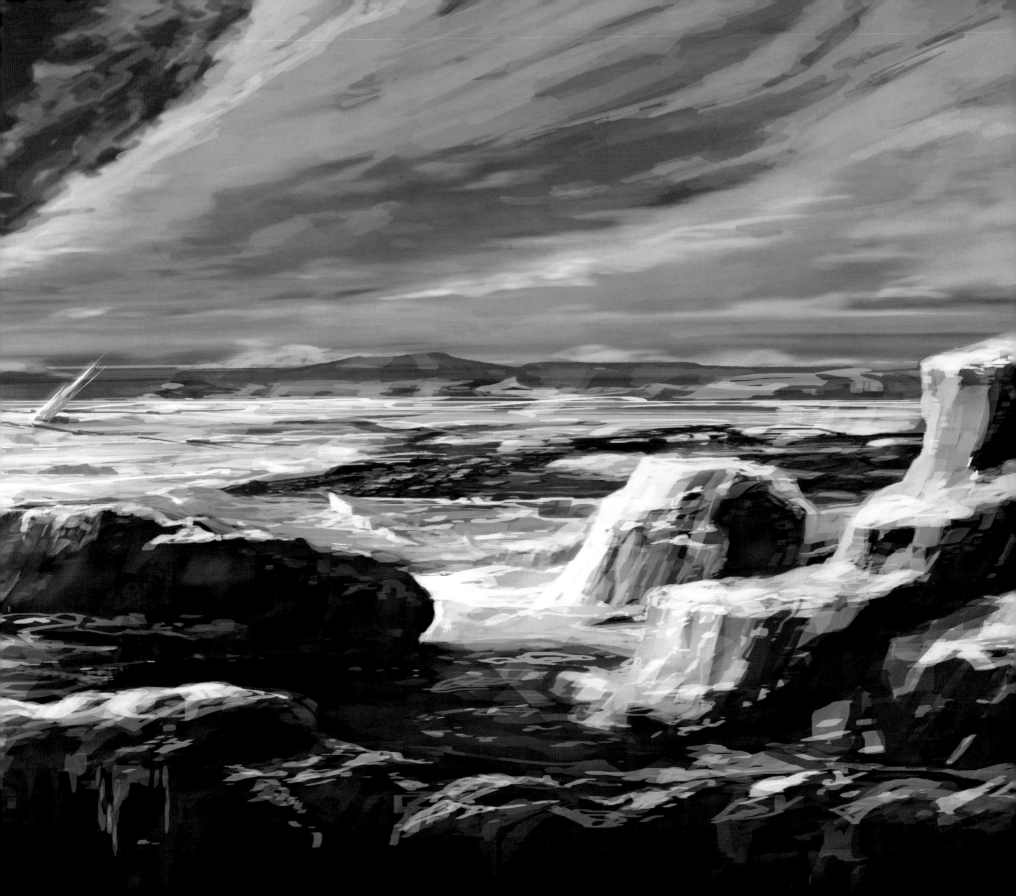

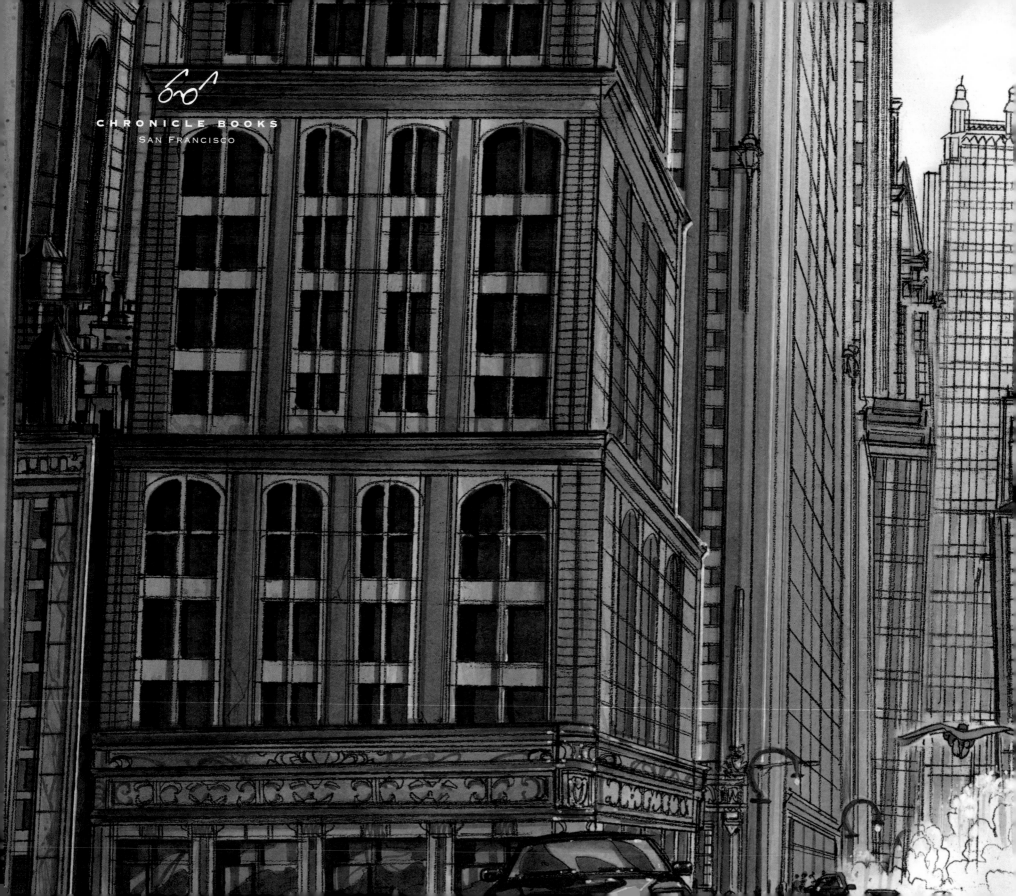

CHRONICLE BOOKS
SAN FRANCISCO

Screenplay by Michael Dougherty & Dan Harris
Story by Bryan Singer & Michael Dougherty & Dan Harris

THE ART OF
SUPERMAN RETURNS

by Daniel Wallace
Foreword by Bryan Singer
Superman created by Jerry Siegel and Joe Shuster

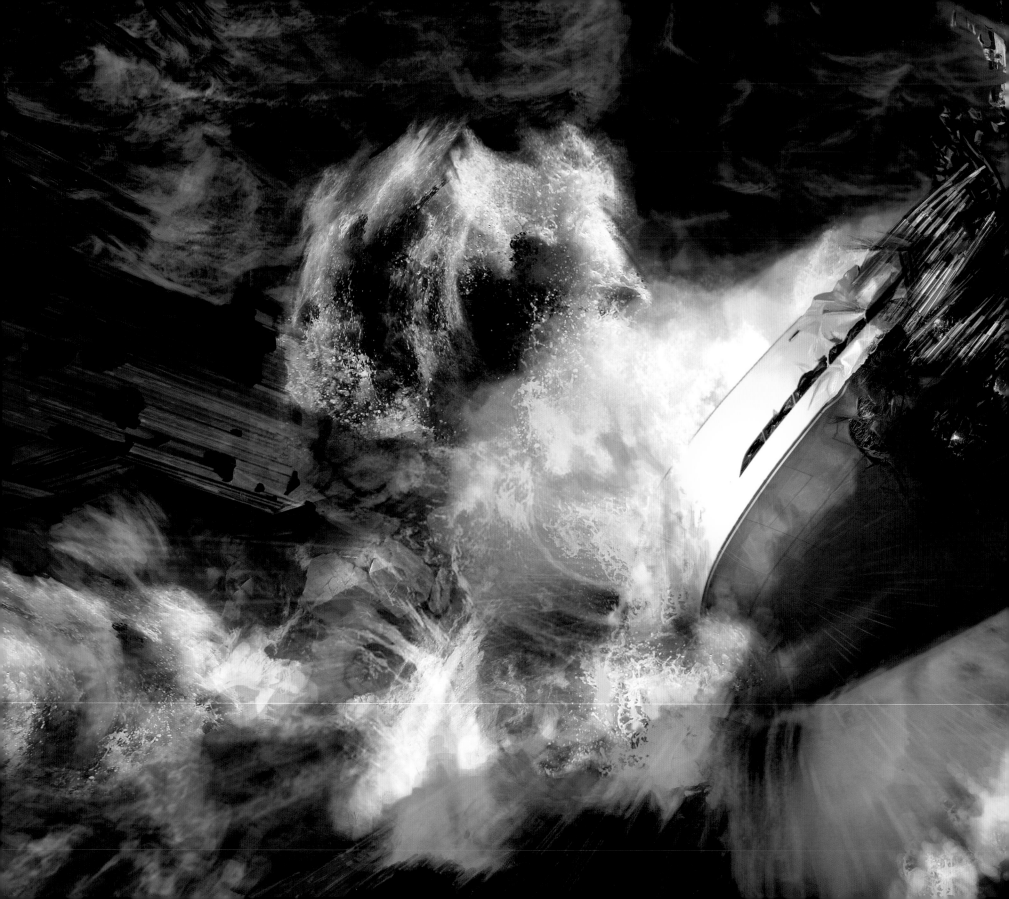

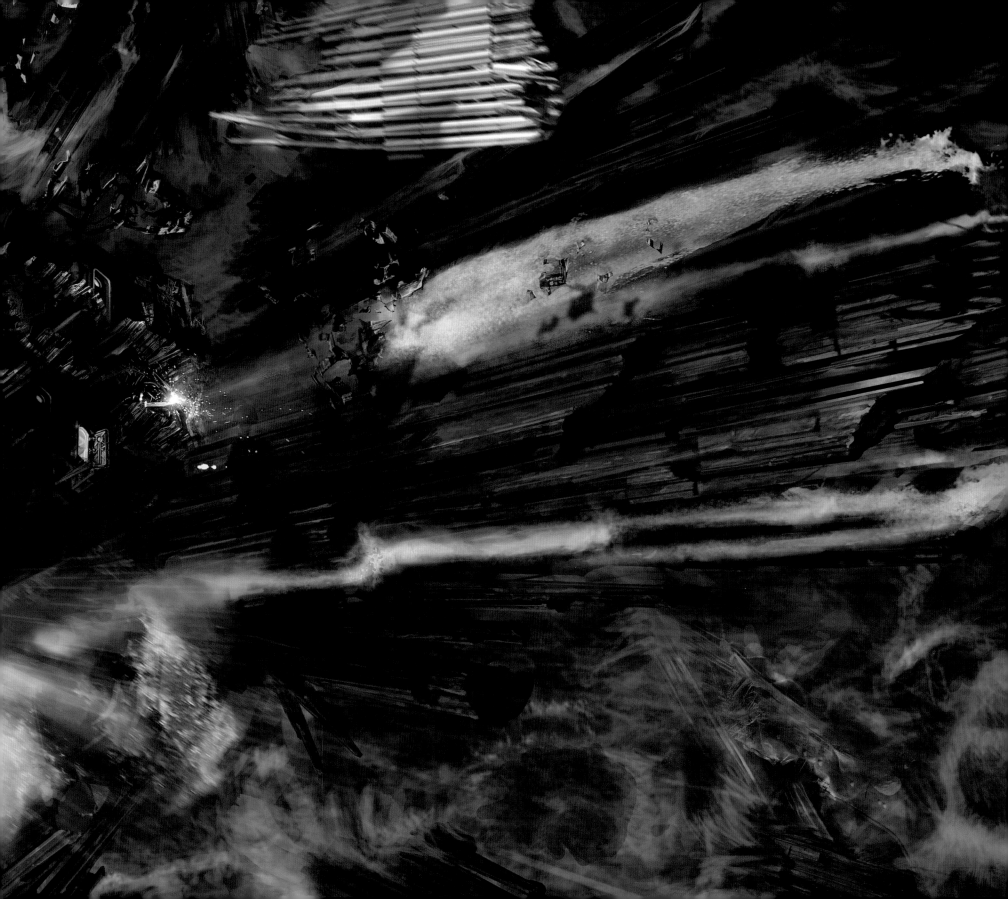

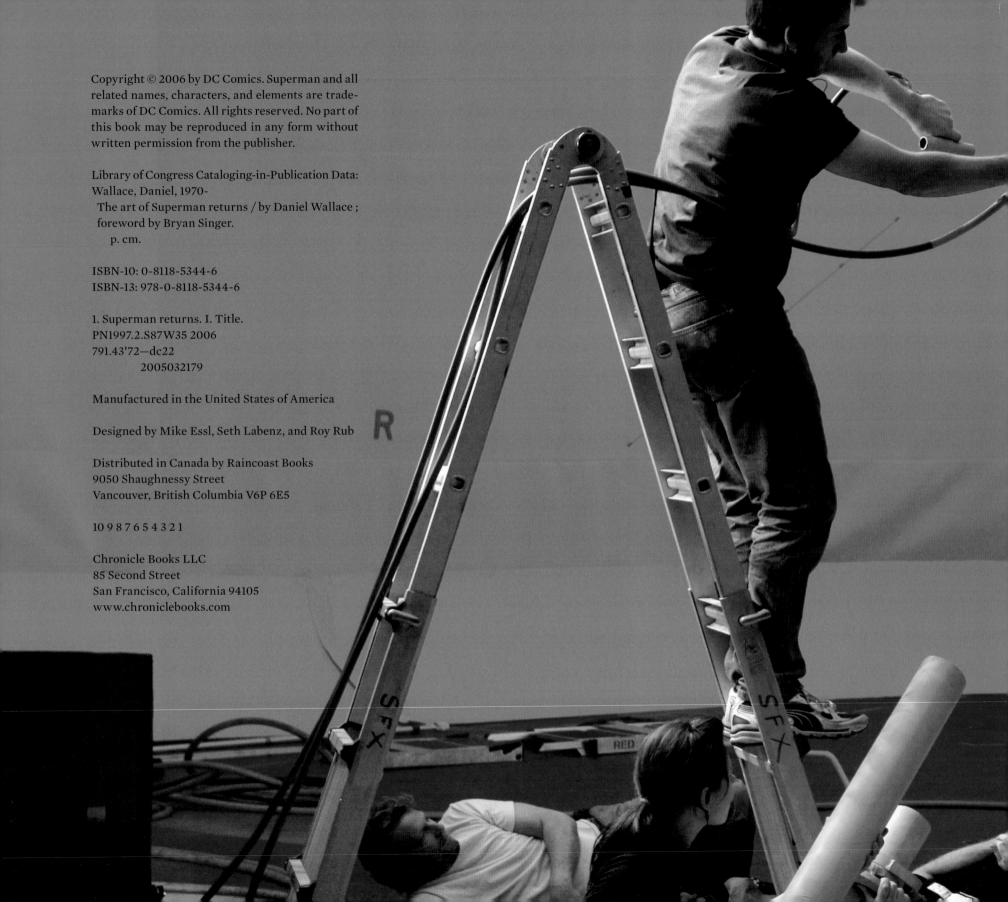

Library of Congress Cataloging-in-Publication Data:
Wallace, Daniel, 1970-
  The art of Superman returns / by Daniel Wallace ;
 foreword by Bryan Singer.
    p. cm.

ISBN-10: 0-8118-5344-6
ISBN-13: 978-0-8118-5344-6

1. Superman returns. I. Title.
PN1997.2.S87W35 2006
791.43'72—dc22
            2005032179

Manufactured in the United States of America

Designed by Mike Essl, Seth Labenz, and Roy Rub

Distributed in Canada by Raincoast Books
9050 Shaughnessy Street
Vancouver, British Columbia V6P 6E5

10 9 8 7 6 5 4 3 2 1

Chronicle Books LLC
85 Second Street
San Francisco, California 94105
www.chroniclebooks.com

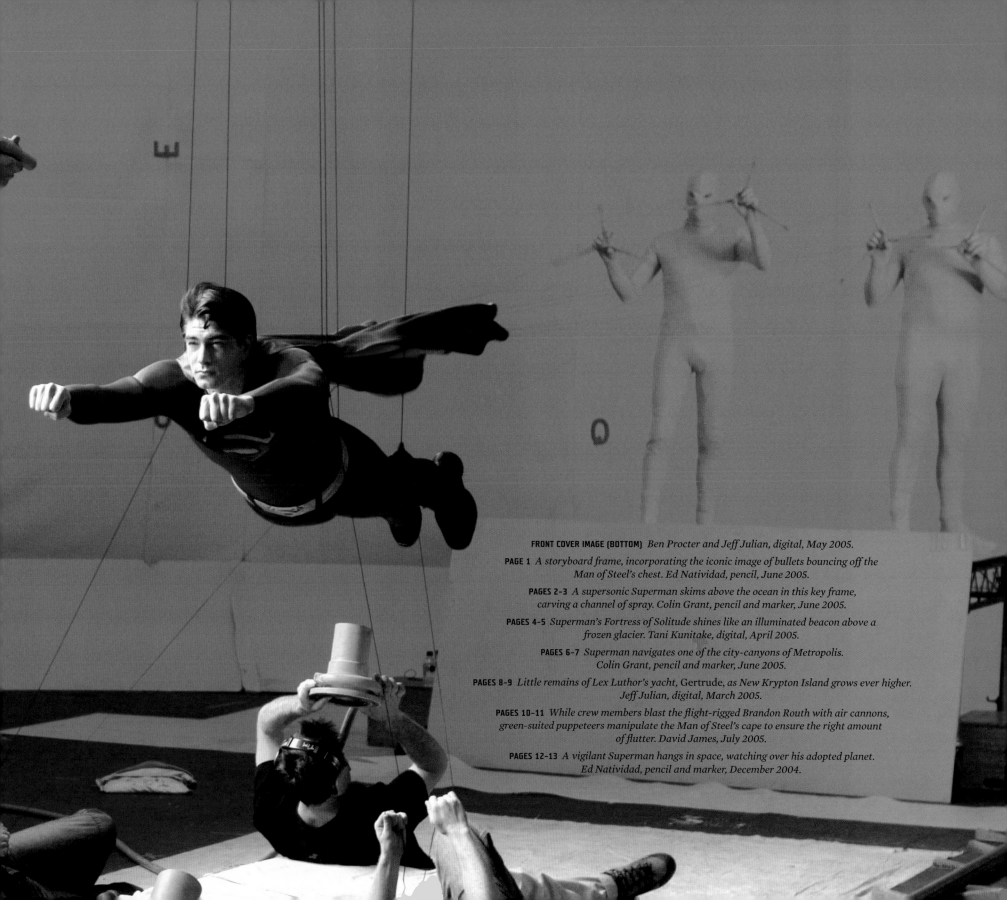

FRONT COVER IMAGE (BOTTOM) *Ben Procter and Jeff Julian, digital, May 2005.*

PAGE 1 *A storyboard frame, incorporating the iconic image of bullets bouncing off the Man of Steel's chest. Ed Natividad, pencil, June 2005.*

PAGES 2-3 *A supersonic Superman skims above the ocean in this key frame, carving a channel of spray. Colin Grant, pencil and marker, June 2005.*

PAGES 4-5 *Superman's Fortress of Solitude shines like an illuminated beacon above a frozen glacier. Tani Kunitake, digital, April 2005.*

PAGES 6-7 *Superman navigates one of the city-canyons of Metropolis. Colin Grant, pencil and marker, June 2005.*

PAGES 8-9 *Little remains of Lex Luthor's yacht, Gertrude, as New Krypton Island grows ever higher. Jeff Julian, digital, March 2005.*

PAGES 10-11 *While crew members blast the flight-rigged Brandon Routh with air cannons, green-suited puppeteers manipulate the Man of Steel's cape to ensure the right amount of flutter. David James, July 2005.*

PAGES 12-13 *A vigilant Superman hangs in space, watching over his adopted planet. Ed Natividad, pencil and marker, December 2004.*

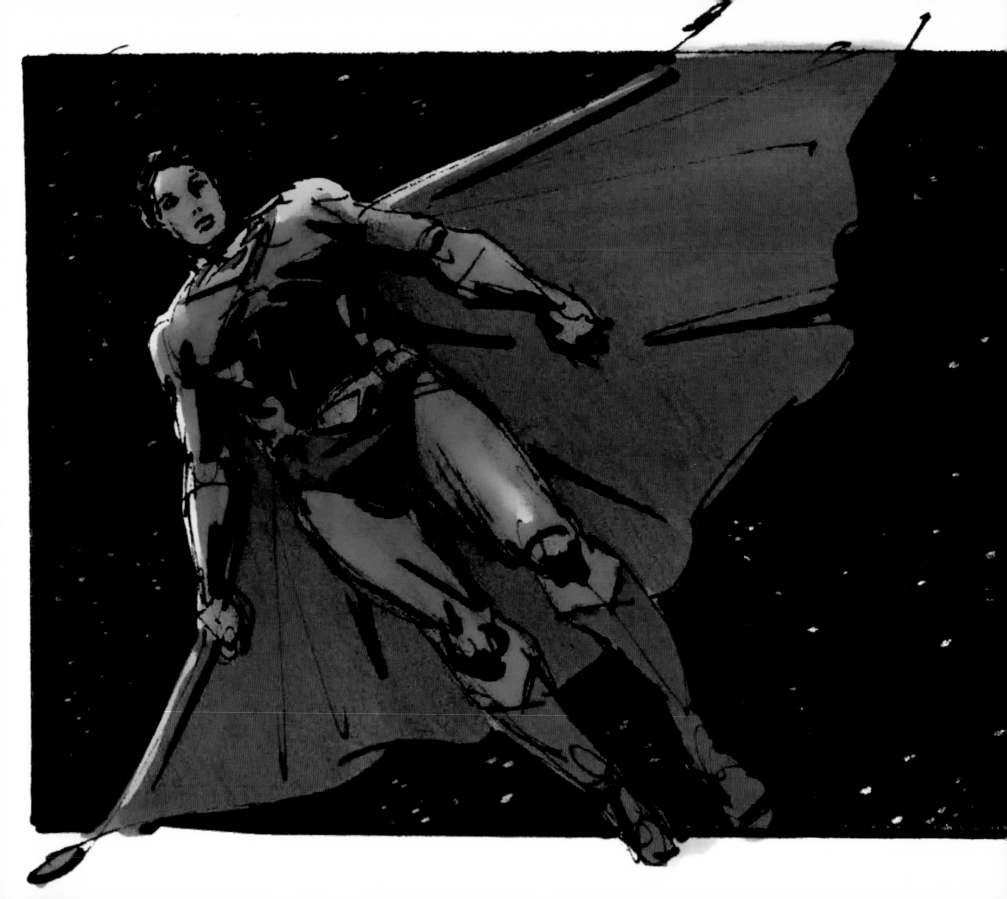

FOREWORD

From the very beginning, *Superman Returns* has been about the blending of old and new—the mixing of history with the state of the art.

I have always been inspired by the character. Like Clark Kent, I'm an only child who was adopted. There's something about Superman being the "ultimate adopted kid" that appealed to me at an early age. Clark's Smallville upbringing is the key to his personality. The character has three distinct faces: the young man who was raised on the farm, the bumbling cover identity used in the Daily Planet, and the larger-than-life heroism represented by Superman. These facets are every bit as much the products of Martha and Jonathan Kent as they are products of his Kryptonian heritage.

I'm a fan, and I grew up as a fan—first of the original George Reeves television series, and subsequently the 1978 Richard Donner film adaptation. Enough time had passed since the close of the previous film series that it seemed right to make a return visit to Superman's world. But it's not the same world it was when Clark left it. He can no longer rely on the security of the familiar, which supplies new challenges for the Man of Steel.

The following is a glimpse of the outstanding work of production designer Guy Dyas, cinematographer Newton Thomas Sigel, costume designer Louise Mingenbach, visual effects supervisor Mark Stetson, set photographer David James, writers Mike Dougherty and Dan Harris, and an army of artists and friends, old and new.

—Bryan Singer

RIGHT *Director Bryan Singer on the set. David James, August 2005.*

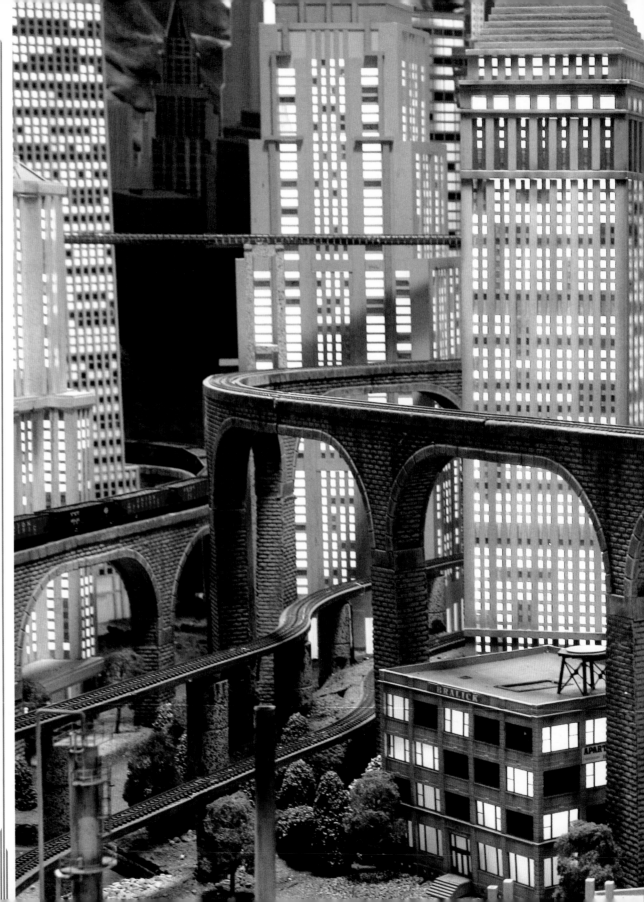

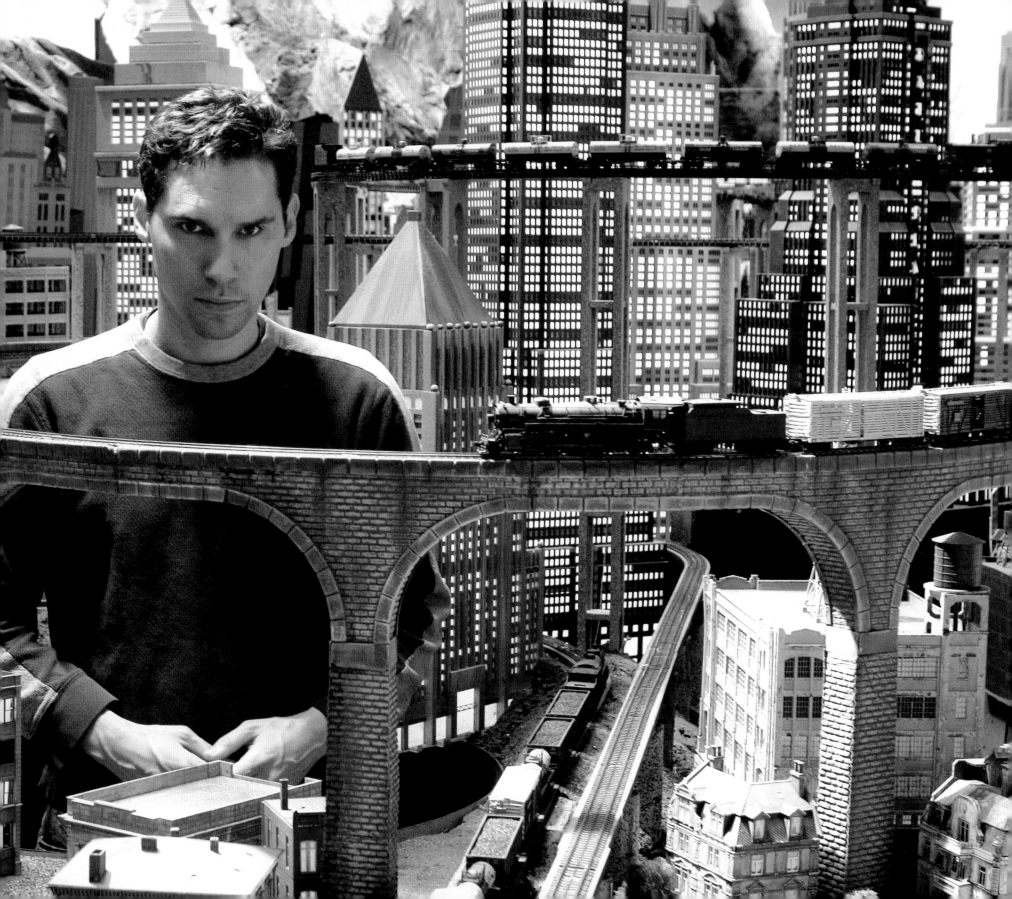

INTRODUCTION

Jerry Siegel and Joe Shuster ◇ Richard Donner
It's Not a Remake ◇ He's Searching for Answers ◇ A Pig Shed
1,000 New York Buildings ◇ A Blending of References
Legions of Supermen

Everyone knows the story of Superman. A strange visitor from the planet Krypton, he was raised in Smallville as Clark Kent and moved to Metropolis to work at the *Daily Planet*. His love interest—unrequited when he is posing as the mild-mannered reporter—is Lois Lane; his arch-enemy is Lex Luthor. Created by science fiction fans Jerry Siegel and Joe Shuster in the 1930s, Superman is a supremely adaptable icon, embodying the virtues of valor and nobility yet comfortable being name-dropped by Eminem.

DC Comics has published Superman adventures continuously since *Action Comics* #1 in 1938. The Man of Steel has bent other media to his will, inspiring productions that include radio plays, movie serials, and a Broadway musical. Among the most memorable offerings are Fleischer Studios' 1940s cartoon shorts, the 1950s TV show *The Adventures of Superman* starring George Reeves, and *Smallville,* the TV series that has been chronicling the exploits of a teenage Clark Kent since its debut in 2001.

For many, however, the definitive telling of his story came in 1978. *Superman: The Movie* presented the visions of director Richard Donner and production designer John Barry and introduced Christopher Reeve in the title role. Among the movie's devotees are *Superman Returns* director Bryan Singer and co-screenwriters Michael Dougherty and Dan Harris. "To us, *Superman: The Movie* hit every [nail] on the head," says Harris. "The iconic beats of young Clark throwing the crystal to create the Fortress, of Krypton being a planet built from crystals, of Lex being a criminal businessman interested mainly in land, of Jonathan Kent dying on the Kent farm gave us the material to create the plot of *Superman Returns*."

Singer grew up as a fan of the George Reeves series and of Donner's cinema adaptation. "I felt that enough time had gone by that it was right to make a film like this," he says. "It's not a remake. It puts the original film into a vague history, [and also incorporates] elements of the second film related to Superman and his relationship to Lois Lane."

"*Superman Returns* is about Superman returning to the big screen," Dougherty puts in, "but also in the film he's returning to the world. He's searching for answers about who he is and where he came from, and when he comes back, he's forced to confront the past. All the things that he expected to be steadfast and true, everything has changed."

The nerve center for production of the new film is Fox Studios Australia, a busy hive in the heart of Sydney encompassing soundstages, workshops, and production offices. "Our art department used to be a pig shed," remarks production designer Guy Dyas, explaining that the state-of-the-art studio occupies buildings that once housed the showgrounds of the Royal Agricultural Society. The stages are built on exhibition areas where cows and sheep were put up for auction. "Some of the stages have a very slight taper," he continues, "so the exhibitors could hose down the floor and it would all go down the drain.

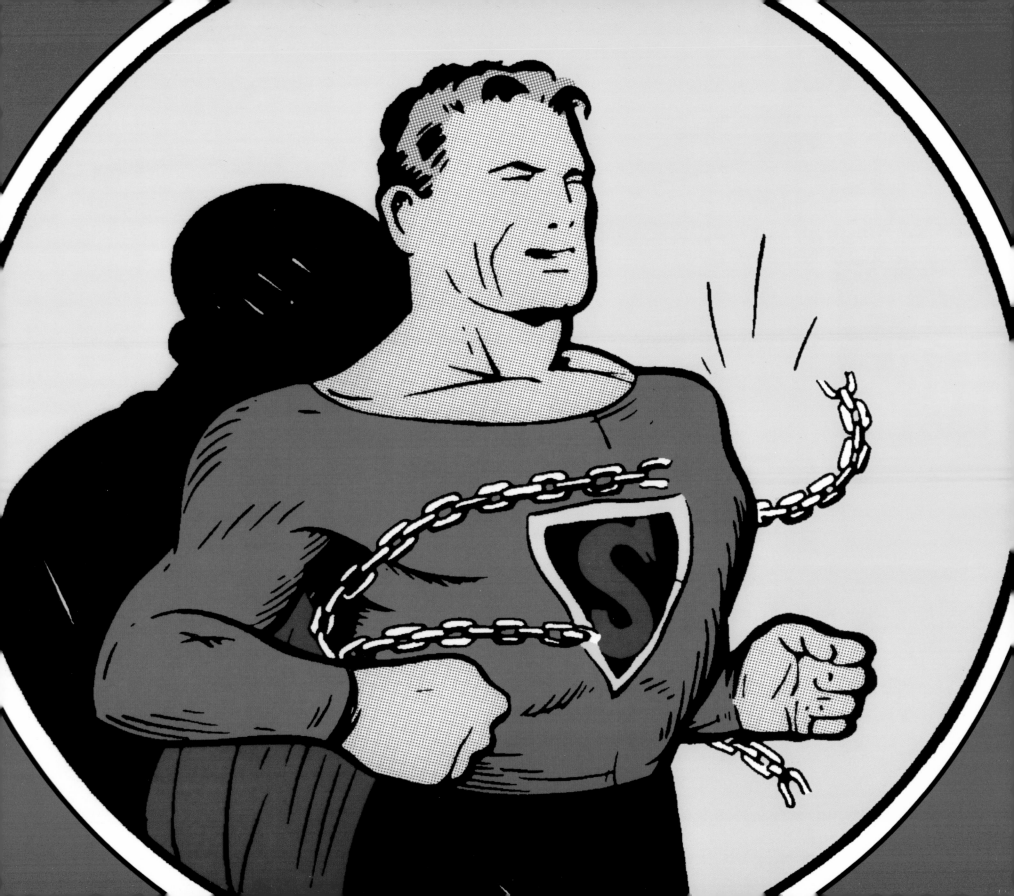

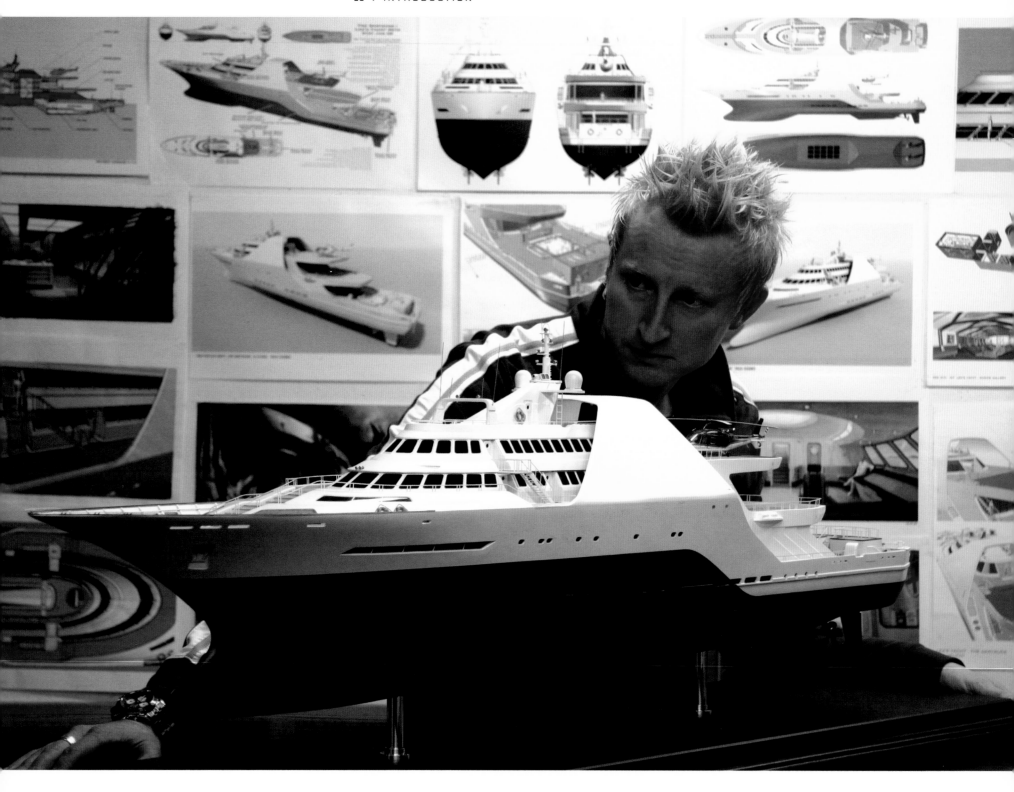

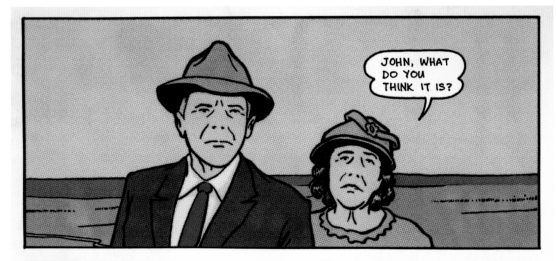

JOHN, WHAT DO YOU THINK IT IS?

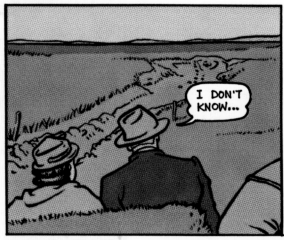

I DON'T KNOW...

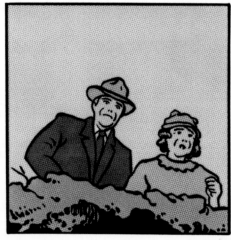

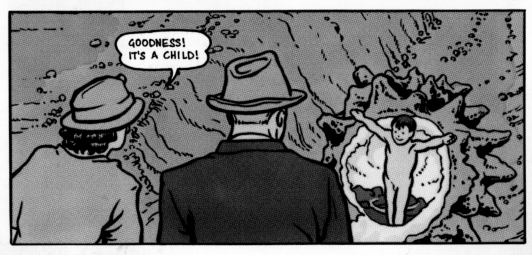

GOODNESS! IT'S A CHILD!

That was one of the biggest headaches I had to face when I came here, because it means that some of the sets we build have to be on an uneven floor."

The architecture of animal waste disposal wasn't the only challenge for the *Superman Returns* art department. As the first feature film to star the Man of Steel in nearly twenty years, *Superman Returns* required the crew to conjure wonders. Within the Fox Studios buildings, Dyas and his team created everything from the humming hub of Metropolis to the lonely reaches of outer space.

At the top of a wooden staircase sits a room packed with so much imagery that the eye can't take it all in at once. This is Guy Dyas's office, its walls plastered floor to ceiling with sketches, paintings, storyboards, and photographic composites. Miniature models sit on shelves. A bookshelf groans with heavy tomes including *1,000 New York Buildings, Earth From Above, American Art Deco,* and the *DC Comics Encyclopedia.*

Dyas drops an artifact on his desk. It's a comic book that was created solely as a concept for the opening scenes of the movie. It bears the same cover as *Superman #1* from 1939, but the interior pages depict key elements from the 1978 film, carefully illustrated in a period technique as if drawn by Joe Shuster.

The blending of references on the comic-book page is a microcosm of the *Superman Returns* style philosophy. The movie is designed to look ageless, mixing forms from decades past into a pleasing visual gestalt. "We didn't want to design a period film," says Dyas, "but we did agree that there are some amazing things that have happened through the ages with Superman that we wanted to capitalize on." Among them are a 1930s art deco look for Metropolis and a broadening of the 1970s version of a crystalline Fortress of Solitude.

OPPOSITE PAGE *Guy Dyas and a* Gertrude *model. Dan Harris, March 2005.*

LEFT *Superman arrives in Kansas. The opening comic book illustrates key scenes from* Superman: The Movie, *using a period style that evokes the original comics from the 1930s. Chew Chan, pen and ink with markers, January 2005.*

PAGE 17 *Superman as he appeared in his original incarnation, as conceived by Jerry Siegel and Joe Shuster.*

"Superman's a part of American culture now, and I think it's important that that's respected," says Dyas. "Bryan was very strict that we follow that folklore." Everywhere on set, there is a deference to the character that is palpable. "Bryan wants us to do our homework," says Dyas. "We have to go and read a huge amount of the backdated comic books, as well as some of the classic DC Comics books that lay out the law of the Superman universe."

But there's a fine line between respecting the source material and reinforcing clichés. Fortunately, the art department is no taxidermy shop. *Superman Returns* presents a completely new Superman in a fresh environment, yet everything about the production feels familiar, as if assembled from dream fragments.

It is, in fact, a very comic-book notion. Throughout his four-color existence, Superman has been refashioned numerous times. He has undergone an evolutionary shift from bare-knuckled defender of the poor to cosmic protector of the planet, and several revolutionary retoolings at the hands of new writers. In these cases, reality-warping villains would send Superman back in time to his early beginnings, conveniently eliminating decades of knotty backstory and allowing a fresh start. Throughout booms, busts, and the turning of a millennium, Superman has endured.

Dyas looks around at the art that wallpapers his office. "I've got to please the fans of the past, and I've got to please the fans of the future," he says. From every surface, legions of Supermen stare back at him.

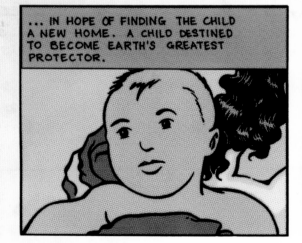
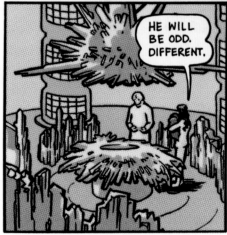
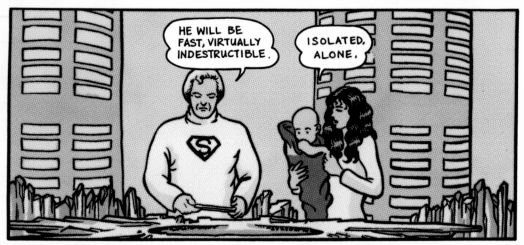
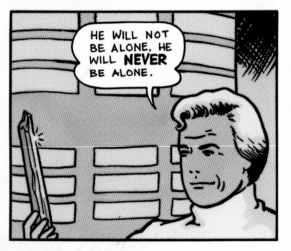
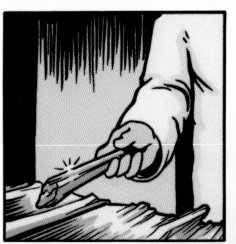

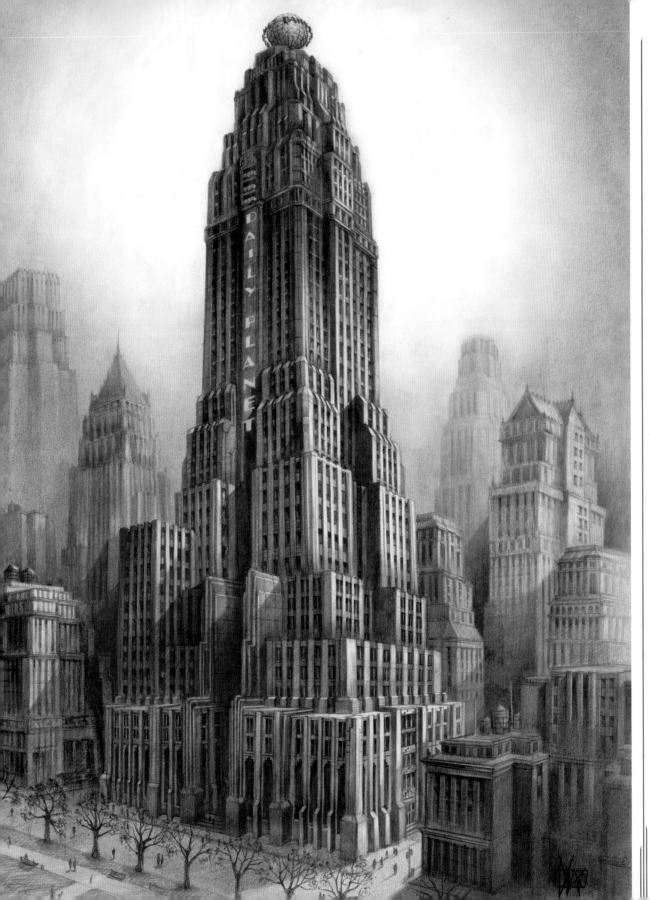

OPPOSITE PAGE *Jor-El and Lara send their son to Earth in this comic book page that recaps the origin recounted in the 1978 film. Chew Chan, pen and ink with markers, January 2005.*

LEFT *One of the earliest pieces of art created for Superman Returns, this black-and-white sketch by Guy Dyas captures the grandeur of prewar architecture exemplified by the Daily Planet Building. Guy Dyas, pencil, November 2004.*

SUPERMAN

An Extroverted Explosion ◇ Canceled Brainstorms
Seventy Years of Mythology ◇ A Calling Card in Every Footprint
He's So Tall ◇ What Being Invulnerable Really Means
Someone Who Never Lies

Superman is more powerful than a locomotive. His skin is bulletproof. He has X-ray eyes; his heat vision can melt iron. These abilities make him humanity's protector, a role the Man of Steel advertises with his attire. In contrast to his drab Clark Kent wardrobe, Superman's costume is an extroverted explosion, complete with cape, boots, and a Kryptonian crest that resembles a stylized S. From the moment of its introduction in 1938, Superman's suit ushered in the age of the skintight super hero.

"The story is, when he was an infant he was wrapped up in these three primary colors and sent away in the baby pod with this fabric. And Ma Kent made the suit." With those words, Louise Mingenbach, costume designer for *Superman Returns,* summarizes the in-universe backstory of the iconic costume. Mingenbach and costume supervisor Dan Bronson are responsible for dressing everyone in the movie, from Metropolis police officers to the Last Son of Krypton.

As Mingenbach notes, this is one point where mythology butts up against reality—and wins. The suit created for *Superman Returns* devoured reams of cutting-edge fabric. The money spent to design it could have bought the Smallville farm several times over. In short, it's far beyond anything Martha Kent could have stitched together on a sewing machine. "Audiences have become so sophisticated about what a super-hero suit is supposed to look like," says

Mingenbach. "Now, seeing a *wrinkle* is a bad thing. There has to be a suspension of disbelief. If we had made a suit that looks like Ma Kent could have made it, that would have been the end. You would have walked out of the theater."

Talk like this seems to imply that Superman has gone high tech. Far from it. When the first photos of Superman actor Brandon Routh in costume hit the Internet in April 2005, the fans reacted with surprise at how *traditional* the outfit looked.

Director Bryan Singer didn't want to reimagine Superman's suit. "There's been a history to Superman," explains Mingenbach, speaking of earlier, aborted attempts to relaunch the Superman franchise, "and there have been directors who have tried to reinvent the suit." These canceled brainstorms were available for Singer to review when he started work on *Superman Returns.* In fact, all the discarded conceptual work is still kept in an auxiliary warehouse. Says Bronson: "It's kind of like the 'boneyard of Superman.' "

"It got crazy," Mingenbach says. "Armored suits." (As production designer Guy Dyas notes, "He doesn't need the Batman armor. He's the Man of Steel.") "Suits where it was really low cut and his chest hair popped out the top. Pretty much everything had been tried," she continues. But, as Bronson observes, "Bryan always wanted a classic."

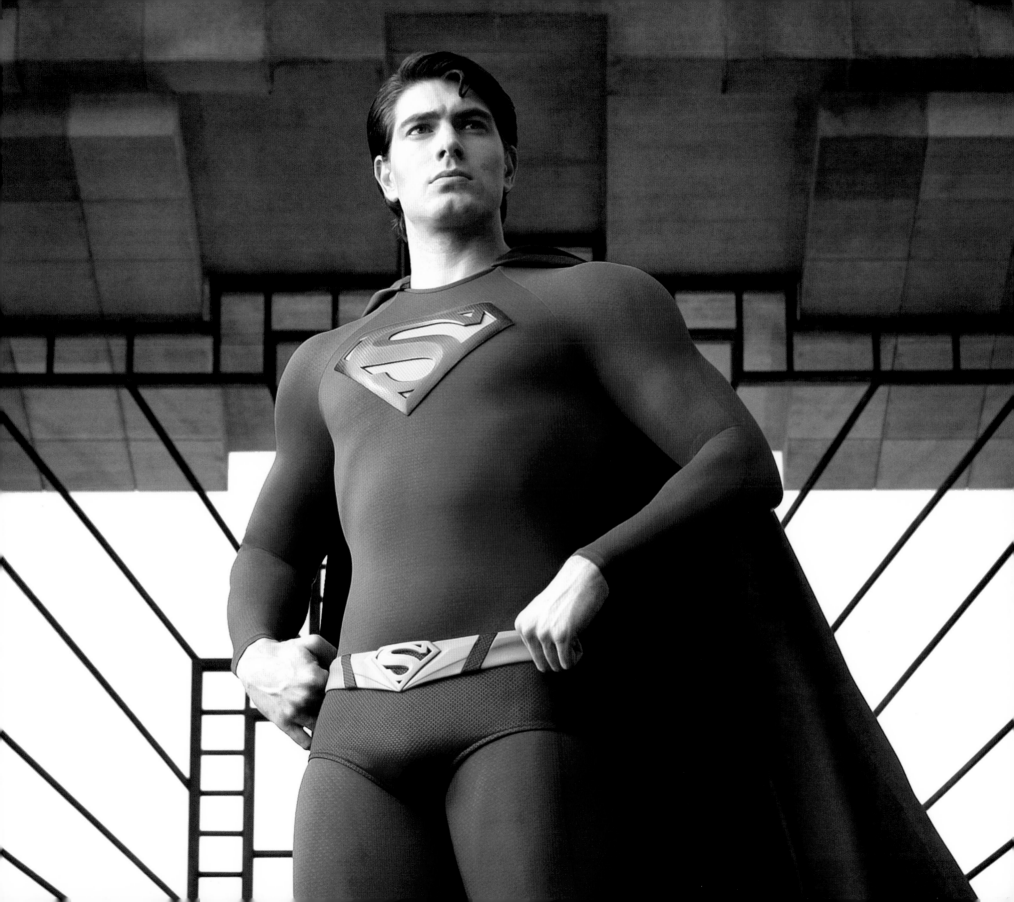

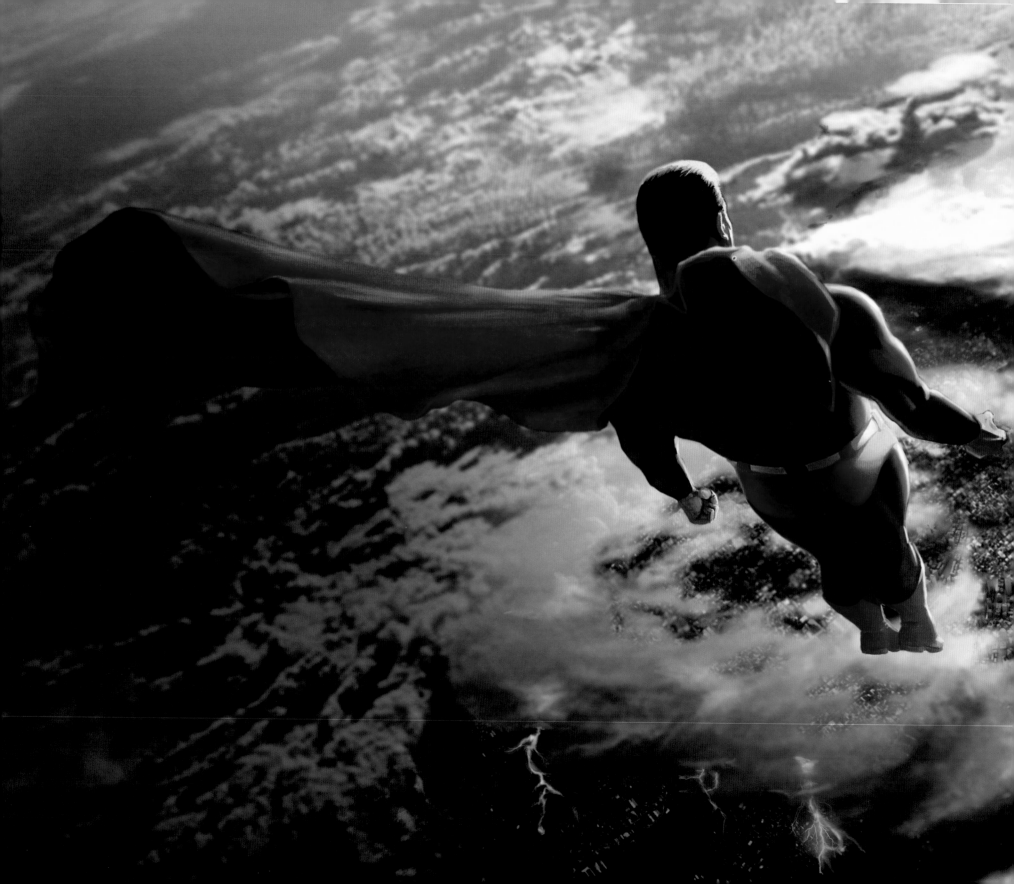

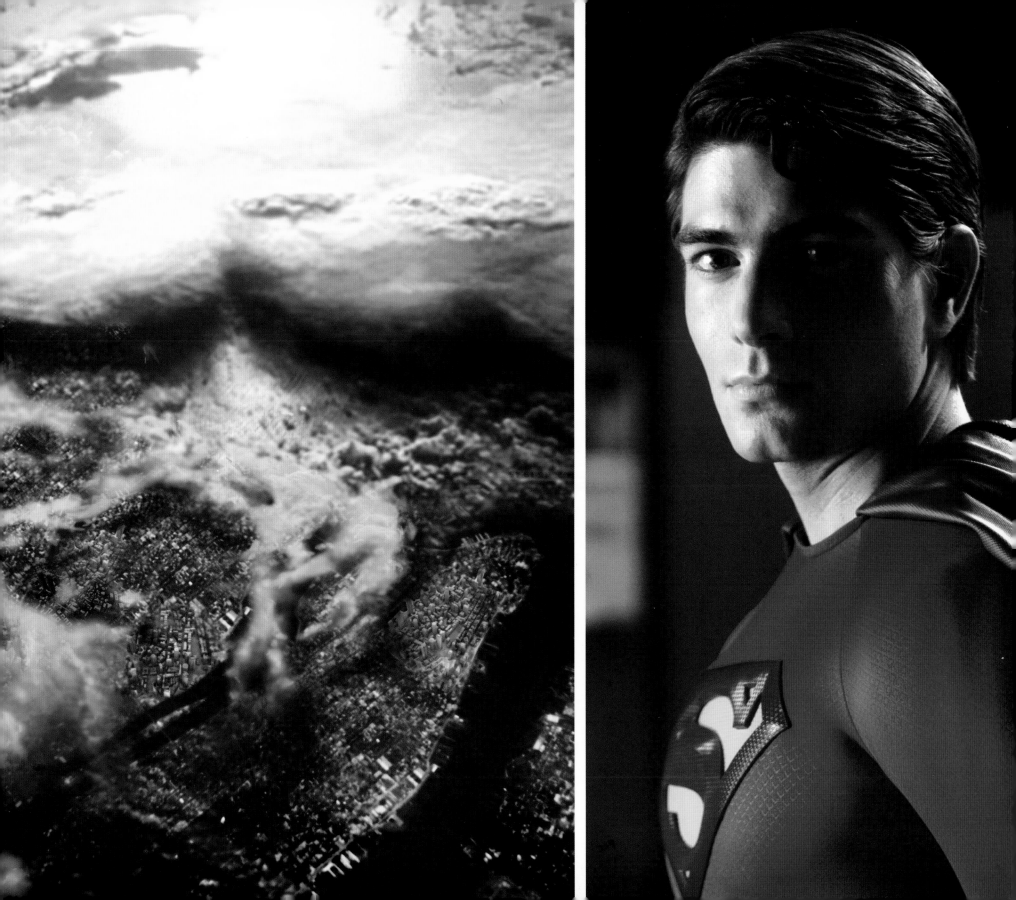

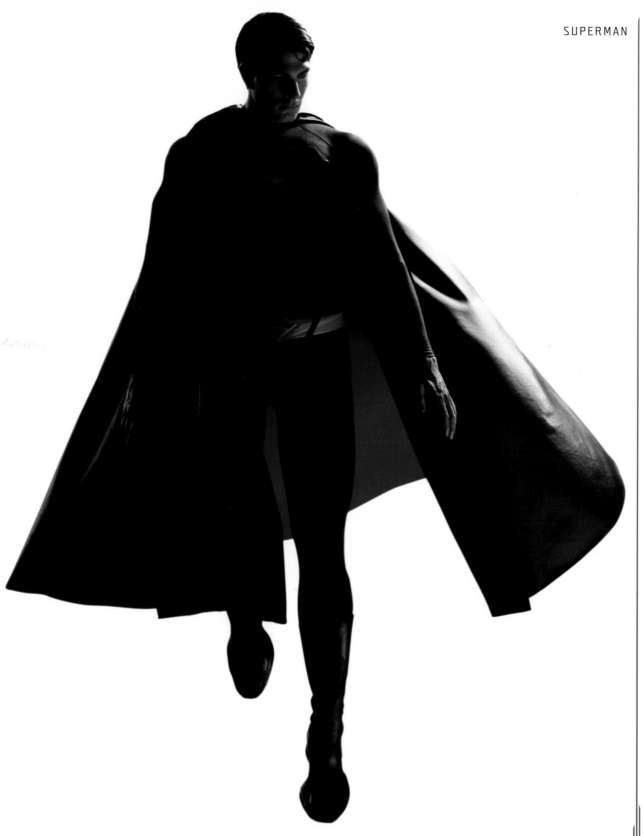

"Basically when we started we had zero development time," Bronson recalls, with an air of relief that the costume's backbreaking gestation period is behind them. Previous Superman productions, he recounts, had a year or two to develop the suit. "We started out with nothing but deadlines." Mingenbach adds, "I think we benefited greatly from all those past developments, because they were so extreme. It got so crazy and out of hand." But many were ideas that would logically come to mind. "Until you see how wrong it is, you think maybe it's right."

The office of the costuming department is a comfortable space filled with couches and computers. Stairs lead down to a warehouse area, and the opposite wall is a showcase for dozens of black-and-white costume sketches. One illustration holds a special meaning. Drawn by artist E.J. Krizer, it is the sketch Bryan Singer presented to pitch Brandon Routh to the studio. The image shows a costumed Routh hovering in the air—in fact a "head swap" reworking of an earlier image, made before any casting details were known. What's remarkable about the illustration is how closely it matches the finished product. Except for subtle tweaks made by the costuming perfectionists (another illustration shows a half-dozen minor variations in the leather on Superman's boots), the crew's first take was right on the mark.

The suit is secure in a fitting room downstairs. Though it's mounted on a headless mannequin, the costume delivers the amassed power of seventy years of mythology, and to all who enter, it packs quite a punch. *That's really Superman's suit.*

The costume is visibly darker. Superman still wears the primary colors of red, blue, and yellow, but the palette has a slightly darker mix. The red is more of a rich maroon, and what was lemon yellow is now a mustard color. There's an S insignia on the chest, of course, but this time it's a raised medallion, and it's smaller than the chest-plastering S common to recent interpretations of the Superman costume.

"It's an aesthetic decision," says Mingenbach, referring to the chest insignia. "I sat with Bryan and asked, if you want a smaller S or a bigger S, what does that do to his chest, and what does that do to Brandon? Ultimately we were dealing with [Routh's] proportions, and what looks best on him." Dyas at first favored a smaller S shield similar to the one used in early issues of *Action Comics* and in the Fleischer cartoons. In the end, "I actually felt that Bryan had made a good compromise," he says. "He'd chosen something that was somewhere between the '30s and the modern ones."

Hundreds of tiny S shapes have been screen printed into the background of the chest shield. These can be seen only when the viewer is a few inches away from the actual item, and even then, it takes some squinting.

The leathery cape is made of a gluey plastic material that calls to mind the stuff used to keep bath mats from slipping. Its hefty weight gives the garment body and form, Mingenbach explains: A cape made from lightweight fabric "just looks like a towel." The cape is a single uniform color, with no yellow S embellishment on the back. "That's more practical than anything else," she clarifies. "When he's flying, the cape folds in on itself, and an insignia ends up looking distracting."

The fabric used for the suit's body is a very fine synthetic milliskin that feels almost like a diaphanous wetsuit. Although the costume is fixed in place on its mannequin frame, Bronson divulges that were it removed, it would shrink like woolen socks in a clothes dryer. "It's made for a nine-year-old boy, stretched onto a six-foot-three frame," he laughs.

Bronson also reveals one of the dirty little secrets of the Superman suit. While it's true that this is a classic costume without molded plastic muscles, the tightness of the outfit tends to squeeze out whatever natural definition the wearer might possess. "The blue suit compresses the muscles," admits Bronson, bringing out a light, see-through mesh suit designed to be worn as underwear, featuring strategic padding on the biceps, shoulders, and pectorals. "So we had to enhance the body to keep the cuts and shapes in there." Worn by Routh, the body-hugging muscle suit gives back everything the outer costume takes away.

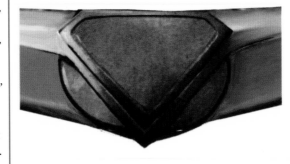
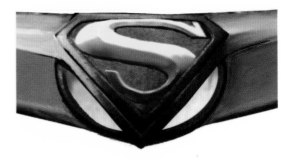
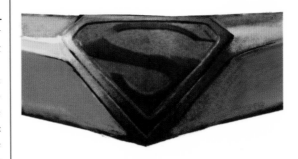
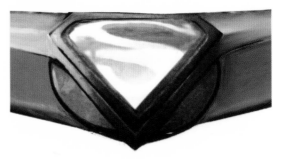
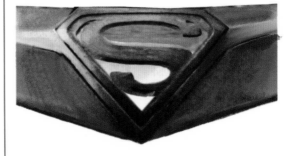
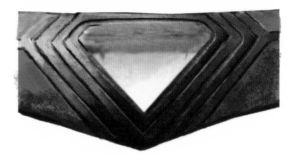

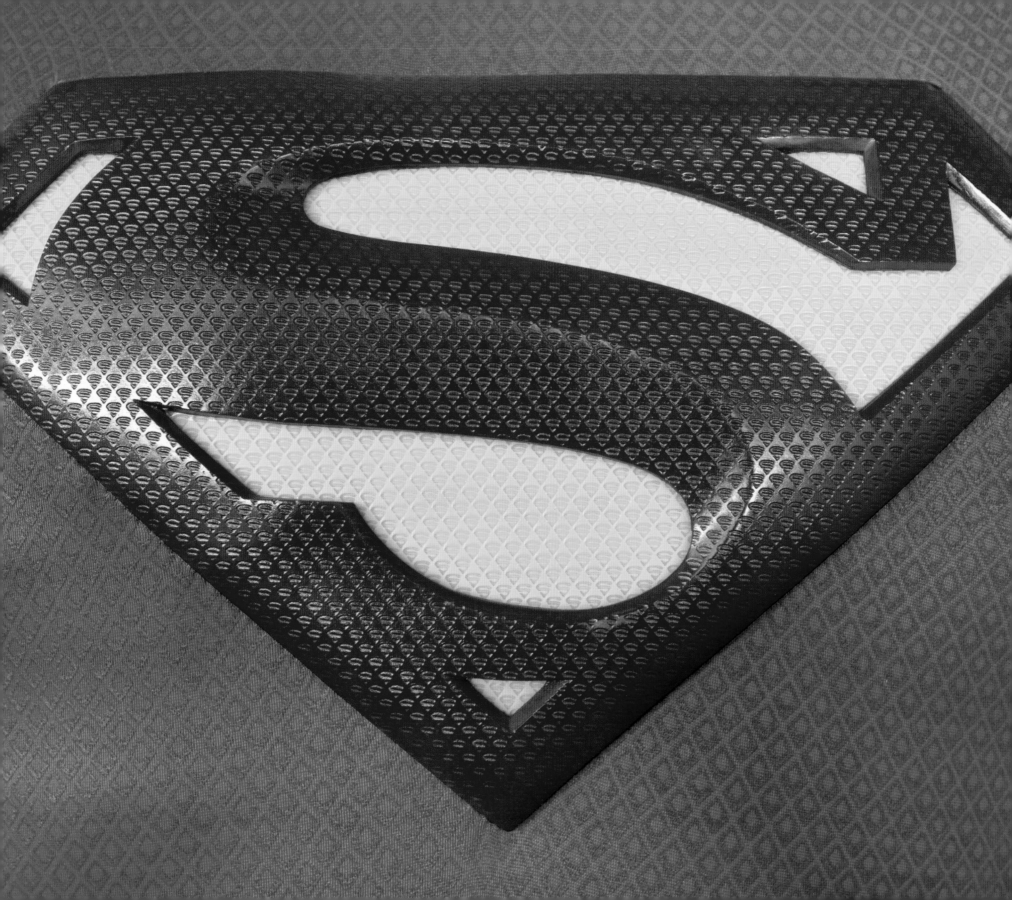

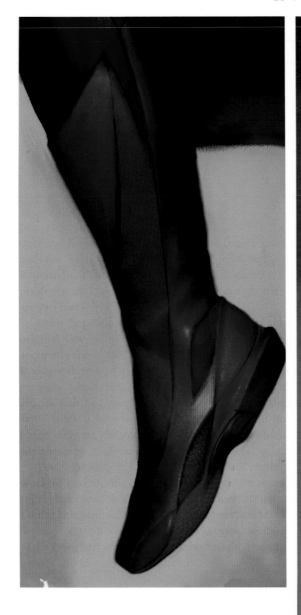

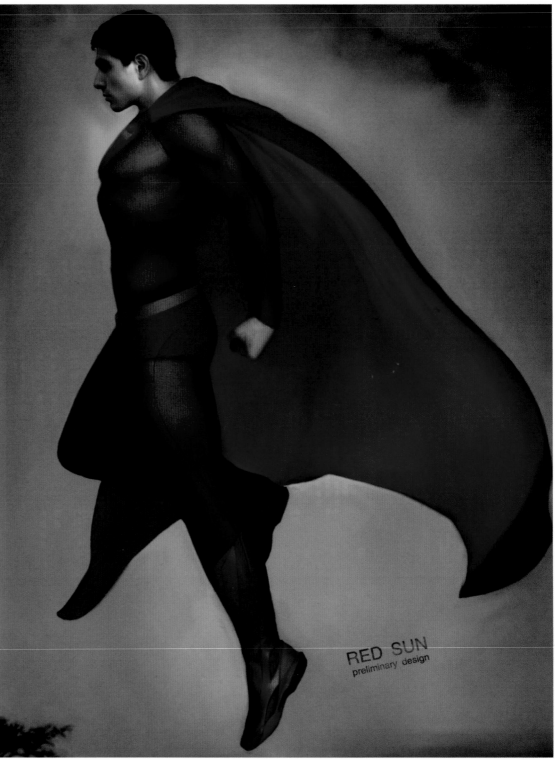

RED SUN
preliminary design

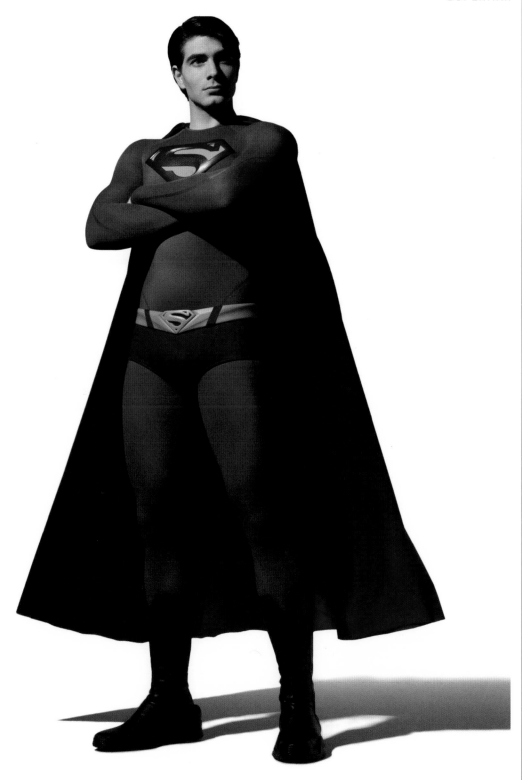

The costume displayed on the tailor's dummy is what is known as a "hero suit," a perfect (and expensive) version designed to look good in publicity stills. But there are nearly eighty Superman suits in all, ranging from resilient stunt versions to variants with extra-long sleeves, created to keep the cuffs from riding up Routh's forearms when he assumes Superman's classic flying pose.

An adjacent storage chamber is filled with cardboard crates and wheeled clothes racks. Bronson pulls down a few boxes and peeks in on their contents. "We've got hero suits, we've got water suits, we've got arms-up suits, we've got different water capes, water boots . . . " The water items he mentions aren't made to keep the wearer dry—they are constructed of special material to prevent liquid from darkening the fabric and changing its color during filming.

Bronson finds the capes. Like the suit itself, the capes are provided in a multiplicity of fabrics and measurements. "The beauty capes are twice as big as the performance capes, which we use on the flying rigs," he says. Size, length, and weight all come into play to produce "the right amount of flutter."

Other boxes hold Superman's boots. At least twelve different pairs were made. Tiny S insignias have been laser cut into the leather, and each boot has a prominent S shield on both the heel and the tread (meaning that Superman leaves his calling card in every footprint). The first boot designs had a thinner sole, more like a wrestler's shoe, until the costumers met Brandon Routh. "He's so tall," says Mingenbach, "and with this cape . . . he looked top-heavy." A bulkier boot style added the necessary counterbalance to Routh's muscular silhouette. "It grounds him," Bronson says.

OPPOSITE PAGE LEFT *One of many boot concepts considered by the* Superman Returns *costume department. E.J. Krizer, digital, January 2005.*

OPPOSITE PAGE RIGHT *Alternate angle of the Brandon Routh pitch illustration. An earlier, black-and-white version of the same illustration featured a generic Superman actor inside the costume. E.J. Krizer, digital, January 2005.*

LEFT *Routh in costume. The weighty material chosen for the cape gives it form and presence. David James, June 2005.*

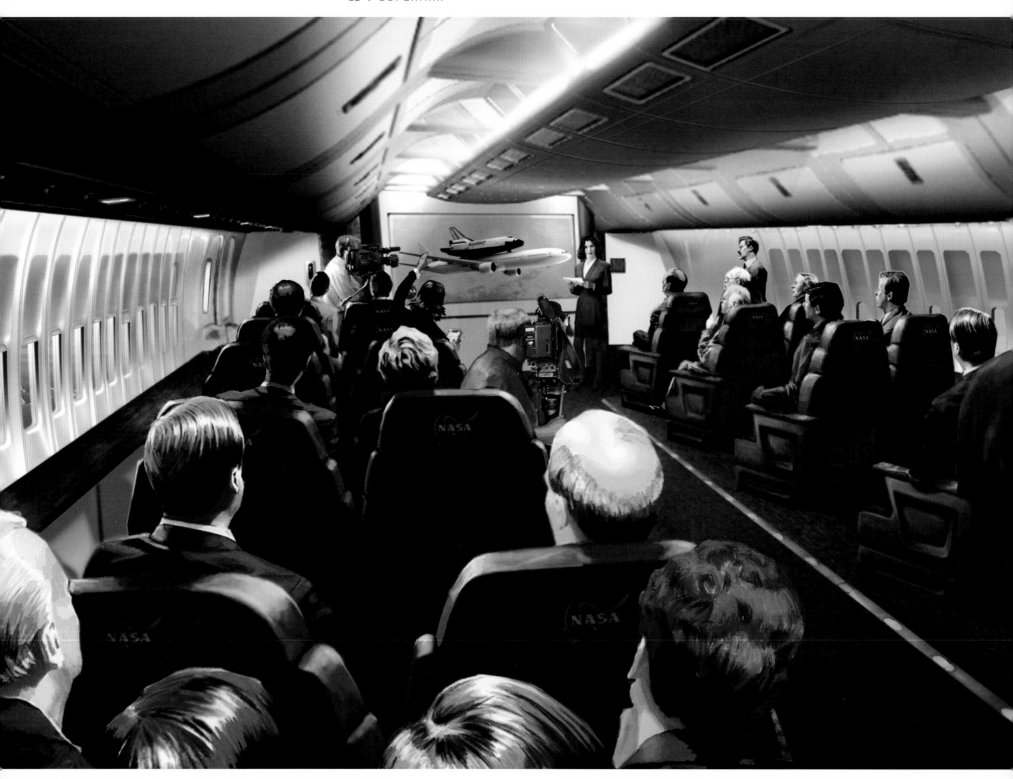

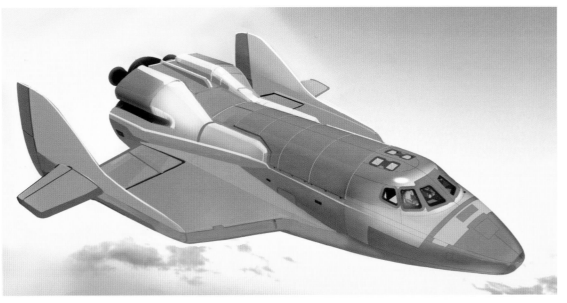

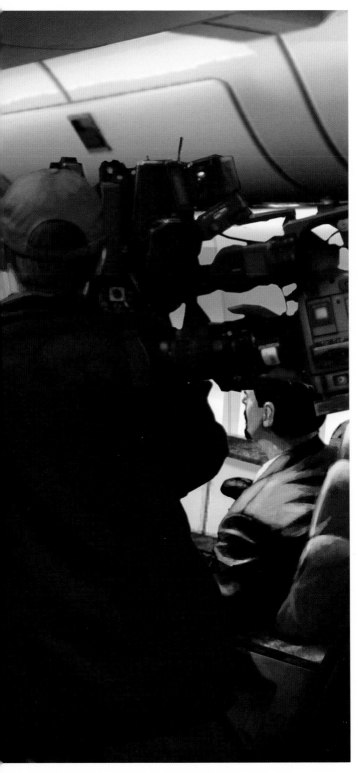

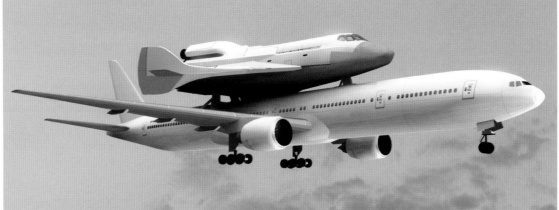

TOP *Rejected shuttle concept, with variations to the wings and engine bank. Paul Ozzimo and Tani Kunitake, digital, May 2005.*

ABOVE *Rendering of the jet in flight, carrying its piggyback shuttle. Paul Ozzimo and Tani Kunitake, digital, May 2005.*

LEFT *Early concept of the press jet interior. The first-class seating would later be swapped for more cramped quarters. Jeff Julian, digital, February 2005.*

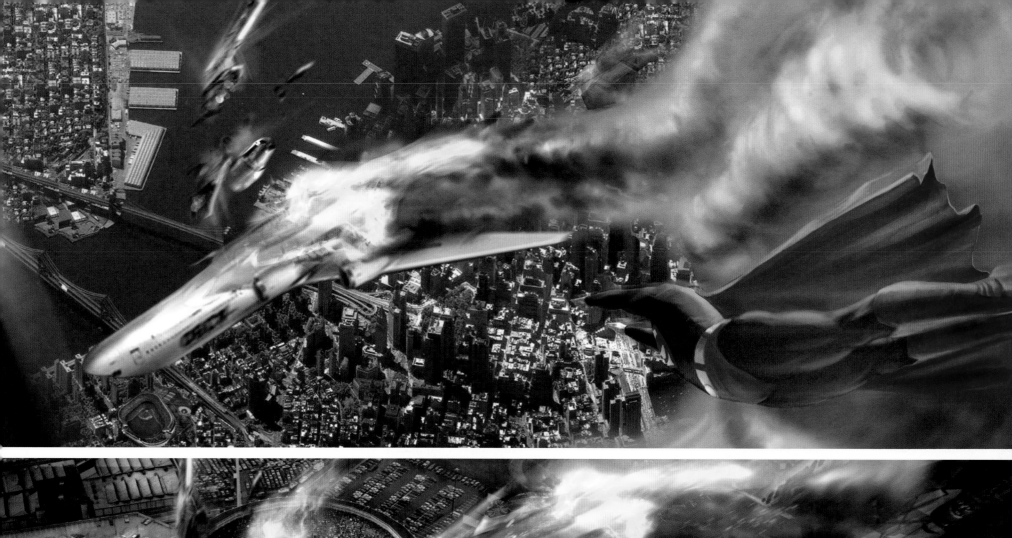
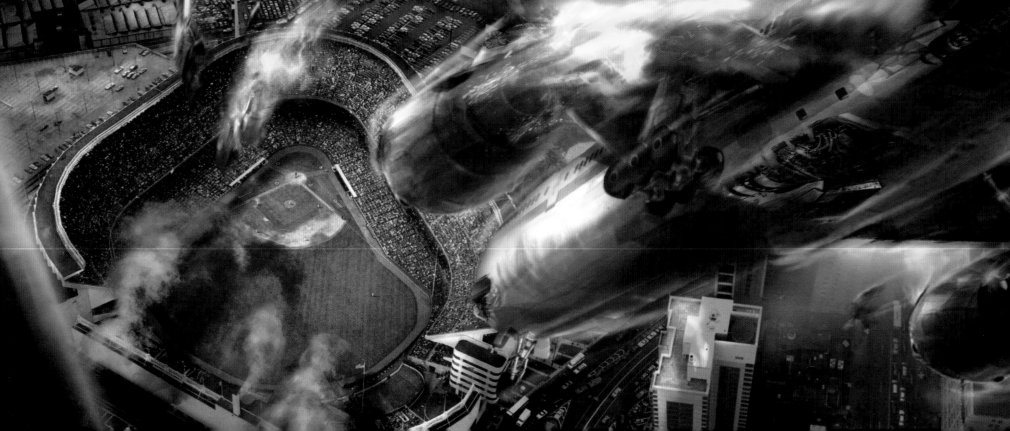

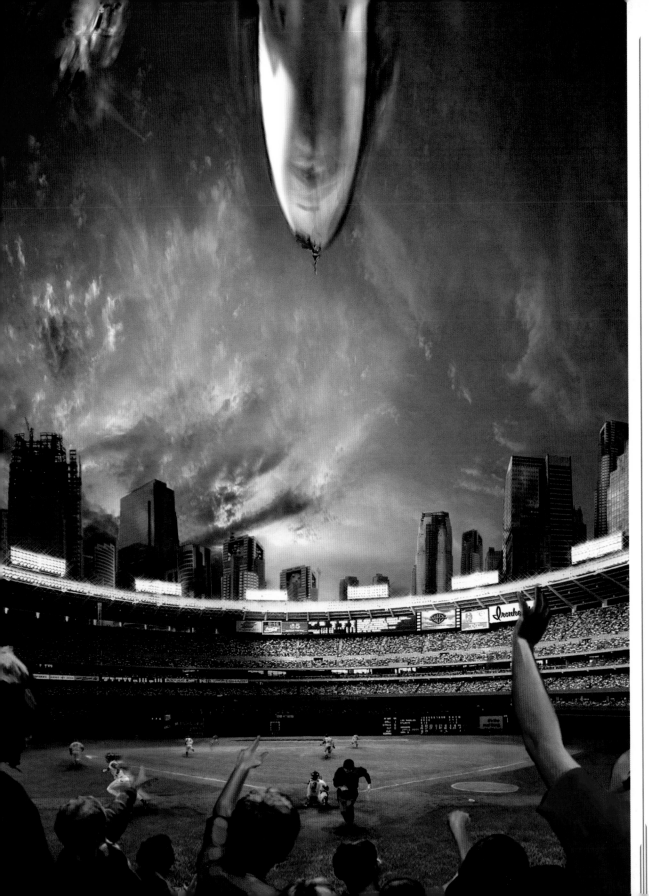

One of the key moments of *Superman Returns* is, well, Superman's return. After his arrival back on Earth at the start of the film, the exiled hero adjusts to a changed world until a crisis involving a jet and a space shuttle induces a rousing return to form. Many variants on the sequence were considered and rejected, all traces of their passing confined to Guy Dyas's office.

Tacked to the wall are a half-dozen iterations of the NASA shuttle, evidence of the art department's struggles to refine a craft that could piggyback on a Boeing 777 past the boundaries of the stratosphere. Other amendments were smaller in scale, such as Bryan Singer's decision to change the interior of the press jet from business class to coach. The military chase planes in the sequence are top-of-the-line F-35s—actual aircraft not to be deployed to the world's fighting forces until 2008, although the film was shot in 2004.

After Superman rescues the stricken jet and sets it down safely on the infield of a packed baseball stadium, no one can deny that the Man of Steel's return is a wild success. It must feel good for Superman to stretch his muscles after five years in a space pod, for he quickly tackles even mightier feats. Several of these sequences are on display in Dyas's office as key frames, a step between concept illustrations and full storyboards. Dyas exhibits key frames depicting an oil rig fire that Superman extinguishes with his gale-force breath, as well as storyboards of a spectacular moment where a bullet meets an eye, illustrating what being invulnerable really means.

LEFT AND OPPOSITE PAGE *A flaming jet drops toward a packed baseball stadium in this series of conceptual renderings. Note the way the colors of Superman's costume are used for visual impact. Superman by Alex Ross, background by Jeff Julian; pen and ink with digital composite; February 2005.*

PAGE 36 *Storyboard illustrations from the rooftop standoff sequence. Ed Natividad, pen and marker, June 2005.*

PAGE 37 *Overhead illustration of the rooftop detailing the key elements in play: machine gun, helicopter, and police cordon. Philip Holliday, color pencil and markers, June 2005.*

PAGES 38-43 *More storyboards from the rooftop standoff sequence. The scene begins in outer space, where Superman picks up on the first hints of danger, and incorporates a unique demonstration of Superman's invulnerability. Ed Natividad, pencil and marker, June 2005.*

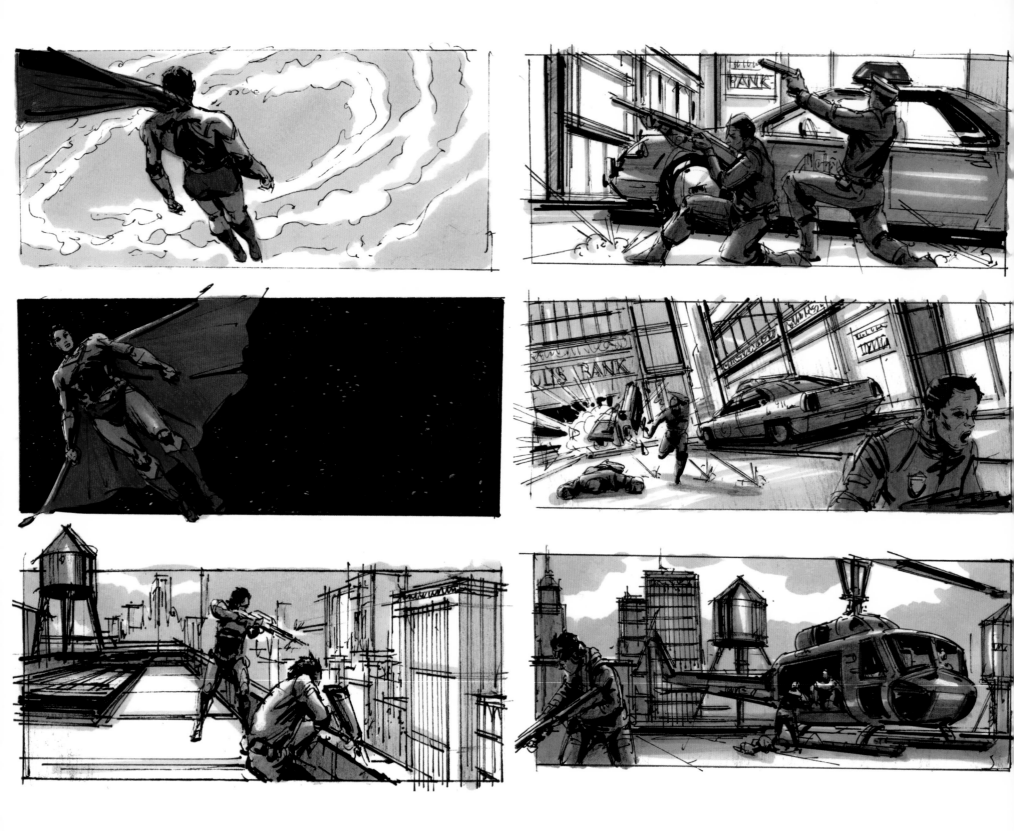

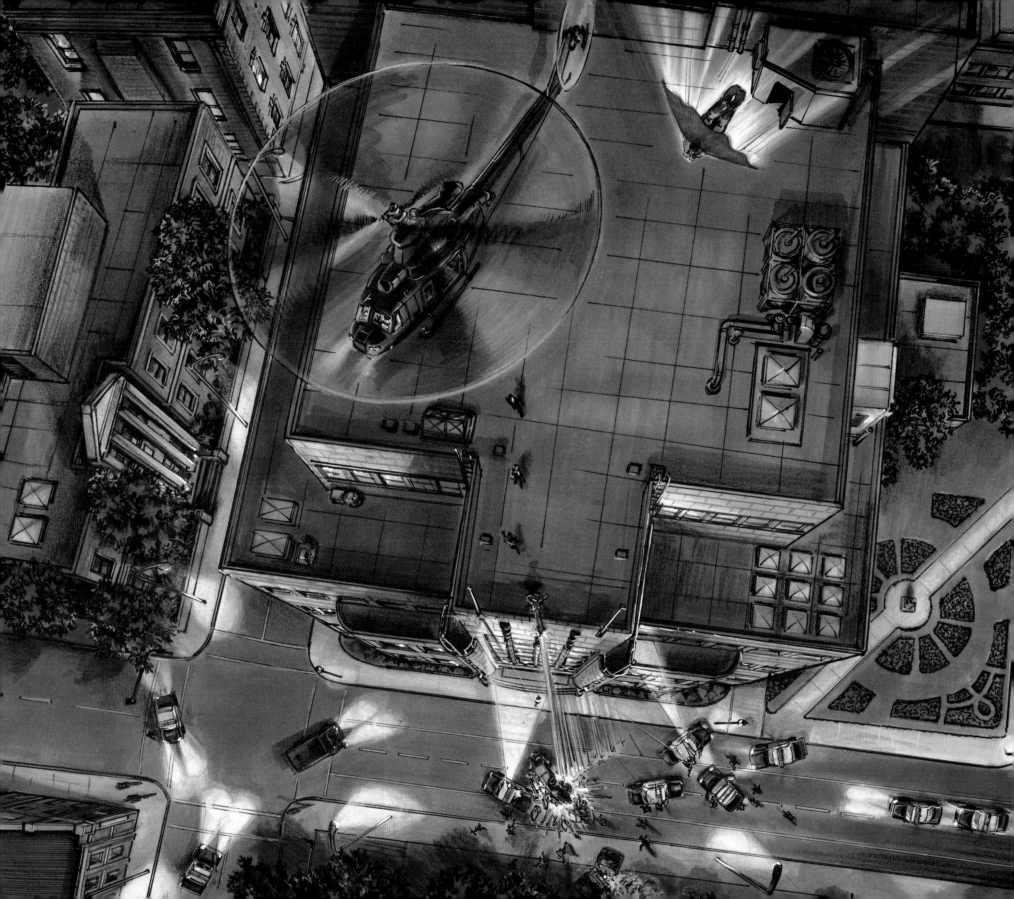

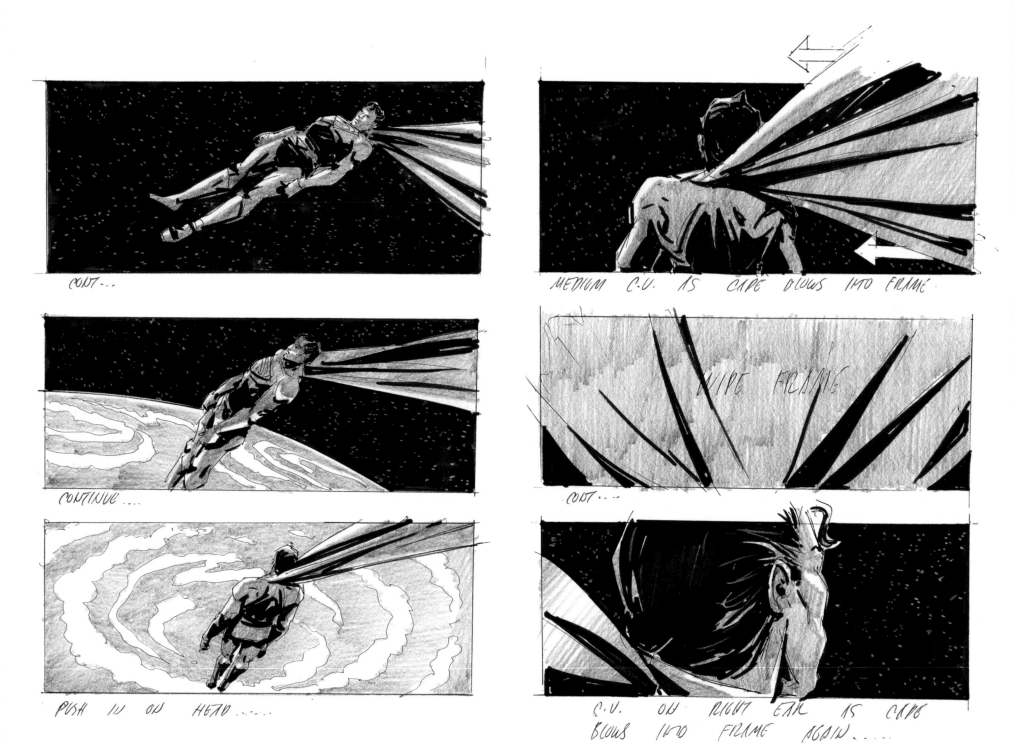

CONT...

MEDIUM C.U. AS CAPE BLOWS INTO FRAME

CONTINUE....

CONT....

PUSH IN ON HEAD......

C.U. ON RIGHT EAR AS CAPE BLOWS INTO FRAME AGAIN.....

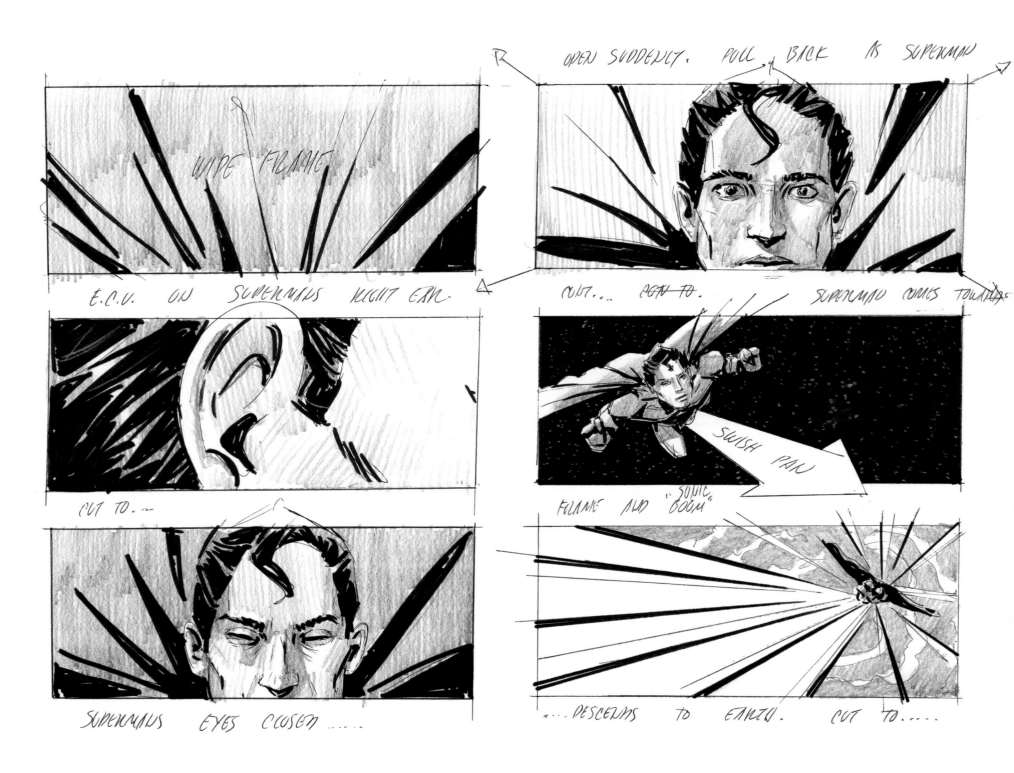

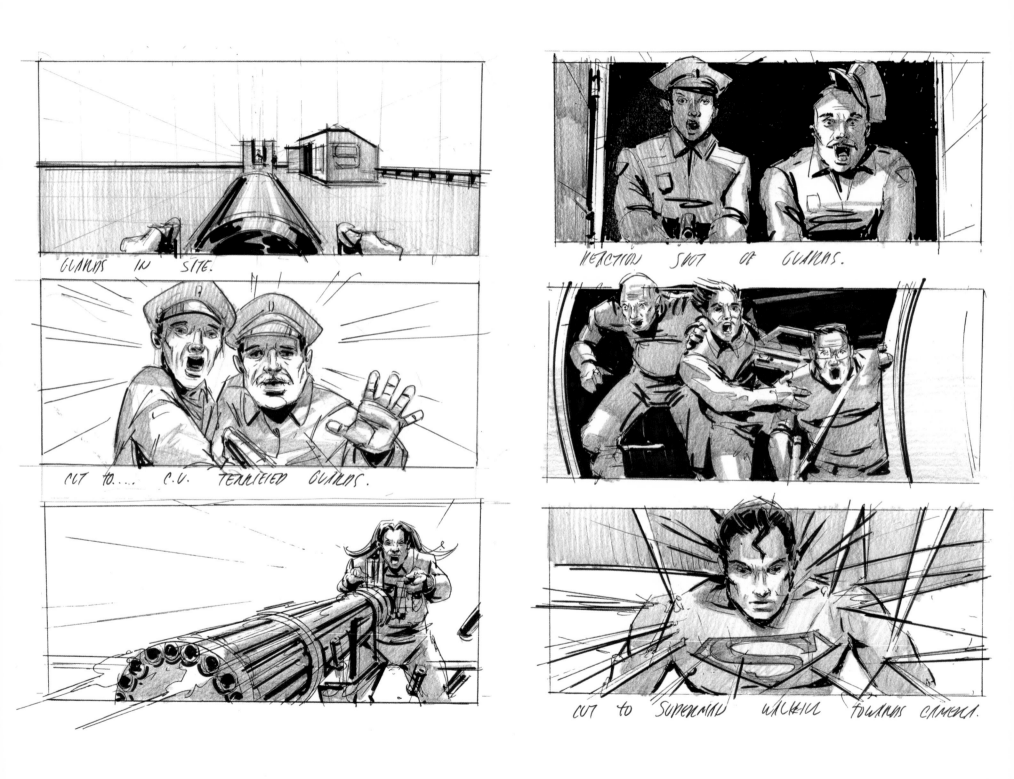

GUARDS IN SITE.

REACTION SHOT OF GUARDS.

CUT TO..... C.U. TERRIFIED GUARDS.

CUT TO SUPERMAN WALKING TOWARDS CAMERA.

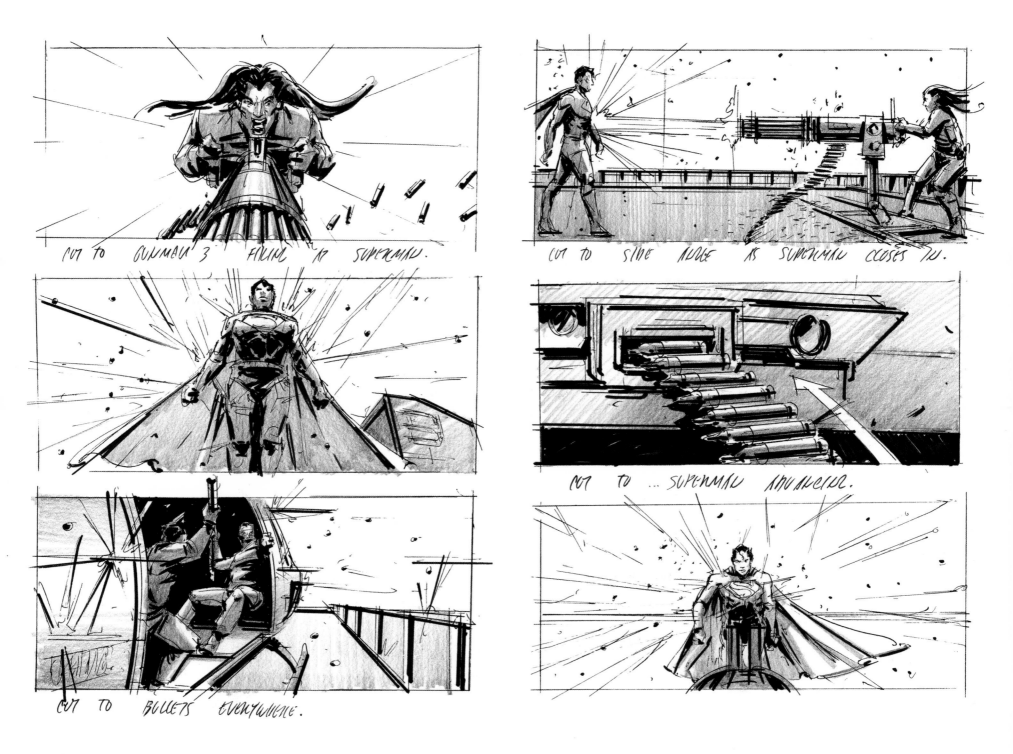

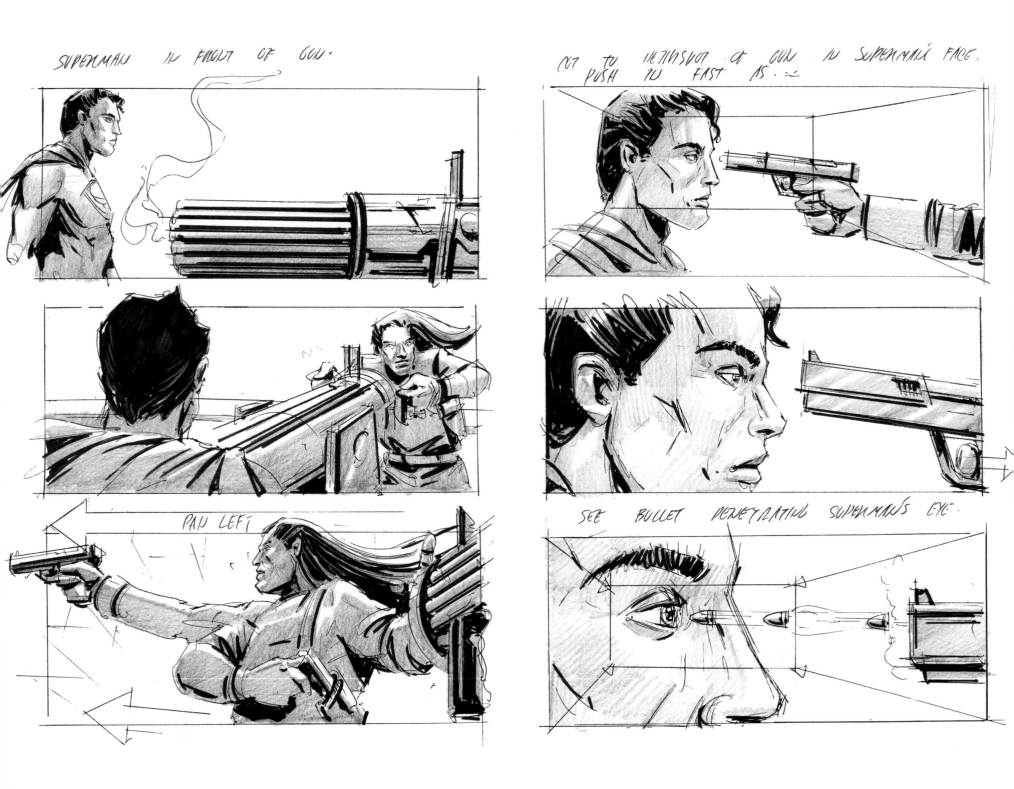

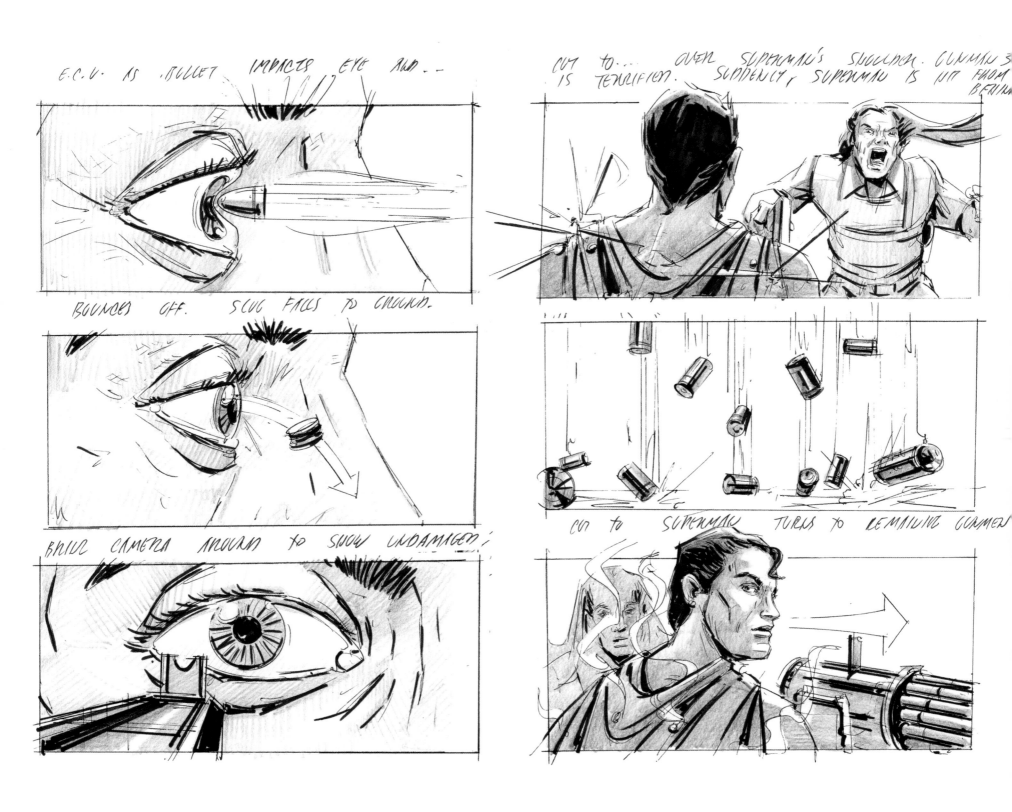

E.C.U. AS BULLET IMPACTS EYE AND ---

BOUNCES OFF. SLUG FALLS TO GROUND.

BRING CAMERA AROUND TO SHOW UNDAMAGED!

CUT TO... OVER SUPERMAN'S SHOULDER. GUNMAN 3 IS TERRIFIED. SUDDENLY, SUPERMAN IS HIT FROM BEHIND

CUT TO SUPERMAN TURNS TO REMAINING GUNMEN

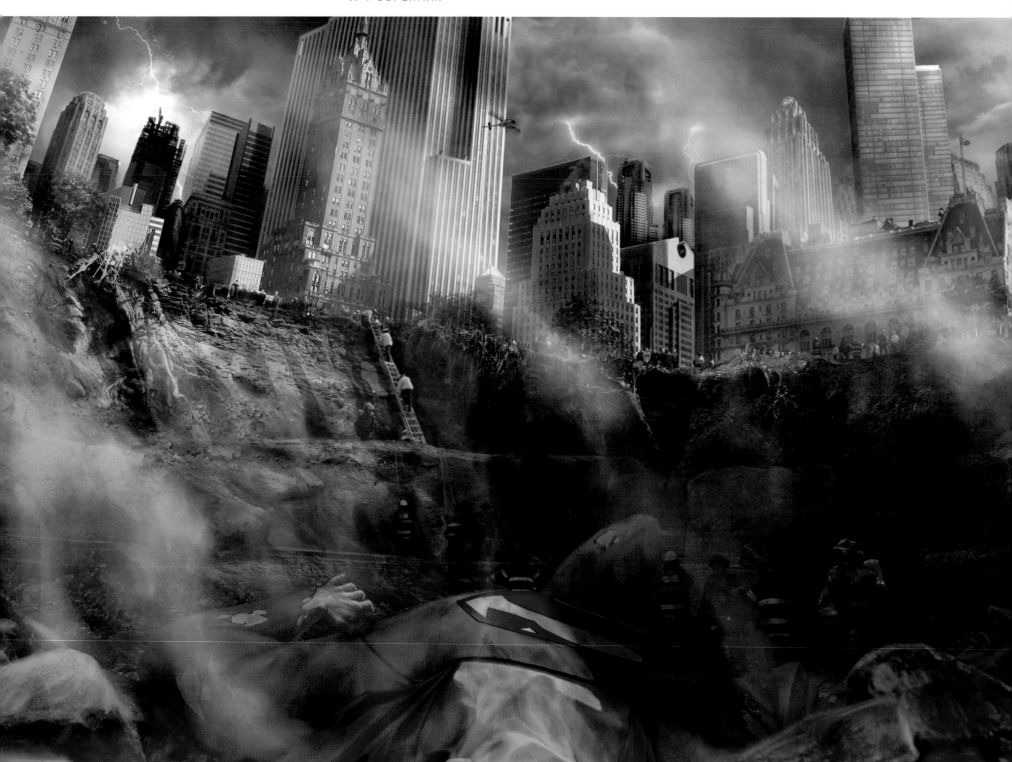

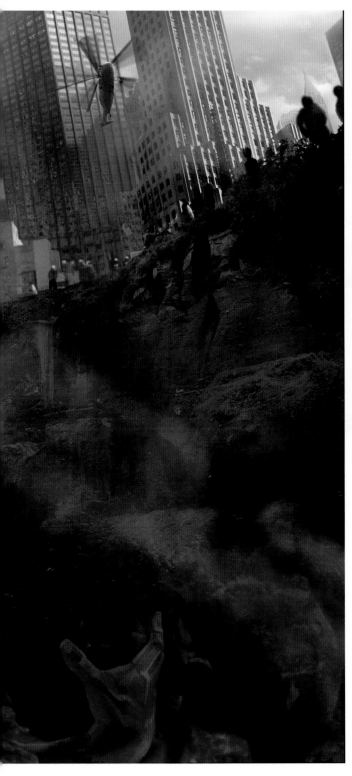

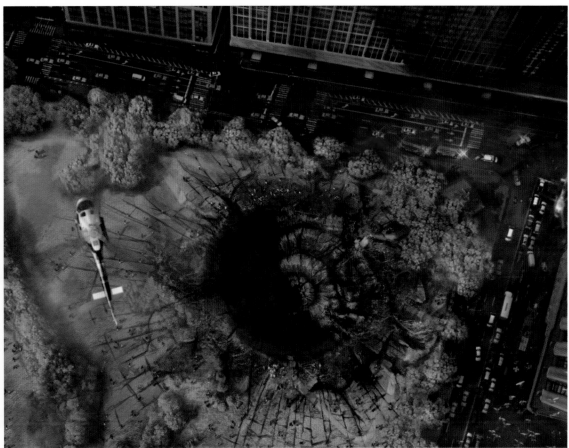

ABOVE *The impact of Superman's fall is sufficient to obliterate much of a city block. Jeff Julian, digital, March 2005.*

LEFT *Street-level view of a fallen Superman at the bottom of an impact crater. Jeff Julian, digital, March 2005.*

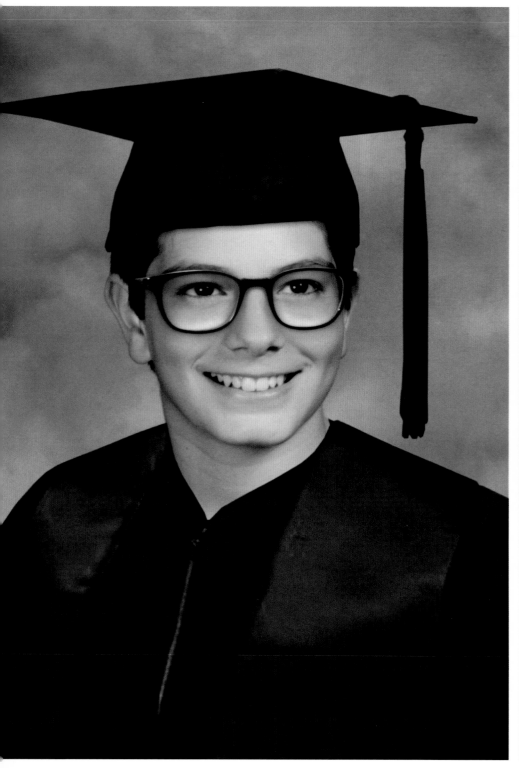

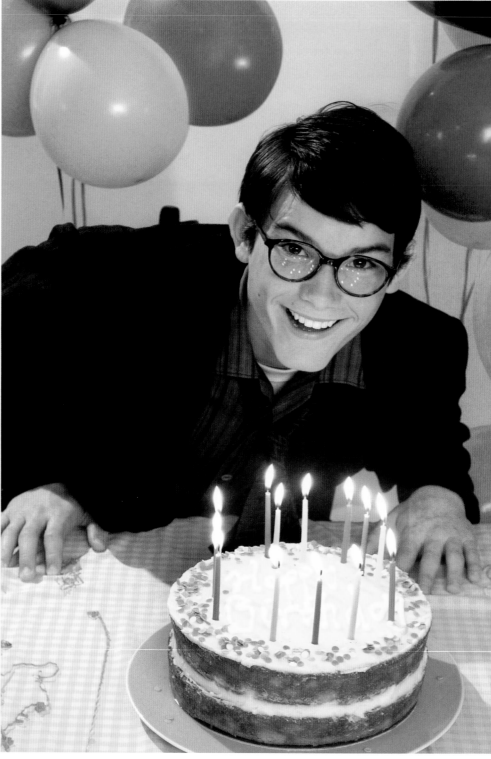

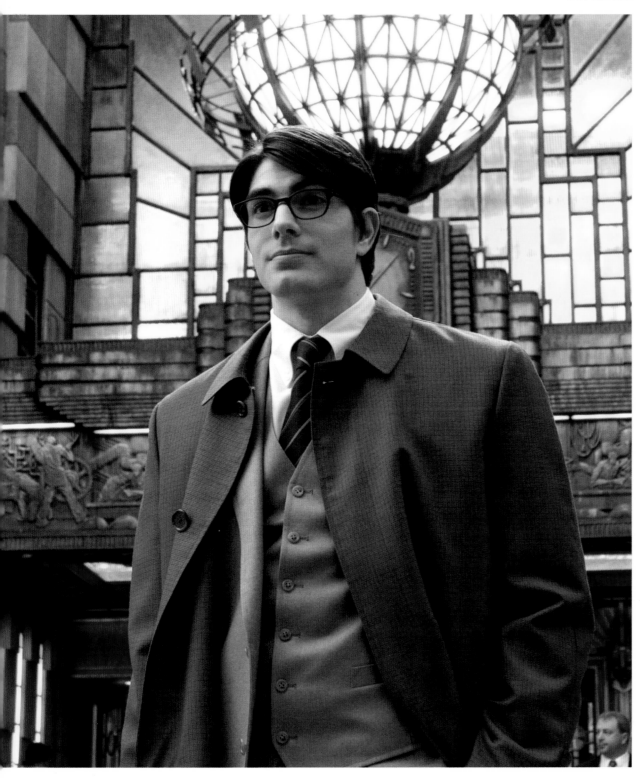

"He's the guy all the guys want to be and all the girls want to marry," says co-screenwriter Dan Harris, ruminating on Superman's perennial pull. "He brings us back to an earlier time, like a bright shining beacon of hope that says there is good in this world." Adds his screenwriting partner Michael Dougherty, "I think that's why he's stood the test of time. Right now we are functioning in an era of edgy, dark super heroes—the X-Men included, and Bryan was the guy who launched that [movie] franchise—but I think you can almost drown in that cynicism. Superman represents that side of ourselves that is brighter, which we might not see enough of."

Singer agrees. "In the *X-Men* movies you had these very complicated people trying to exist in a regular world, and here you have a very regular guy—who happens to have extraordinary superpowers—existing in an ever more complicated world. Superman has a very clear morality, which is very much a product of growing up in the serenity and safety of the Kent farm. In his clear view, he sees beauty and he sees destruction. He sees thriving crops and he sees blight."

"Someone who never lies," Harris ponders. "That simple idea is a relic of the '50s, it's probably something you couldn't get away with now. It's too simple. But that's the thing that's great about Superman. You can always rely on him. And in *Superman Returns,* we throw some serious curveballs at the character and see how he ends up. All we have to do is create the situation, and Superman finds his way through it, with or without our help."

OPPOSITE PAGE LEFT *Graduation photo of Brandon Routh. Digital glasses by Nick Tory.*

OPPOSITE PAGE RIGHT *Birthday party photo of Stephan Bender as Clark Kent. Suzanne Buljan, April 2005.*

LEFT *Brandon Routh as Clark Kent in front of the Daily Planet. David James, June 2005.*

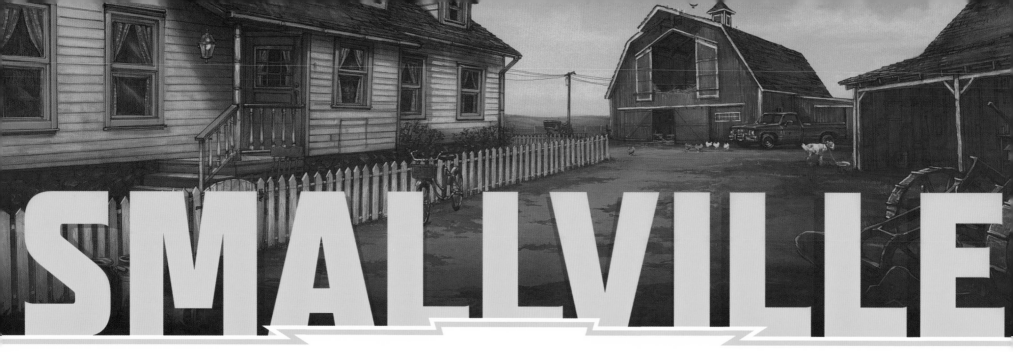

SMALLVILLE

Truth, Justice, and the American Way ◇ Tamworth, Australia
500 Acres of Corn ◇ The Kent Homestead
A Crane-like Flying Rig ◇ A Security Blanket
On a Quest for Identity

As *Superman Returns* opens, the Man of Steel is a million light-years from Earth. His quest for clues to his birth is cut short when he is smacked by the toxic radiation of kryptonite. Weakened to the brink of death, he speaks a single, telling word. Superman's ship swings away from Krypton and redirects its autonavigator to obey his gasped command: "Home."

But wait a minute—isn't Krypton Superman's home? Not at all, despite his perpetual curiosity about his roots. Earth is where Superman lives, but neither the Fortress of Solitude nor Metropolis fills the bill for that evocative word. When he's at his most vulnerable, Superman returns to the place that accepted him for who he was, not what he could do: Smallville, Kansas.

Here, he's not Kal-El or Superman, merely Clark. The values he prizes are the ones he learned in the heartland: honesty, hard work, and fair play. In the original film, Superman, without a drop of cynicism, tells Lois Lane that he stands for "truth, justice, and the American way." That's not Metropolis talking, it's Smallville.

The spaceship arrives in spectacular fashion, screaming through the night sky of Kansas and plowing to a halt in a field behind the Kent farm. The circumstances are similar to those that brought Superman to Earth—Kryptonians don't seem to be big users of landing gear—but this time the wounded leviathan leaves behind a frightening, firelit crash site. Martha Kent is there to greet her son. She is the one who has kept Clark's secret the longest, and who has undoubtedly missed him the most.

Kansas is all about wide-open spaces and amber waves of grain. No one could re-create it on a soundstage, so how do you come up with a Kansas stand-in in the bush of Australia? To an ambitious moviemaker the answer is self-evident— You create your own. In the bare countryside near the town of Tamworth, 250 miles outside of Fox Studios in Sydney, Bryan Singer and crew made something out of nothing.

No computer animation here—just seed, soil, and hard work. Production crews planted 500 acres of corn, timing their labor so that the stalks would be at their fullest when Smallville filming commenced. To reach the remote farm site, the crews laid down their own road.

The main event was the construction of the Kent homestead. Screenwriter Dan Harris describes the Kent farm as "classic and beautiful, [whether] lit under early morning skies or sunsets." Respecting the design used in the 1978 film, the *Superman Returns* crew constructed a main house, a barn, and a tree house in the front yard. The walls of the barn featured gaps between the wooden slats to let in atmospheric shafts of hazy light. Near the farm, space was cleared to accommodate a crane-like flying rig that suspends an actor inside a harness. The scenes shot with teenage actor Stephan Bender inside the rig (appearing in the

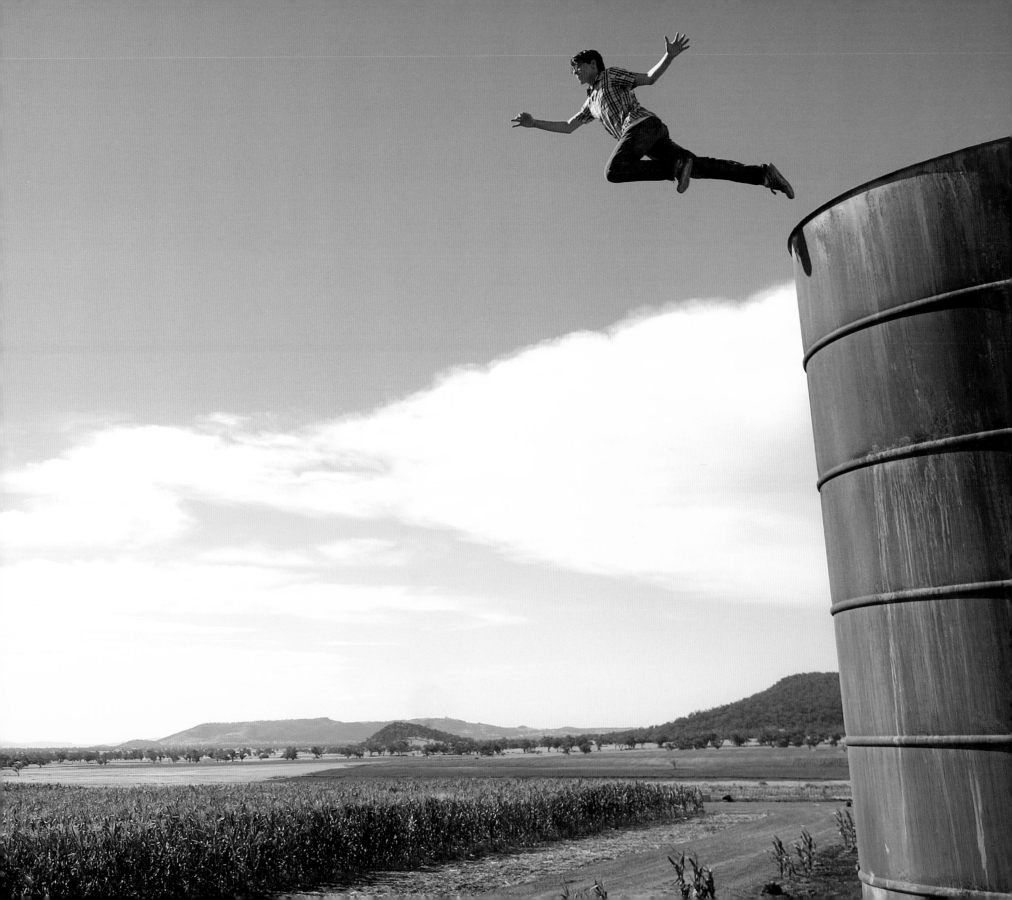

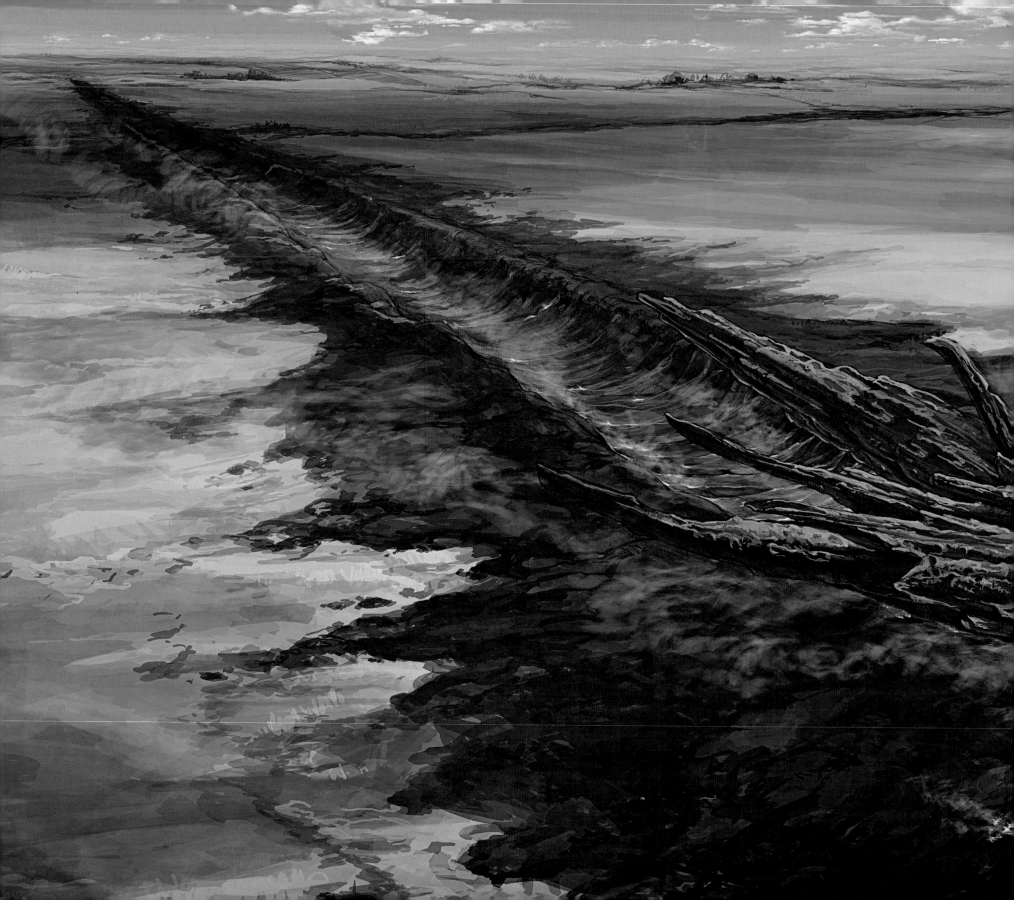

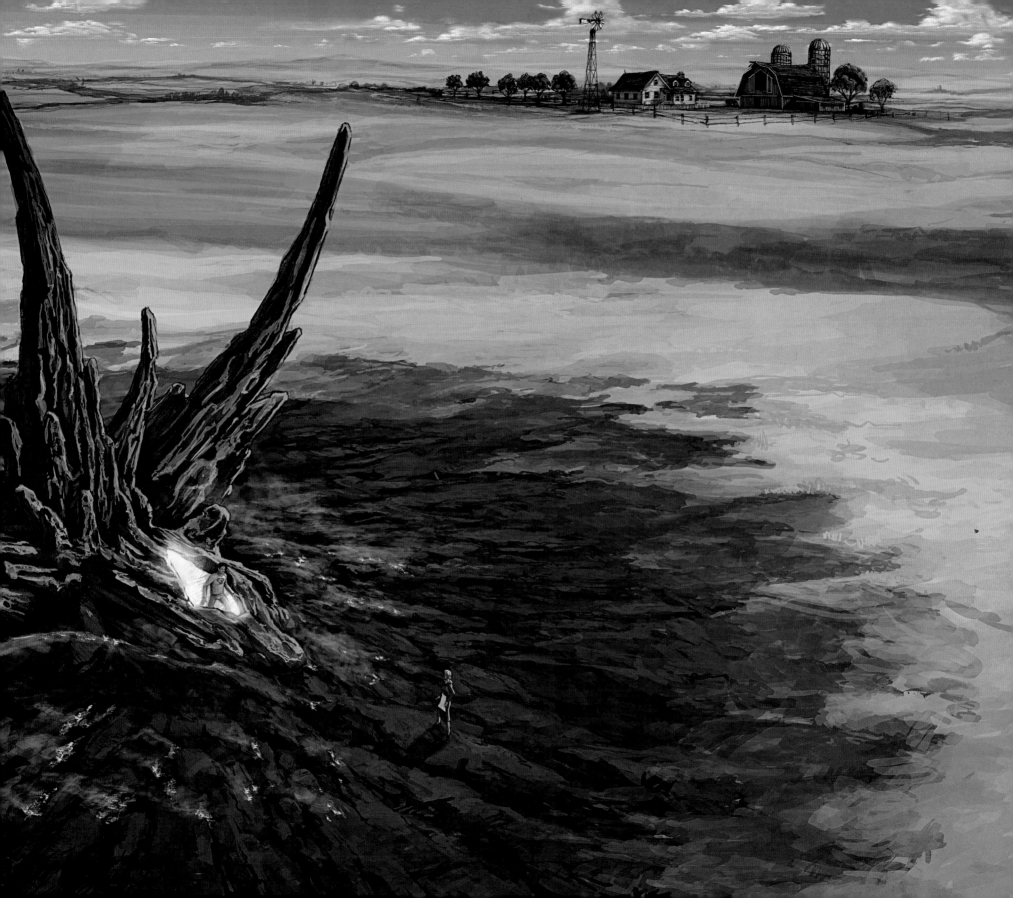

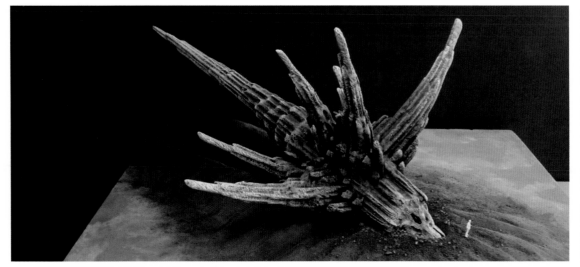

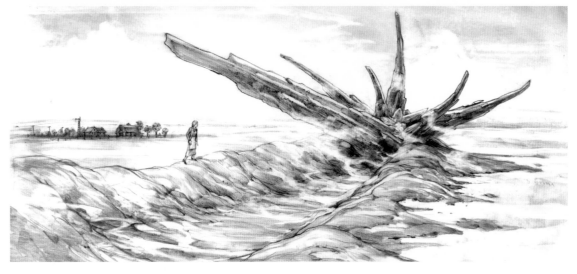

TOP *Model of the starship crash site. Brett Philips and Scott Lukowski, foam and plaster, February 2005.*

ABOVE *Martha Kent approaches the downed alien craft. James Oxford, pencil, March 2005.*

RIGHT *The full-size Kryptonian starship on location in Tamworth. David James, May 2005.*

PAGE 49 *By practicing on grain silos, Clark gained the ability to leap tall buildings in a single bound. David James, May 2005.*

PAGES 50-51 *The alien ship and the violent, black scar of its passage stand in sharp contrast to the sunlit fields of Kansas. James Oxford; pencil, marker, and digital; March 2005.*

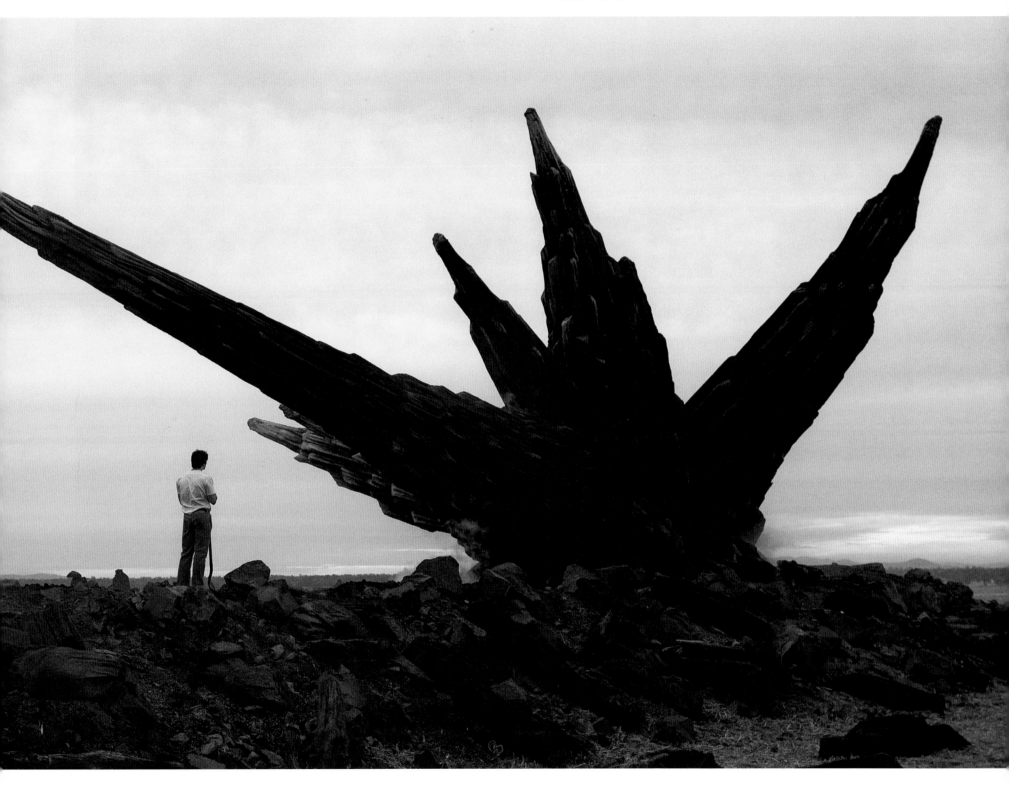

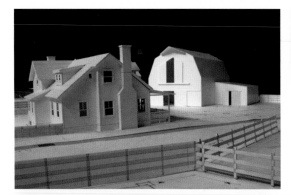

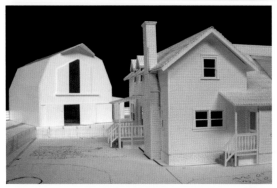

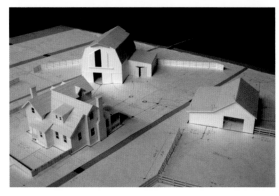

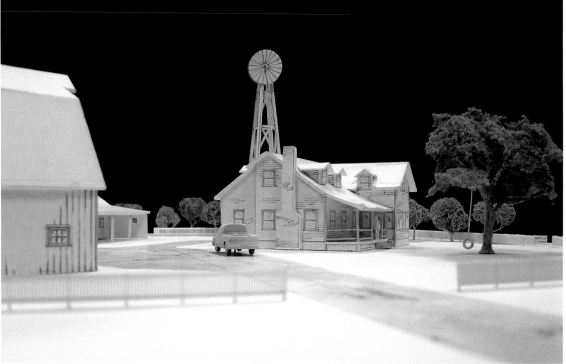

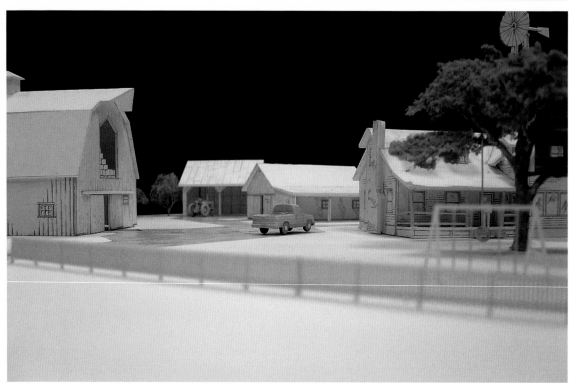

THIS PAGE *Miniature models of the Kent farm, seen from a variety of angles. Brett Philips, Shari Finn, Scott Lukowski, Lewis Morley, and Brad Burnet; card and paper; April 2005.*

OPPOSITE PAGE *The Kent house and barn. David James, May 2005.*

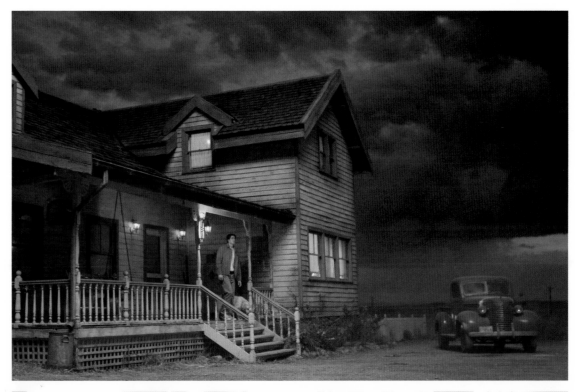

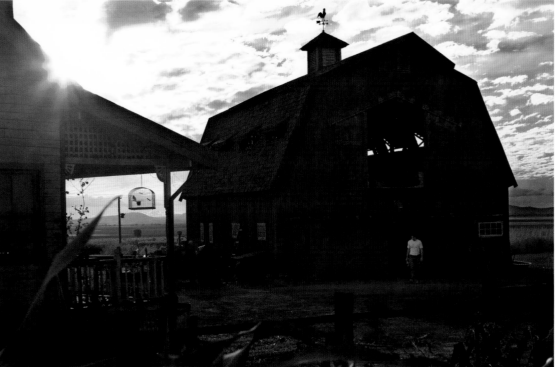

film as flashbacks) show how a fifteen-year-old Clark learned to leap tall buildings in a single bound.

Clark's visit home is bittersweet. Martha, who has found happiness with family friend Ben Hubbard, is planning to sell the farm and move to Montana. It's the first in what will be a string of painful transitions for Clark. "The farm for him is like a warm hearth," says Singer. "It's sort of like when a kid runs away, or goes to war, or goes off on a search for knowledge. Eventually the world seems like a crowded and angry place, and the Kent farm is a security blanket. But in our world *everything's* moved on, and even the farm is not the same secure place that Clark left it."

This sets up one of the movie's key themes. As co-scripter Dougherty puts it, "What is home, where is home, and how do you define home?" One thing is certain—while Clark has been away on a quest for identity, the world has moved forward without him.

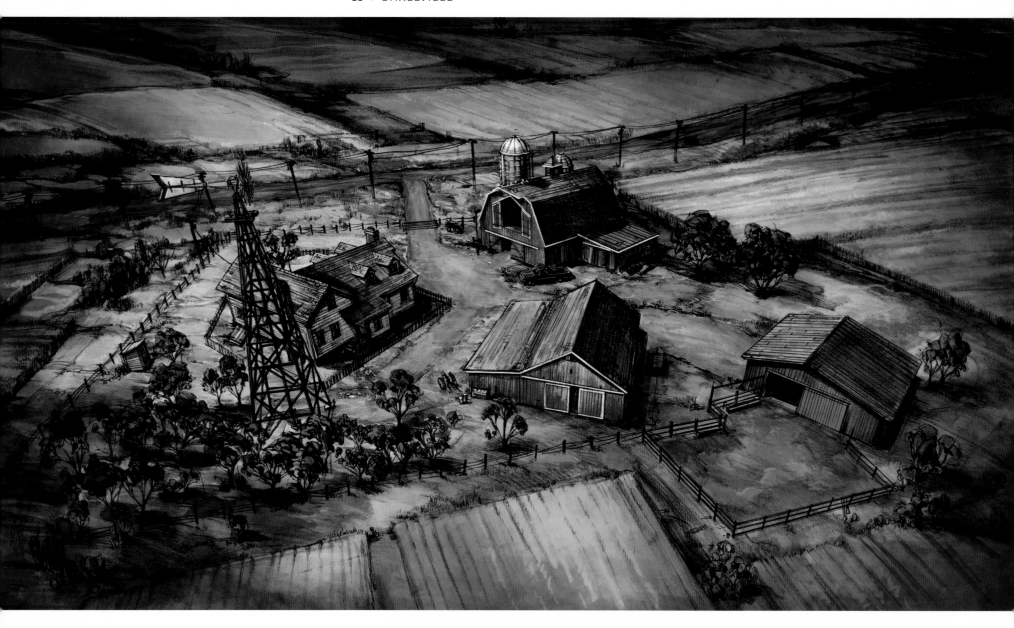

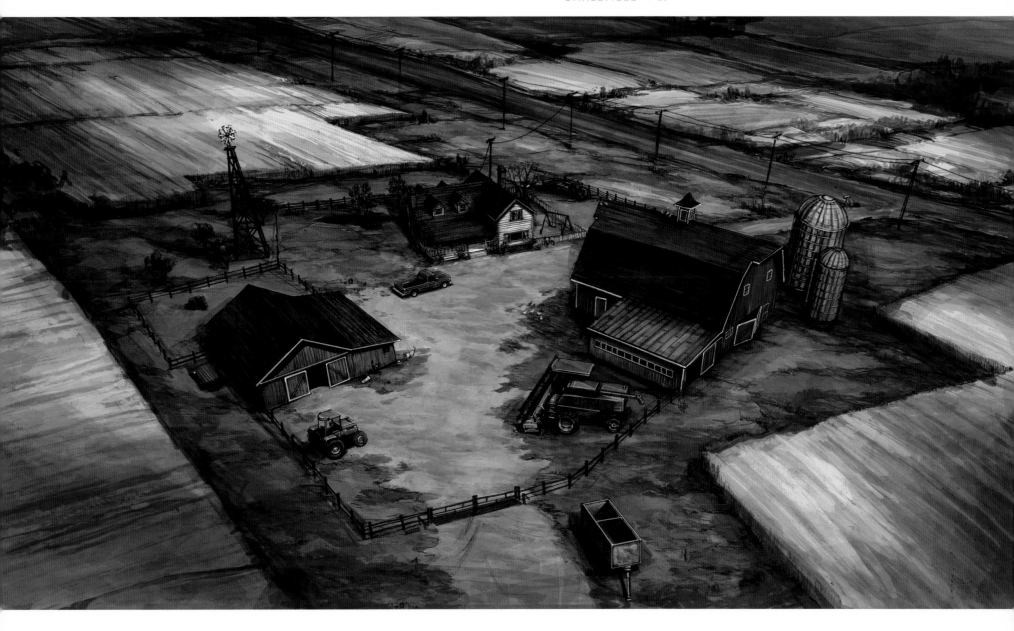

OPPOSITE PAGE AND ABOVE *Two layout variations of the Kent farm as seen from above. James Oxford; pencil, marker, and digital; February 2005.*

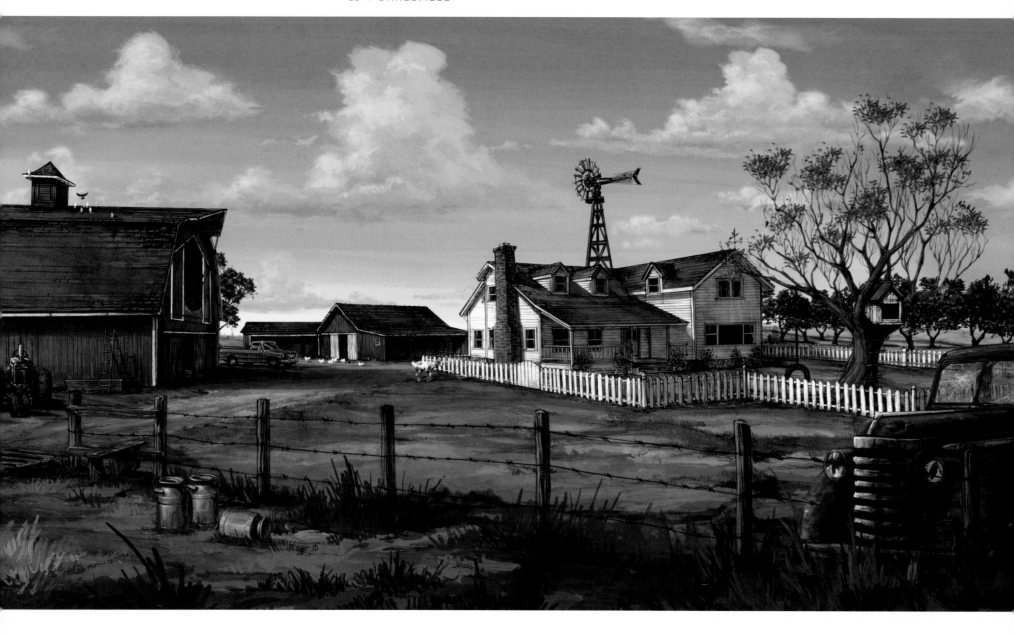

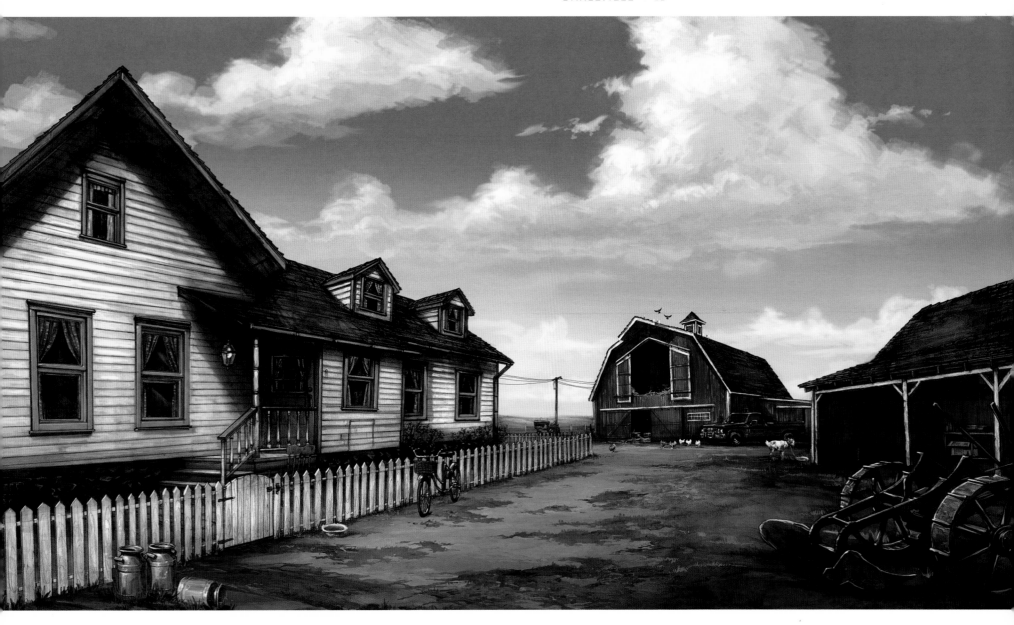

OPPOSITE PAGE AND ABOVE *Two layout variations of the Kent farm as seen from the ground. The Kent farm was designed as Norman Rockwell–like Americana, on the model of the 1978 film. James Oxford; pencil, marker, and digital; February 2005.*

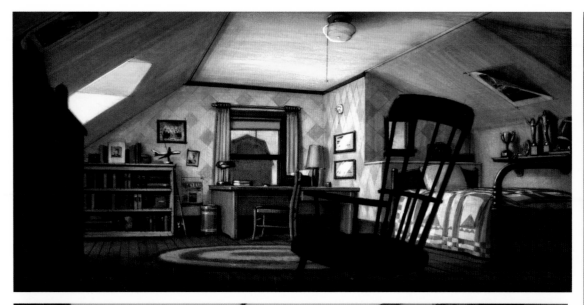

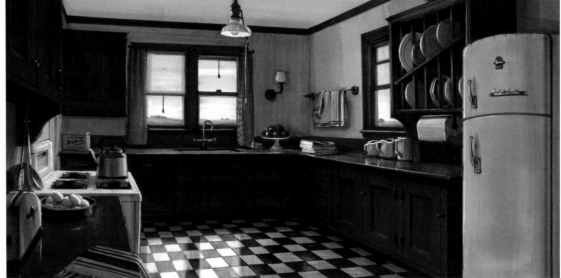

TOP AND ABOVE *The interior of Clark's bedroom; the football on the far right recalls a scene from the 1978 film. The Kent farmhouse kitchen. Jim Feldman, pencil and marker, February 2005.*

RIGHT *The Kent barn. The title of this image during production was "Six Years' Worth of Newspapers." Jim Feldman, pencil and marker, February 2005.*

PAGES 62-63 *The Kent farm buildings, showing varying levels of decay. Dean Woolcott and James Oxford, pencil and digital, February 2005.*

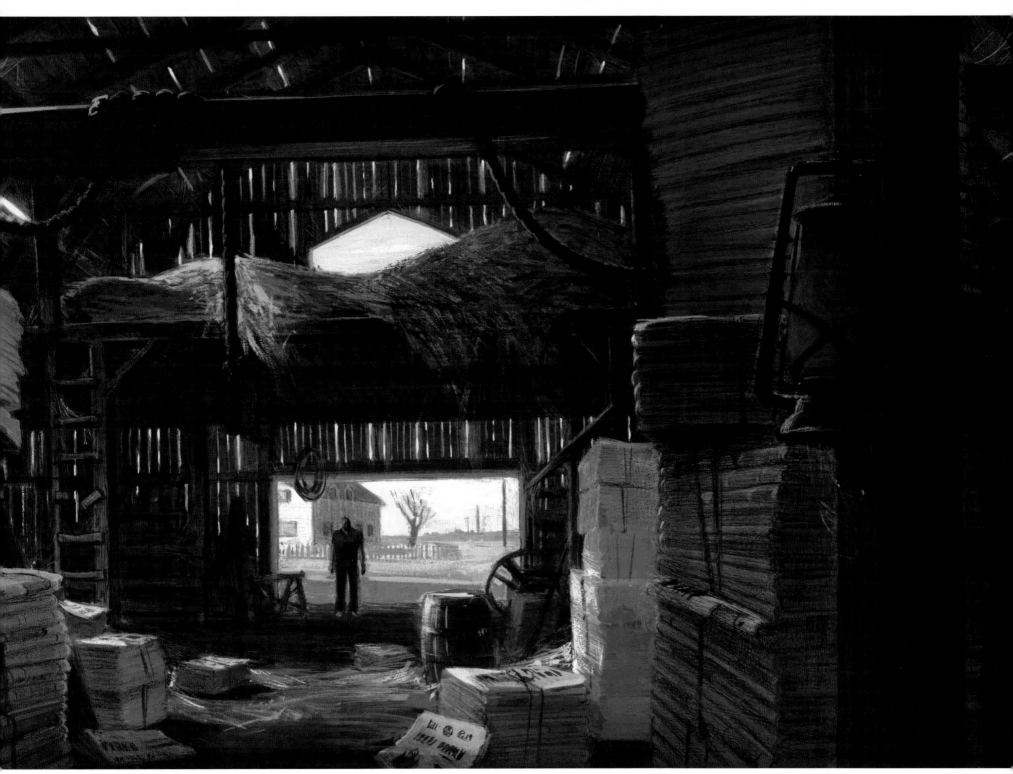

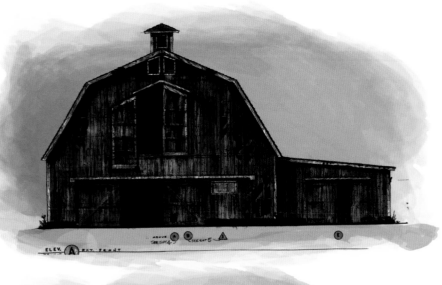

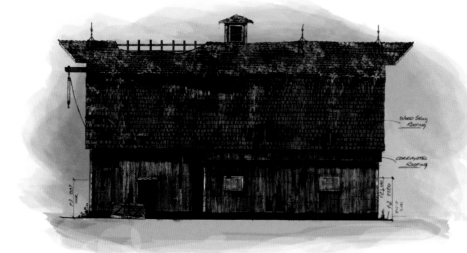

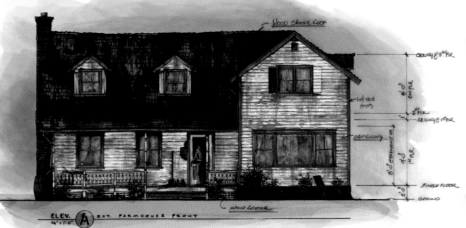

ELEV. Ⓐ EXT. FARMHOUSE FRONT

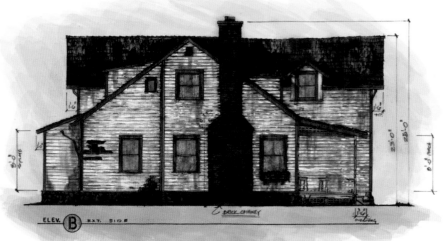

ELEV. Ⓑ EXT. SIDE

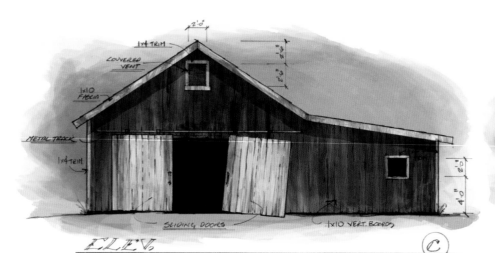

ELEV. Ⓒ

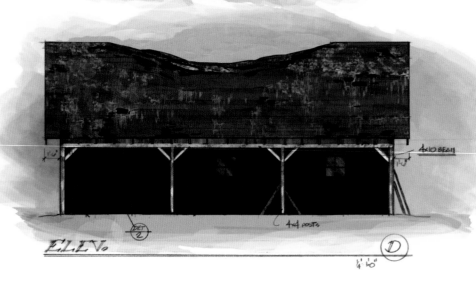

ELEV. Ⓓ

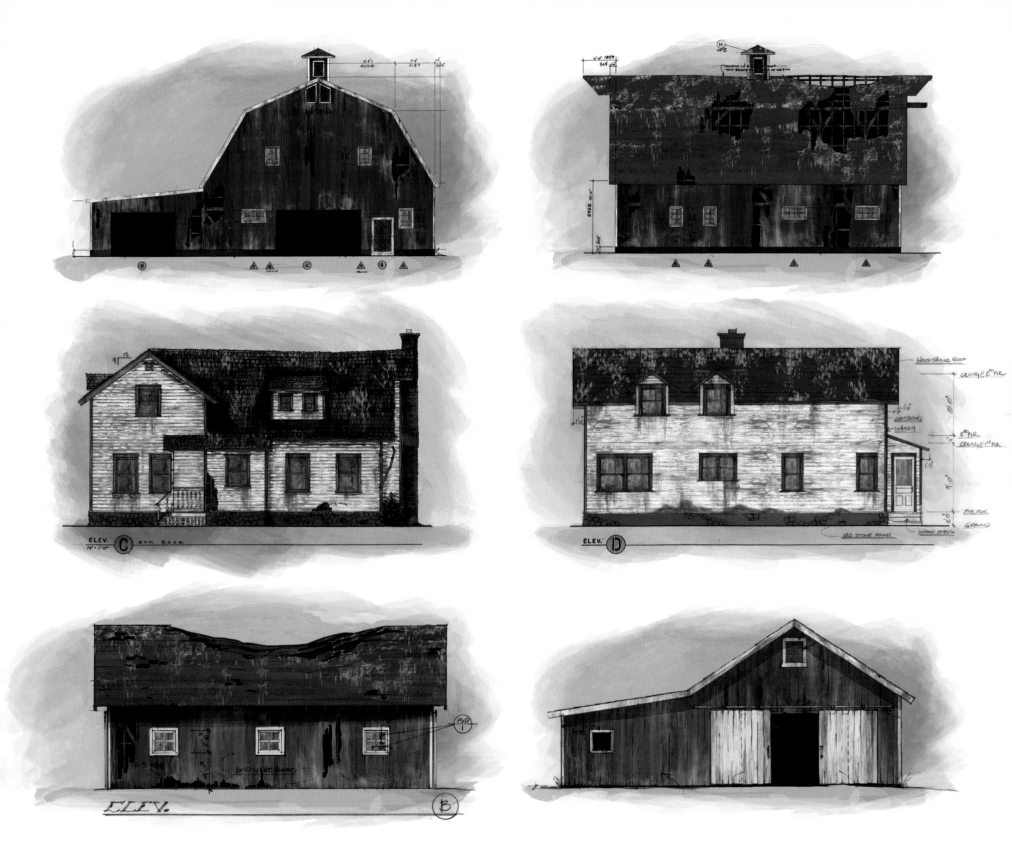

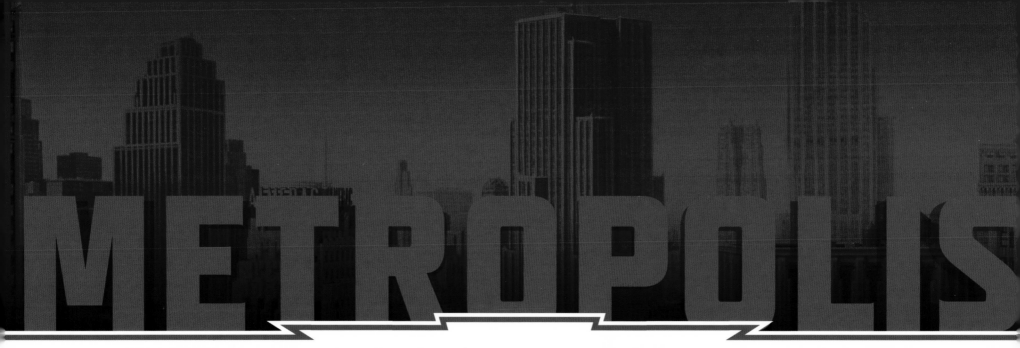

METROPOLIS

New York Above 14th Street ◇ Fantastic Backdrops
Egyptian Artifacts ◇ Shuster Square ◇ The Journalist's Creed
All the President's Men ◇ The Ace O'Clubs
Why the World Doesn't Need Superman

Metropolis is a city of heroic proportions. It is a sunny urban sprawl of optimism, progress, and, as often envisioned in the comics, retro-futurism. Clark Kent toils away at his keyboard as a reporter for the *Daily Planet,* but a swift change in to Superman is just a broom closet away. Buildings stretch into the sky as if to challenge their champion, who is sometimes known here as the Man of Tomorrow.

The locale first appeared by name in 1939's *Action Comics #16.* Usually viewed as a stand-in for New York City, the original Metropolis also incorporated elements from Joe Shuster's birthplace, Toronto, and his hometown, Cleveland, Ohio. Denny O'Neil, writer of Batman comics during the '70s, once said that Metropolis represents New York above 14th Street (whereas Batman's Gotham City envelops the grittier environs below that cutoff point). It has also been said that if Gotham City is New York at nighttime, Metropolis is New York during the day.

Those comparisons are, of course, metaphors. New York exists as a distinct, separate location in the Superman canon. The previous Superman movies, however, muddied the waters by including the Statue of Liberty and other obvious New York landmarks in aerial shots of what was ostensibly Metropolis. Guy Dyas had no intention of perpetuating the confusion. "Do we want to use New York?" says the production manager. "The answer was clearly no."

But Dyas and his crew had a tricky time deciding just where to put the city. Even though their decision had no direct bearing on the movie itself, they tried to plot Metropolis into a zone of existing geography without simply swapping it for New York. On an oversize map, they undertook a wholesale revamp of the Eastern seaboard of the United States. "We wiped out, I think, half of New Jersey to put in Metropolis."

"We will not see any recognizable buildings," continues Dyas, emphasizing the need to make Metropolis both fictional and familiar. "It will have a strong flavor that will very much remind you of central Chicago or Manhattan, and yet it's not [either one]."

To get that flavor, Dyas began collecting images before a single page of the script had been penned. "Bryan, Dan, and Mike went off for a writing session in New York for two weeks," he remembers. The director and screenwriters "basically hid in a hotel and wrote the script. I was invited up to do the legwork of exploring Manhattan north to south, east to west, to catalog the buildings and the atmosphere of New York."

Dyas walks behind his desk and begins pulling sketches off the wall. One two-panel illustration shows a squat building in a classic prewar architectural style, then shows the same building looking as if it's been force-fed growth hormones. "We're going to take pieces of '30s architecture and stretch them like

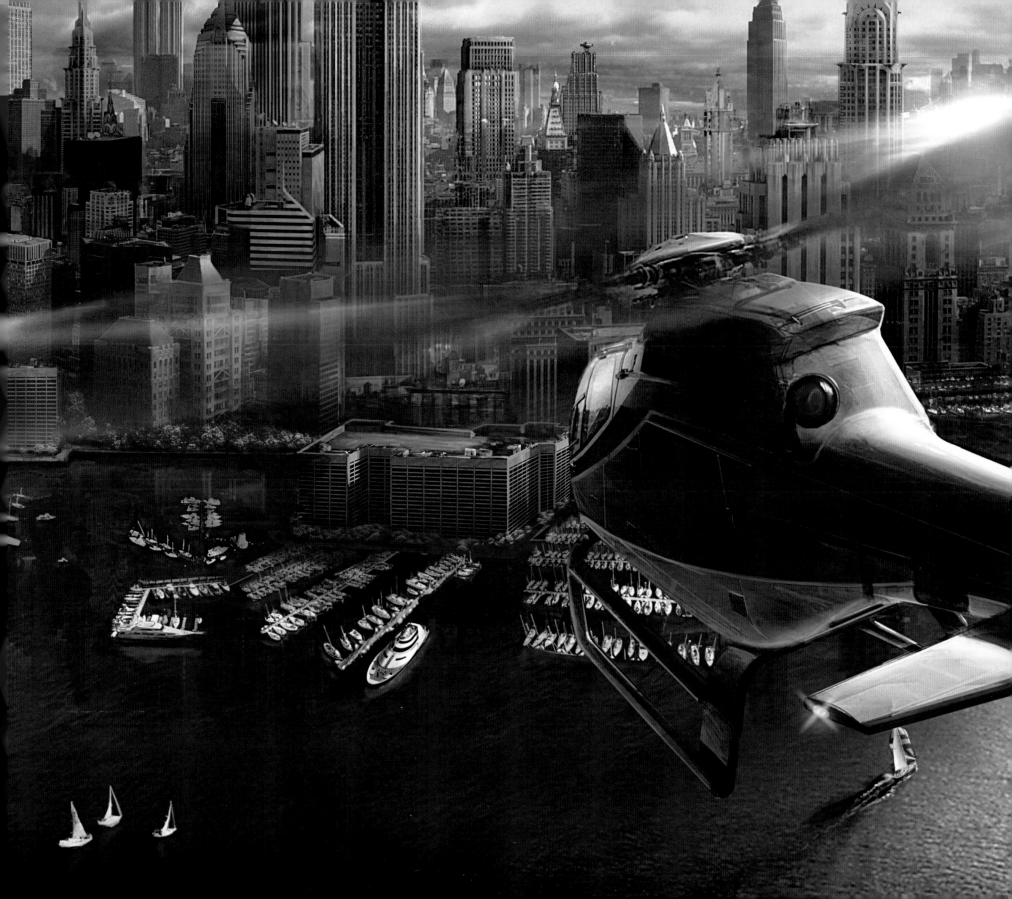

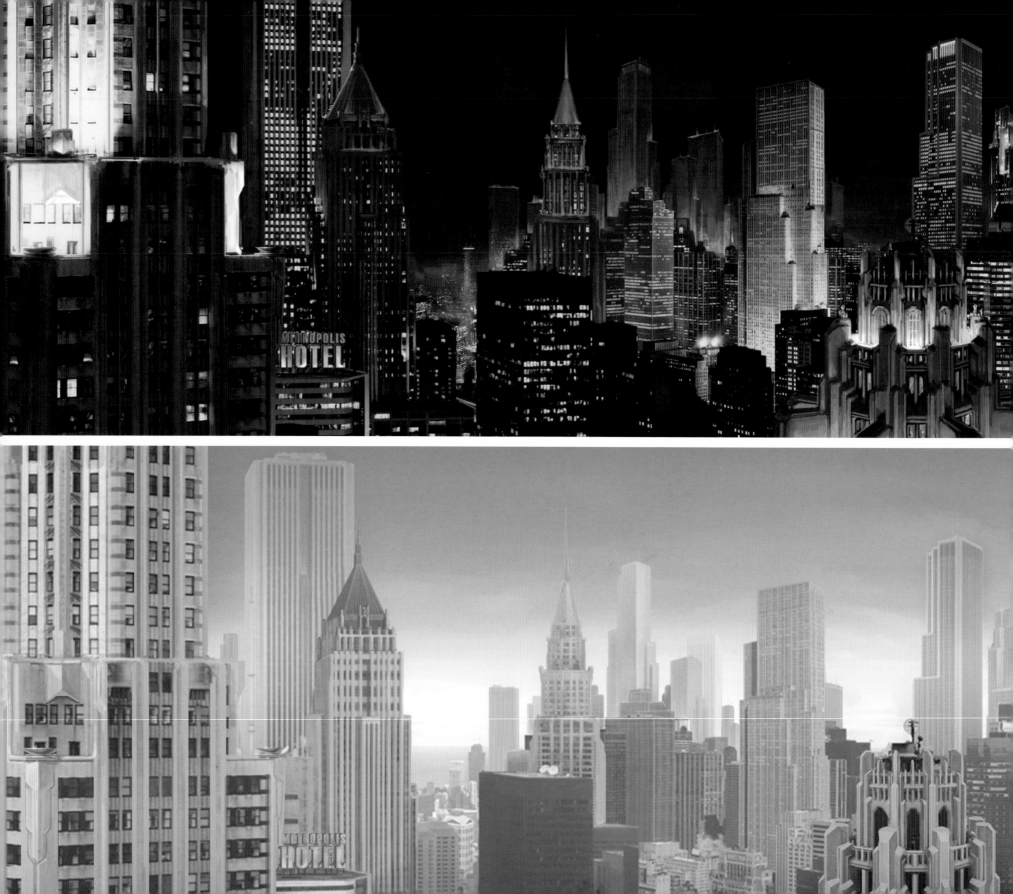

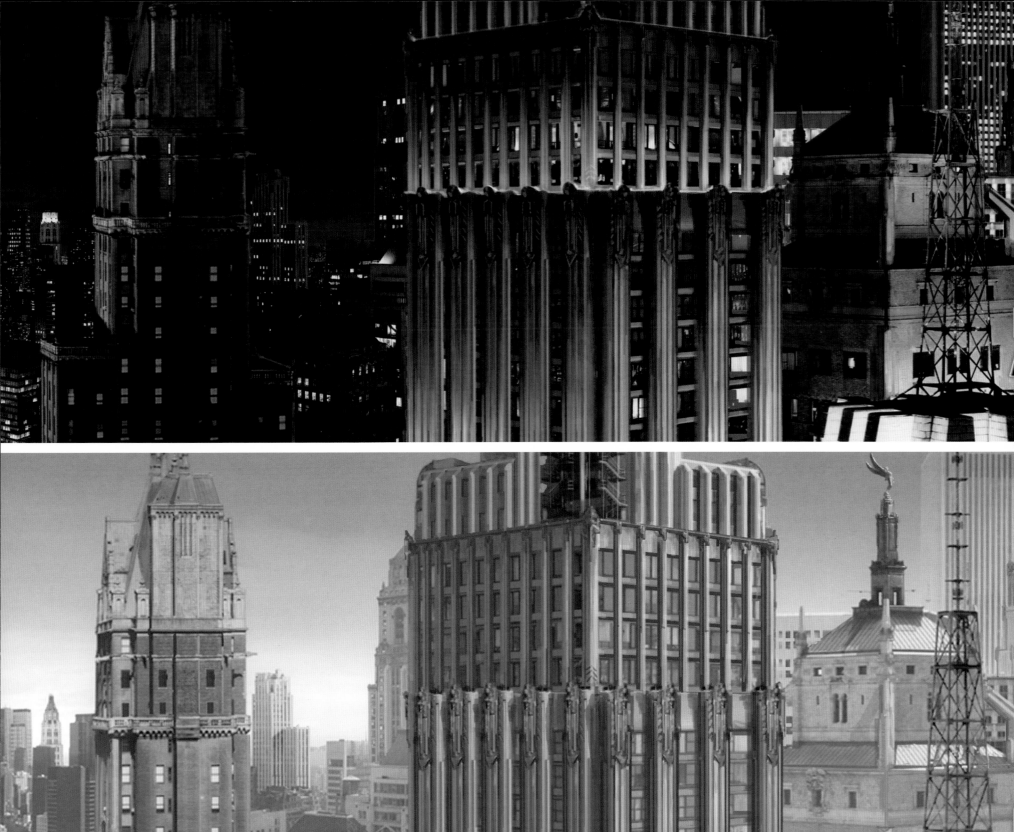

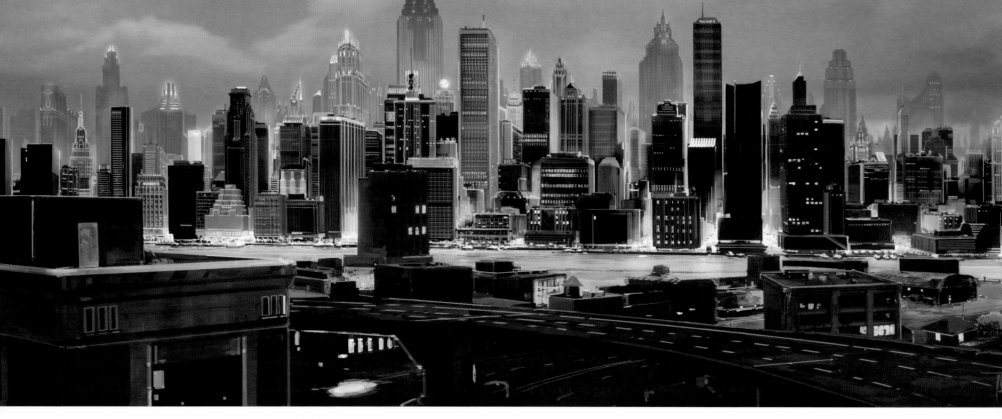

ABOVE   *Metropolis, with a river and freeway in the foreground.*
Tani Kunitake, digital, June 2005.

OPPOSITE PAGE   *The skyscrapers of Metropolis climb to*
dizzying heights. Colin Grant, pencil and marker, June 2005.

PAGE 65   *Lex Luthor's helicopter approaches downtown*
Metropolis. Jeff Julian, digital, May 2005.

PAGES 66-67   *Daytime and nighttime views of the Metropolis*
skyline, as seen from the Daily Planet Building. Jeff Julian,
photographic composite and digital, May 2005.

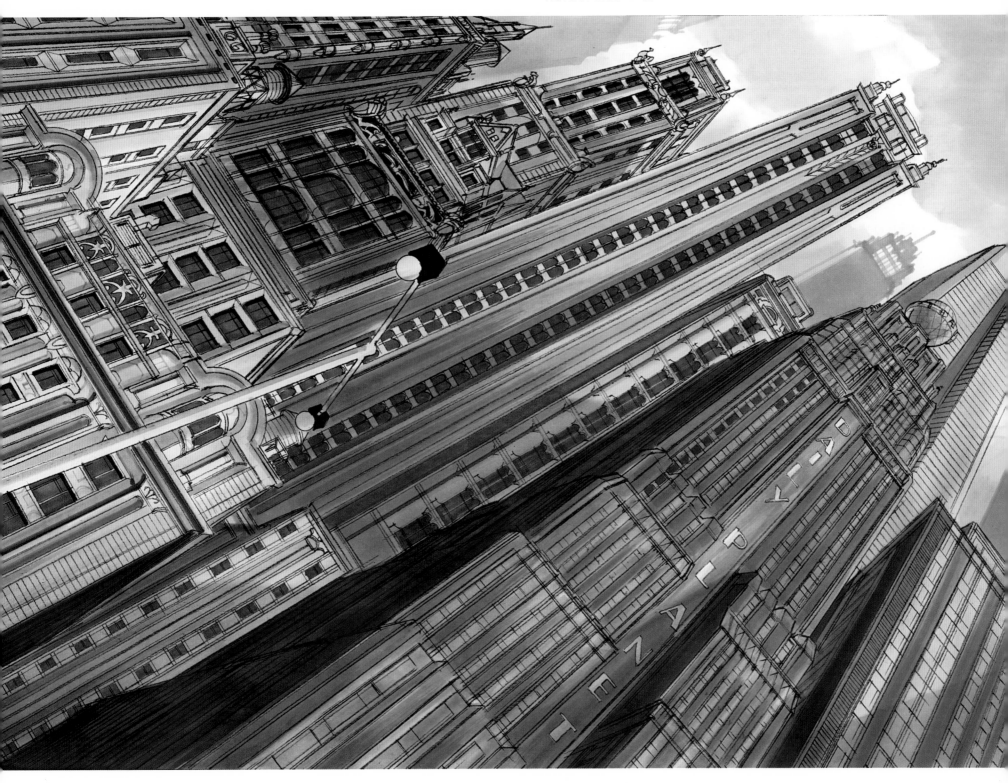

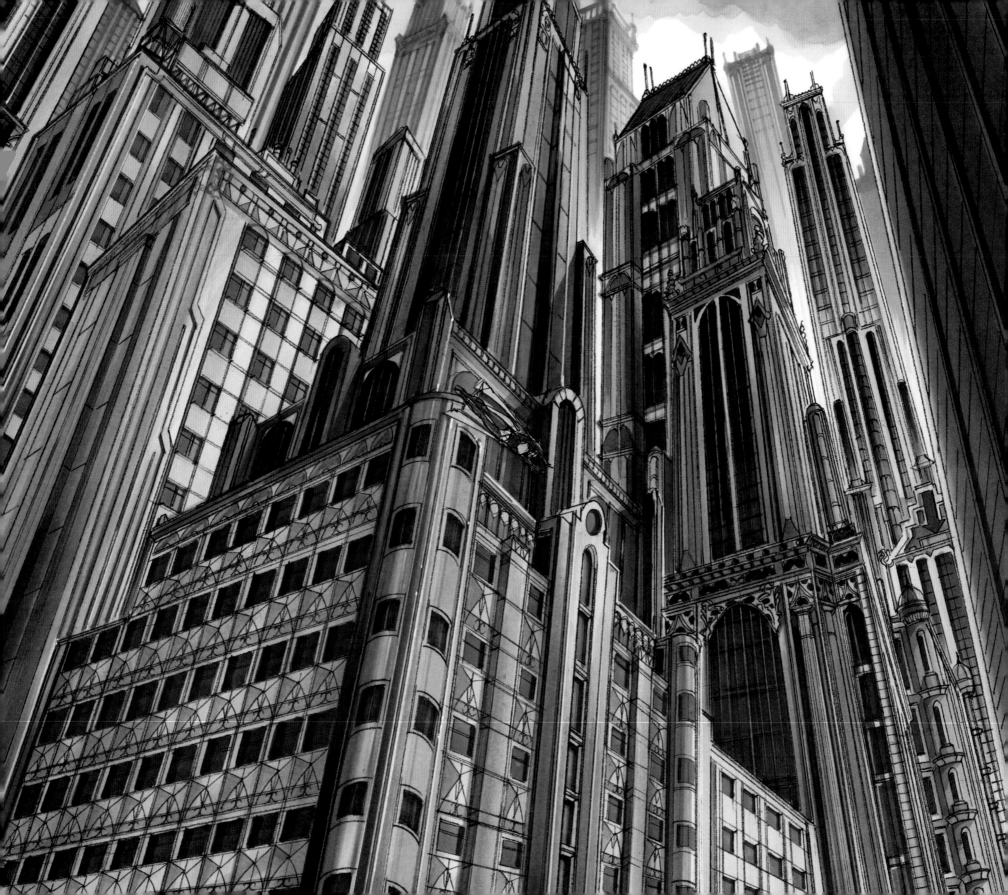

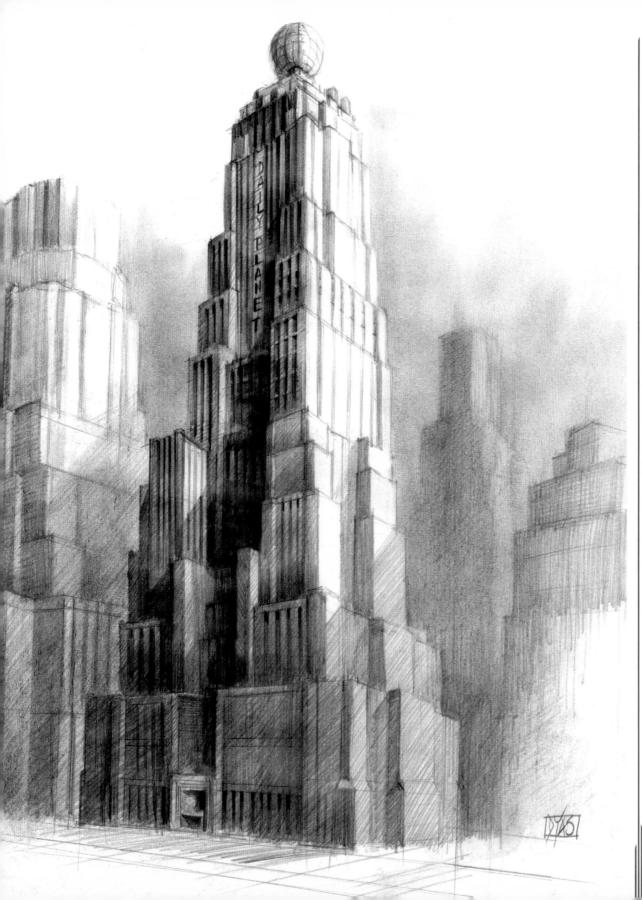

an elastic band," he says. "We add, say, 30 percent to the height of all the architecture, almost as if the engineers could build higher than they really could at the time. So we end up with these elongated walls of buildings as fantastic backdrops."

It is against these backdrops that Superman will soar. The three-dimensional urban canyons of Metropolis couldn't be more different from the flat fields of Smallville. It's an interesting evolution—as Clark's powers of flight mature, he moves from a horizontal to a vertical environment. Dyas agrees. "It's the best place for Superman to live, simply because the height of the buildings gives him a more interesting world to fly around in."

The overall aesthetic for the Daily Planet Building (and much of Metropolis) is art deco, a style developed in the 1920s that drew equally from Jazz Age and Machine Age influences. Art deco incorporates sweeping curves and zigzag patterns inspired by Aztec and Egyptian artifacts. "Deco's a beautiful, very [simple] style that is quite easy to re-create," says Dyas, but adds, "it's hard to do it well. One of the things that I latched on to was this stepping motif." Right-angle zigzags are prevalent in deco hot spots such as the Planet Building's elevator doors and bank of time-zone clocks. "You'll see that a lot in the film."

Metropolis's amalgamated look subtly balances the competing influences of retro and modernism. Bryan Singer oversaw every aspect of the city's appearance. "When you adapt these kinds of worlds that are based on people's collective memory, you try to take the best for yourself from that collective memory," he says. "Superman evolved in the late '30s, and to pay homage to that architecture and place us in a city that's unique to itself just made sense to me."

OPPOSITE PAGE *Vertical Metropolis. Colin Grant, pencil and marker, June 2005.*

LEFT *The first sketch of Daily Planet Building exterior. Guy Dyas, pencil, November 2004.*

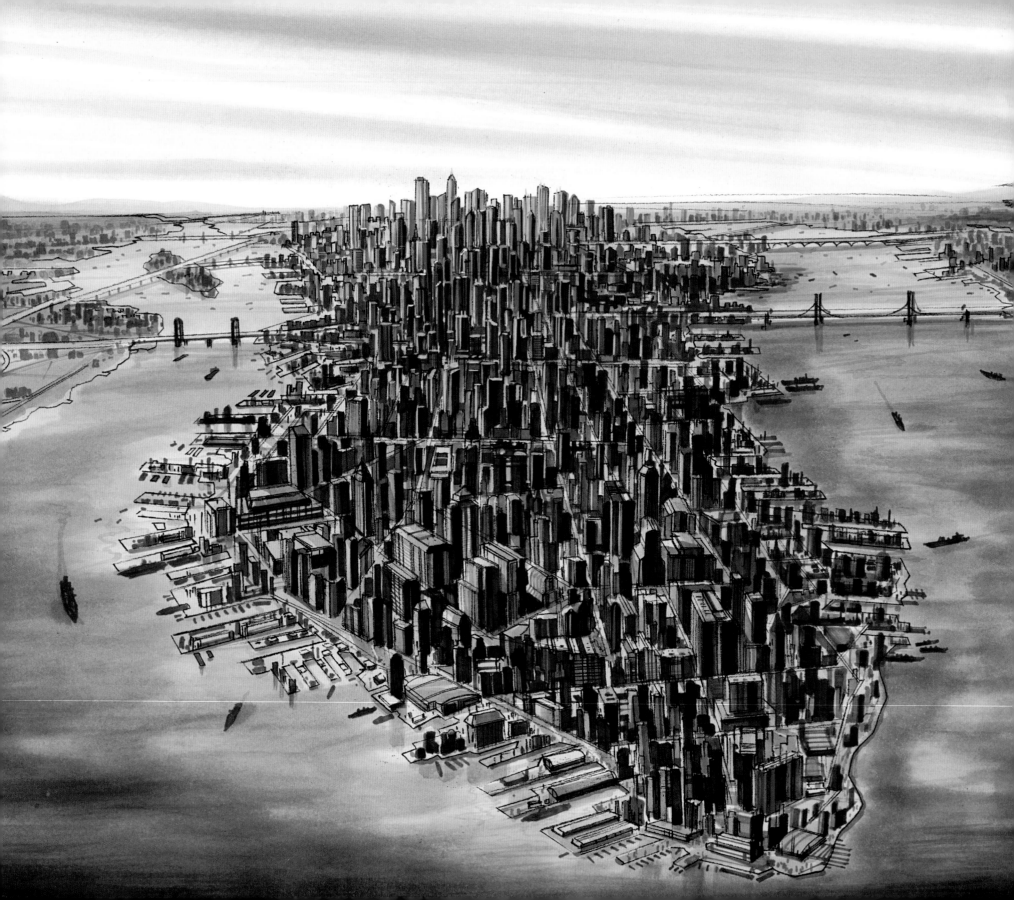

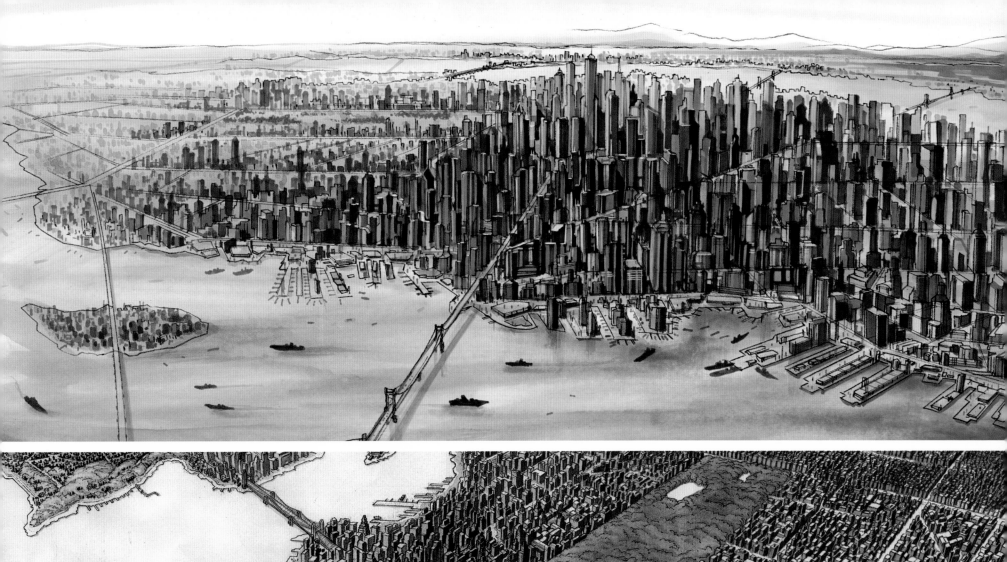
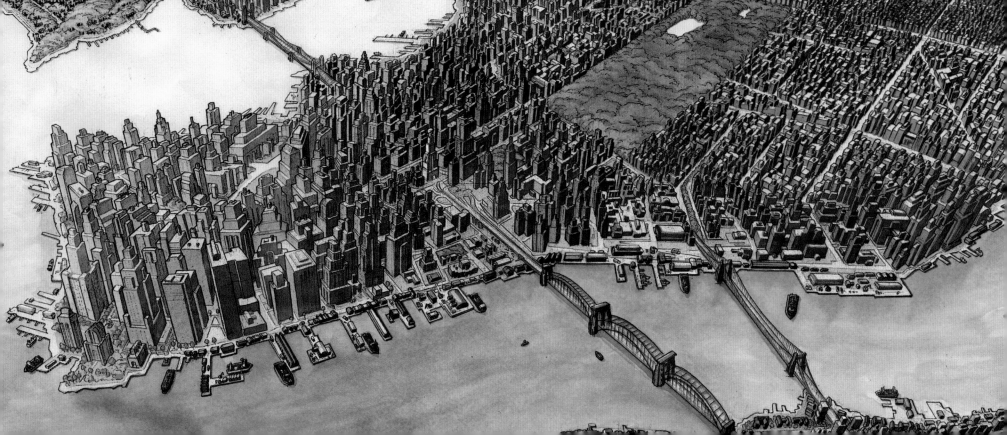

The Daily Planet Building's exterior plaza and lobby is a towering outdoor set, being too large for any soundstage on the Fox lot. Nestled into the gap between Stage 2 and Stage 3, it faces a grassy median that has been dressed up to become a public park known as Shuster Square (named in honor of Superman's co-creator). "Originally Bryan conceived [the entryway] as being on a stage," says Dyas. "We said, well, it's supposed to be an exterior anyway, let's just put it outside between two stages, and utilize the structure of the stages to hold the set up."

Climbing the steps to the *Daily Planet* office and pushing through the gilt-and-glass revolving doors, it's easy to get caught up in the realism of the setting. Dyas and his crew have re-created the foundation of a great period edifice, such as the Empire State Building or the Chrysler Building. Inside the highly elaborate lobby is a gigantic hand-painted frieze depicting heroic workers toiling around a typewriter, in the style of labor painter Diego Rivera. "That's basically our interpretation of Industry," explains Dyas. The words on the frieze are the Journalist's Creed. Not until Dyas points it out does it become apparent that the lobby is too small to easily service a building meant to be 65 stories tall, a result of the limited space available for set construction between the stages.

A separate soundstage holds the *Daily Planet* bureau. It's a long set, anchored on one end by an elevator bank and on the other by editor-in-chief Perry White's roomy office. The elevator doors are adorned with gold inlay, and framed front pages of the *Daily Planet,* marking great moments in history, line the walls of the elevator lobby. In Superman history, "the Daily Planet Building was established in 1932," mentions Dyas, noting that headlines such as THE TITANIC SINKS predate that event by a wide margin. "So you just have to take a leap of faith that the *Daily Planet* was working out of some second-rate building down by the docks for several years before they upgraded. It was probably stories like these that put them on the map."

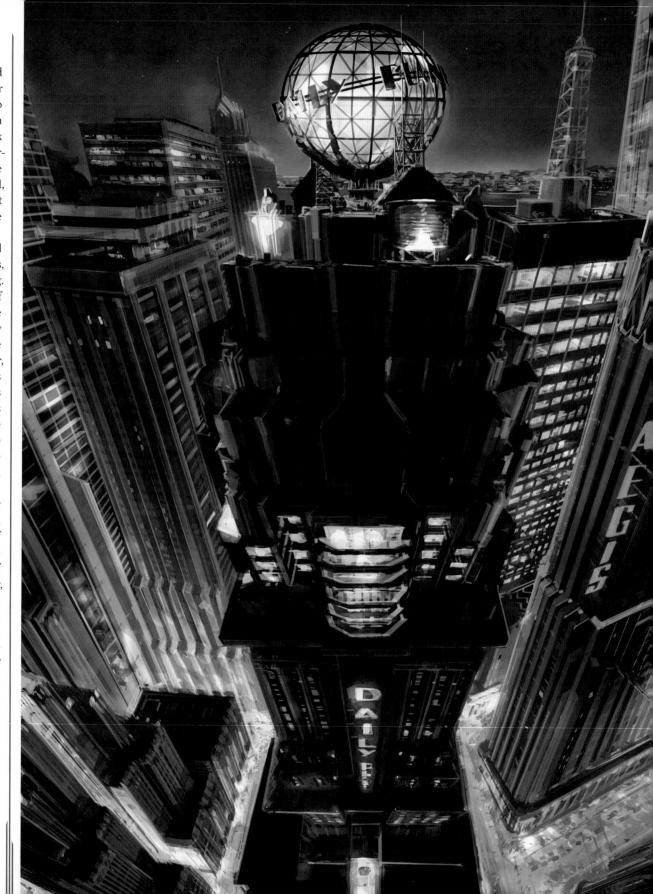

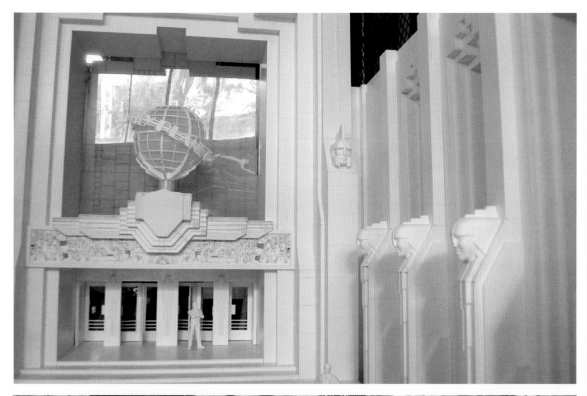

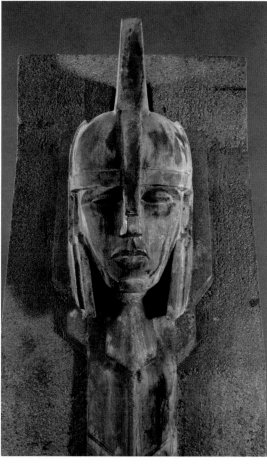

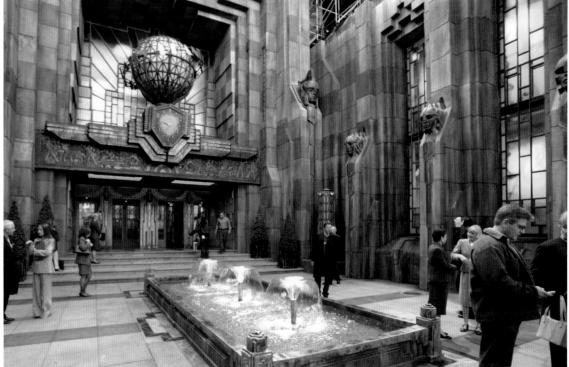

ABOVE LEFT *Unpainted model of the Daily Planet Building's exterior plaza. Shari Finn and Lewis Morley, card and paper, May 2005.*

ABOVE RIGHT *One of the art deco–inspired warrior heads flanking the Daily Planet Building's exterior plaza. Katrina Adams, 2005.*

LEFT *Photograph of the Daily Planet entryway. Note the edge-of-set scaffolding at top of frame. David James, June 2005.*

OPPOSITE PAGE *The luminous Daily Planet globe is the centerpiece of a busy Metropolis night. Tani Kunitake, digital, July 2005.*

PAGES 72-73 *Metropolis borrows its density and structure from Manhattan. Chew Chan and Colin Grant, pencil and marker, June 2005.*

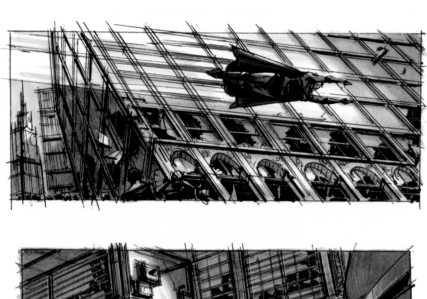

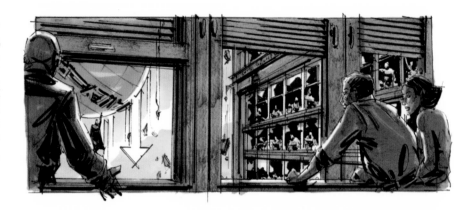

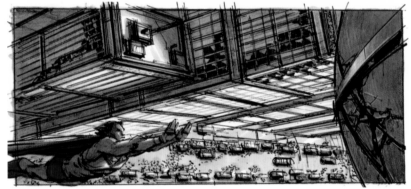

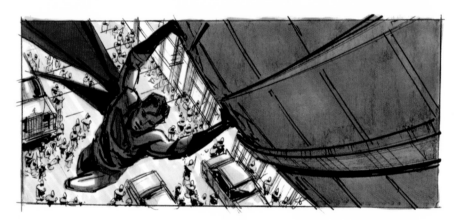

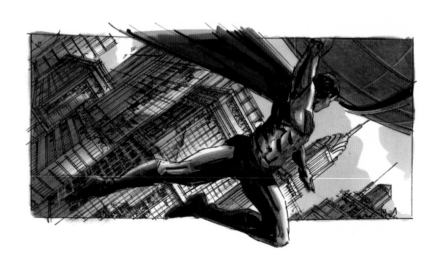

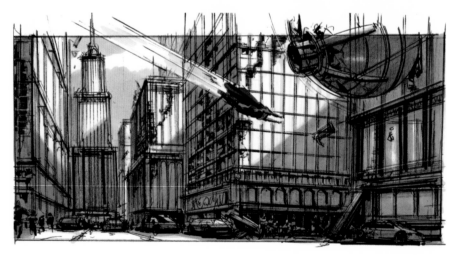

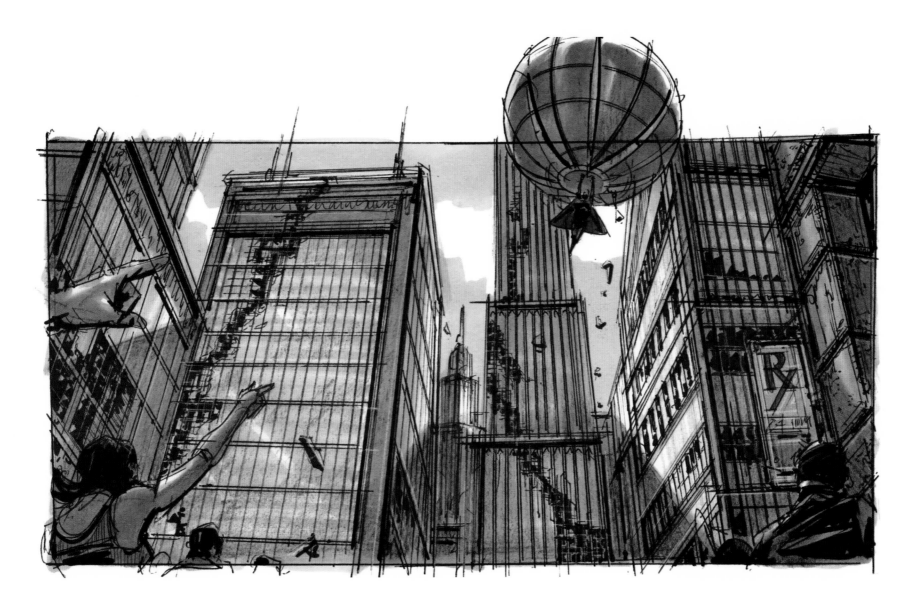

OPPOSITE PAGE AND ABOVE *Superman catches the tumbling Daily Planet globe in these dramatic key frames. Ed Natividad, pencil and marker, April 2005.*

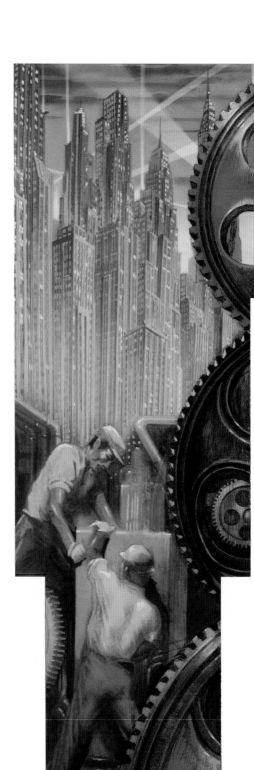

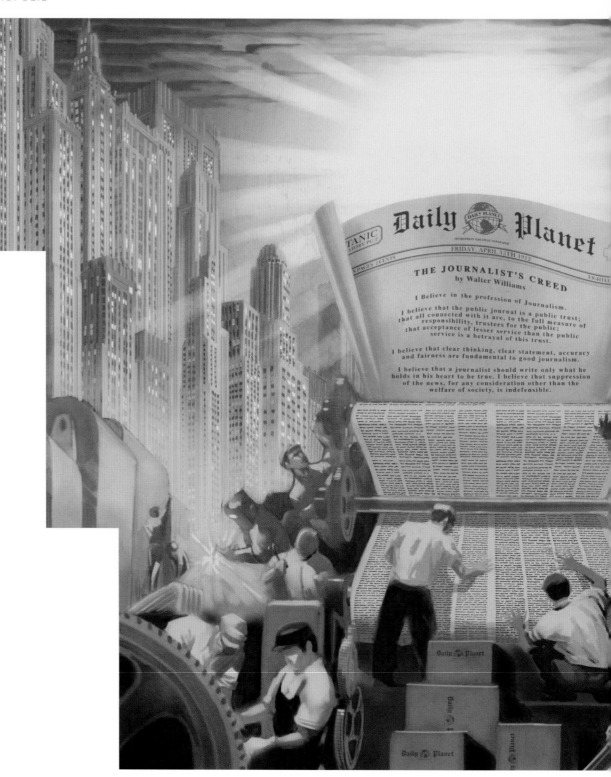

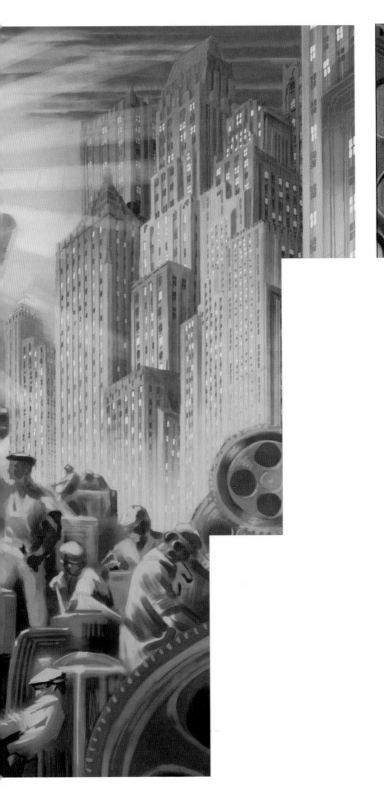

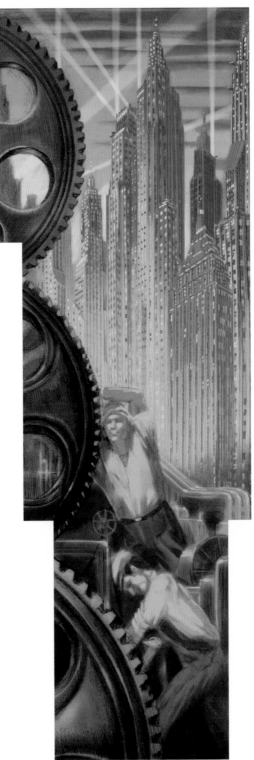

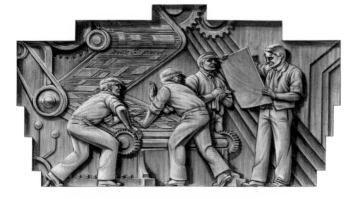

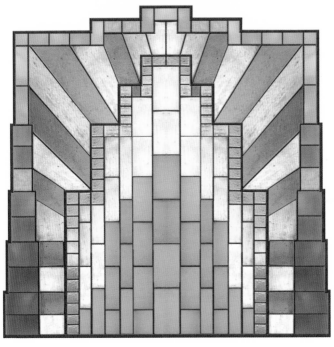

TOP *Daily Planet wall detail. Philip Holliday, pen and ink, May 2005.*

ABOVE *Glass paneling detail from window in the Daily Planet Building's exterior plaza. Matt Hatton, digital, May 2005.*

LEFT *The frieze behind the Daily Planet Building's reception desk is a rendition of "The Journalist's Creed." Matt Hatton, digital, May 2005.*

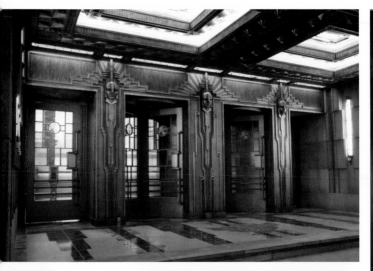

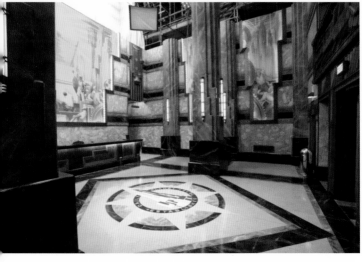

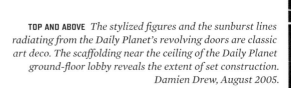

TOP AND ABOVE *The stylized figures and the sunburst lines radiating from the Daily Planet's revolving doors are classic art deco. The scaffolding near the ceiling of the Daily Planet ground-floor lobby reveals the extent of set construction. Damien Drew, August 2005.*

RIGHT *Metallic panel that decorates the interior of the Daily Planet Building's elevators. In art deco style, it highlights the glory of the building. Matt Hatton, digital, May 2005.*

OPPOSITE PAGE *The* Daily Planet *seal decorates the polished floors of the ground-floor lobby. Jim Feldman, pencil and marker, April 2005.*

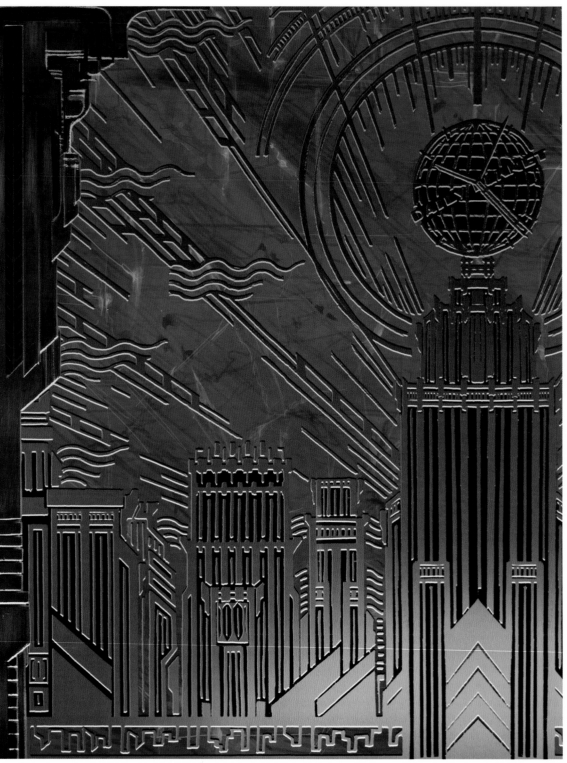

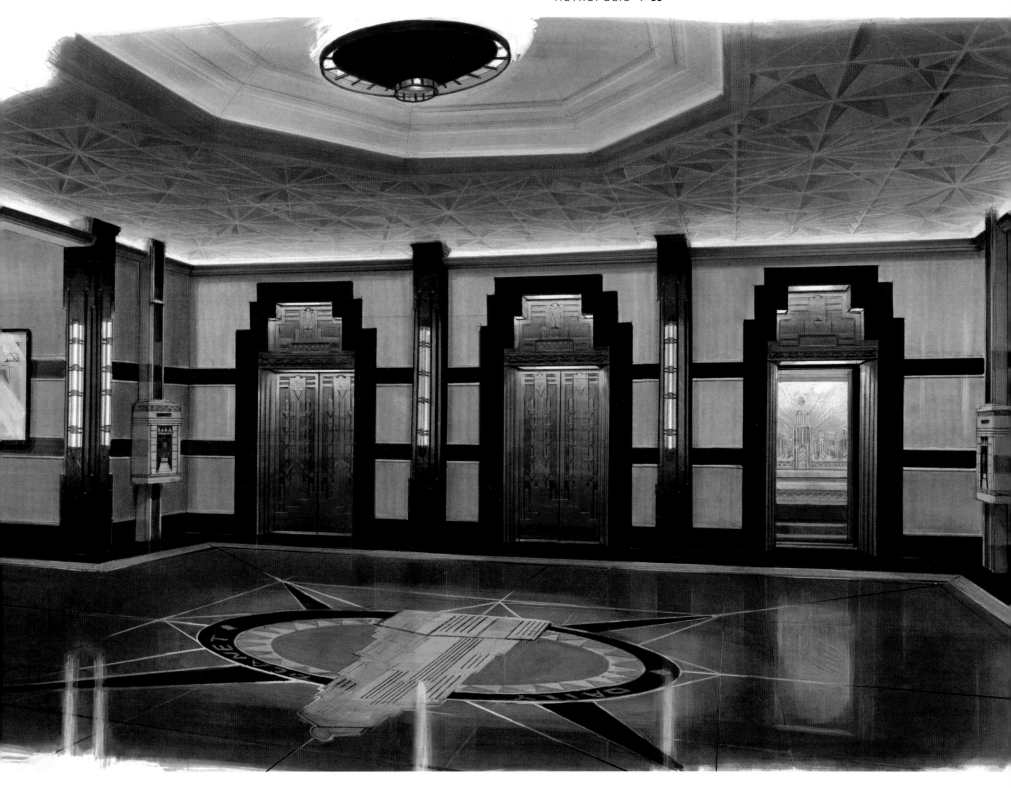

A lane of carpet leads visitors through the reporters' bull pen, which is exceptionally messy as the crew films the aftermath of a Metropolis earthquake. Support columns, inspired by those in Frank Lloyd Wright's Johnson Wax Building, are fitted with dramatically flaring "capitals" a few feet below the actual ceiling. The resulting illusion is that nothing but air supports the roof. "Originally the brief was to make the bull pen look like *All the President's Men*: very basic, square columns and a flat ceiling," says Dyas. However, he points out, a lot of the script is set in the newspaper office. "And it's a very boring space to be in if nothing's going on in terms of the look of the set. We have this floating ceiling, we have these columns, we have these side offices and a lot of glass to create depth. We filled it with lots of detail."

The script's earthquake tremors have made their effects felt on the bull pen set. Shattered coffee cups lie on the floor; fallen picture frames gaze up at the ceiling. "We went to great lengths in the Daily Planet to provide Bryan with a very realistic environment," says Dyas. "There's everything from Lois Lane's business card to fax paper, letterhead, and envelopes that all have the *Daily Planet* logo. There are family photos. Every desk in the Daily Planet has a character that sits there and has their own story to tell." A *Daily Planet* screen saver crawls across the flat-screen computer monitors on many of the unattended desks. Members of the *Superman Returns* production crew installed the same screen saver for use on their personal workstations.

At the far end of the bull pen is Perry White's window office. The walls are decorated with framed honors (one wonders how Perry earned the "Bryan Singer award") and a bookcase holds leather-bound back issues of the *Planet*. Outside the panoramic glass panels are two stylized ram's heads, architectural details that Dyas points out are quite different from the gloomy gargoyles that dominate Batman's Gotham City. "[The ram's heads] are deco style, as opposed to the visually heavier gothic style. If the Daily Planet Building was created in the '30s, it's bound to have some of those embellishments. It's a very grand building."

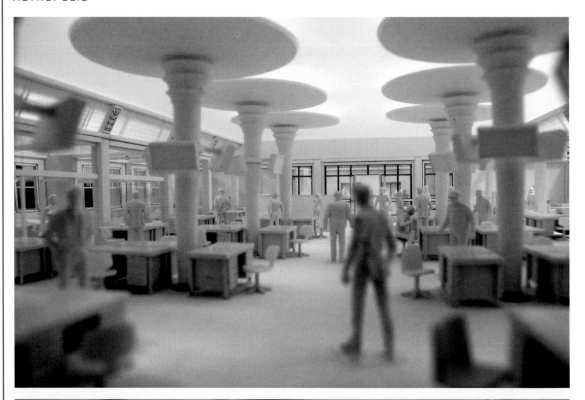

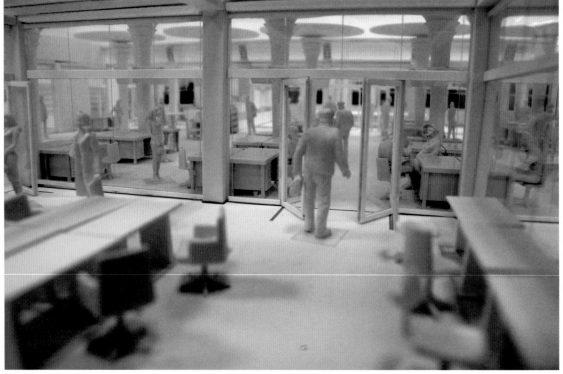

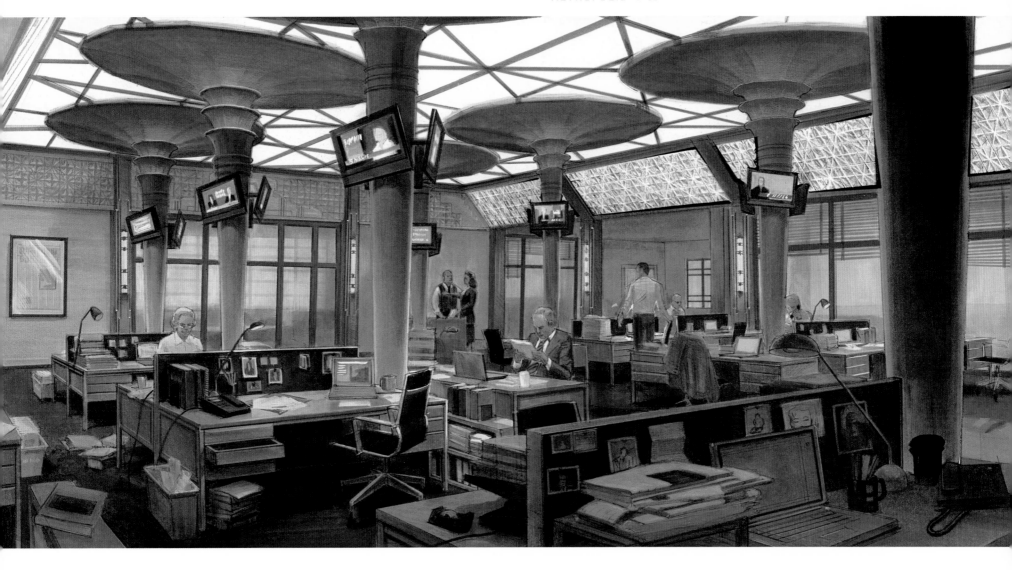

ABOVE *Interior of the Daily Planet bull pen. Flat-screen televisions mounted on the support columns provide live coverage of breaking news, alerting Clark Kent to any situation that looks like a job for Superman. Jim Feldman, pencil and marker, April 2005.*

OPPOSITE PAGE TOP *Interior of the Daily Planet bull pen. The flared pillars, known as dendriform columns, were modeled after those in the Frank Lloyd Wright–designed Johnson Wax Building. Scott Lukowski and Brett Philips; card, plastic, and paper; April 2005.*

OPPOSITE PAGE BOTTOM *Miniature model of the Daily Planet conference room. Scott Lukowski and Brett Philips; card, plastic, and paper; April 2005.*

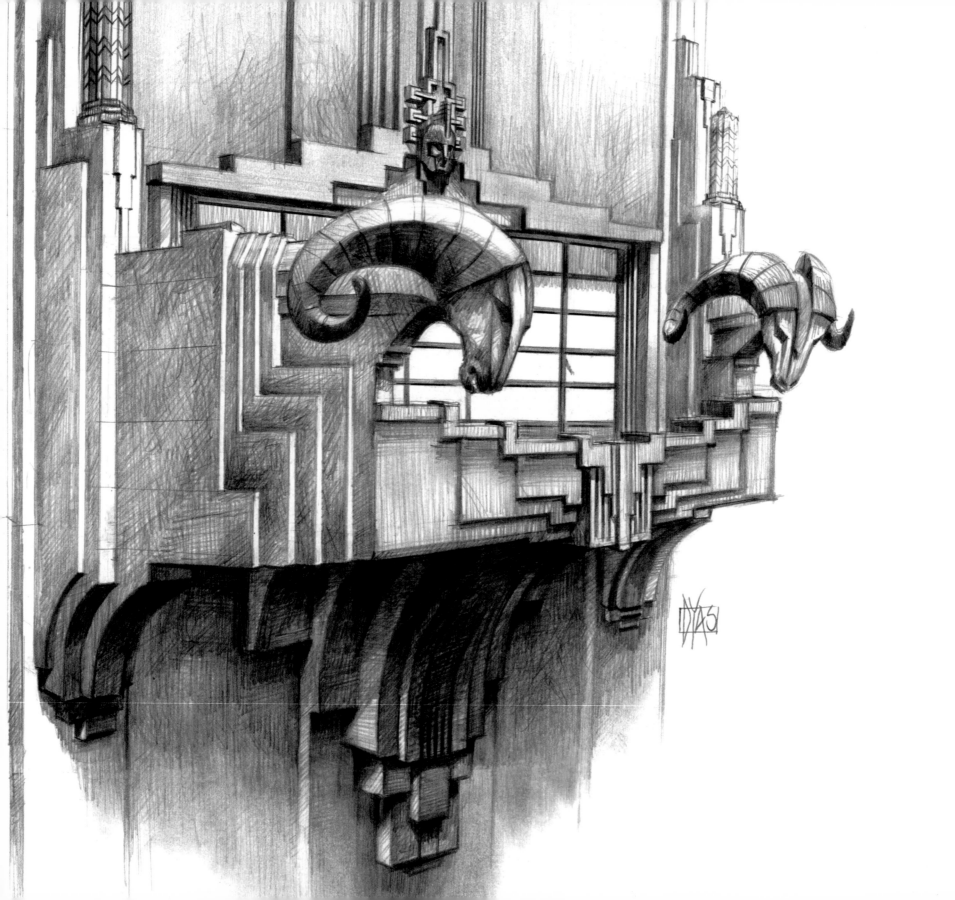

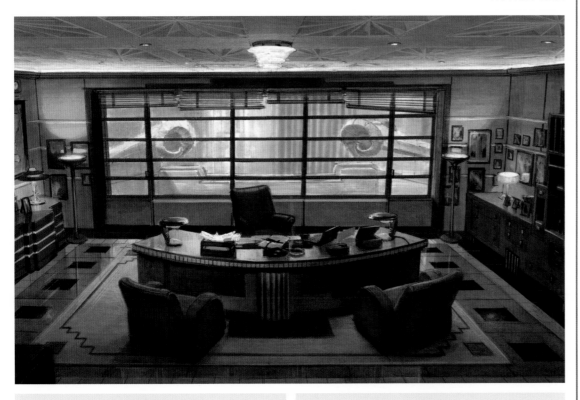

Back in Dyas's office, he flips through a photo book to show off the Metropolis locations that were shot locally in the city of Sydney and its environs. "Sydney is a beautiful city, but it's not New York," he laments. "The basis of the stone that they use here, the scale of the buildings—forget the direction that they drive. Everything's wrong. So it's an enormous task to create Metropolis."

"This is a real place in Sydney," he continues, finding a photo of the Art Gallery of New South Wales. In the film, visual effects will reshape the building's exterior to turn the art gallery into the Metropolis Museum of Natural History. "We suggested to the director and DP [director of photography] the use of a color palette change, growing the urban architecture, losing indigenous species of plants that don't grow on the East Coast, and [taking] the pinky tones out of the stone."

A Belgian beer tavern in downtown Sydney became a setting that Dyas calls "an old boxer's bar," the Ace O'Clubs, which has made occasional appearances in the Superman comics. The actor tending bar is Jack Larson, who played cub reporter Jimmy Olsen in the 1950s television show *The Adventures of Superman.*

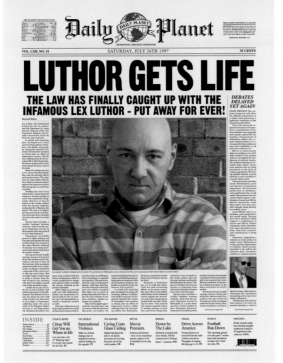

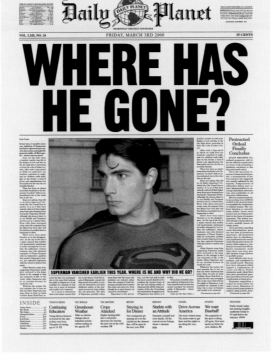

TOP *Editor-in-chief Perry White's office. Jim Feldman, pencil and marker, April 2005.*

LEFT Daily Planet *front-page variations. Suzanne Buljan, Nadia King, and Nick Tory; digital; 2005.*

OPPOSITE PAGE *Pencil sketch of art deco ram's heads that adorn the exterior of the Daily Planet Building. Guy Dyas, pencil, March 2005.*

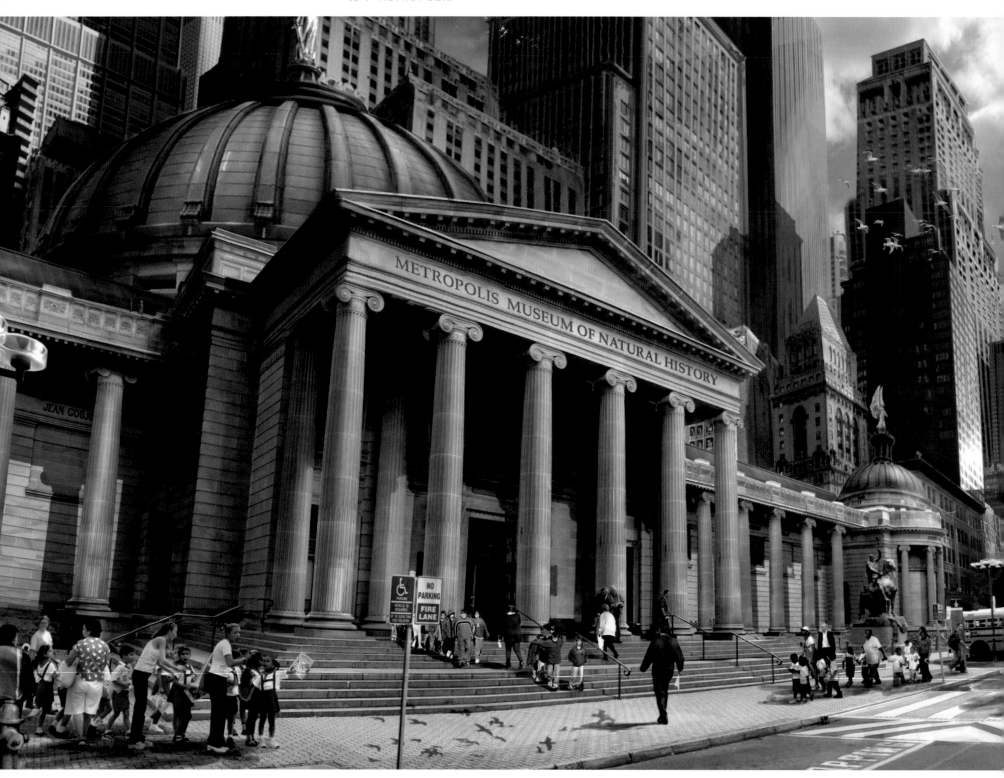

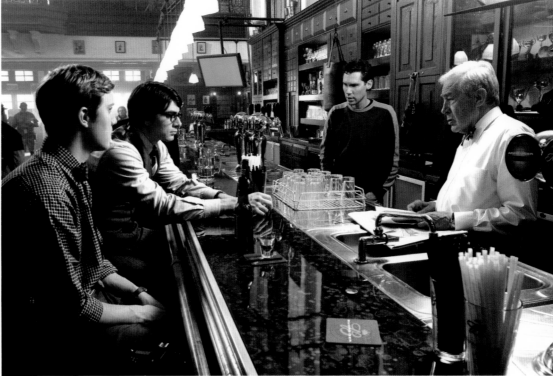

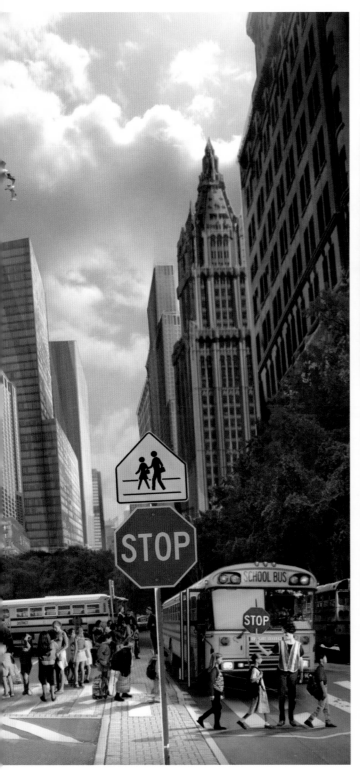

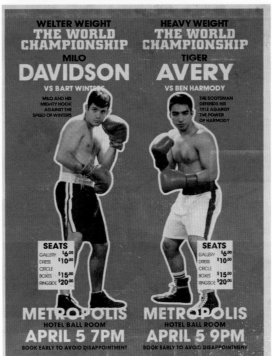

WELTER WEIGHT
HEAVY WEIGHT
THE WORLD CHAMPIONSHIP
THE WORLD CHAMPIONSHIP

MILO
DAVIDSON
TIGER
AVERY

VS BART WINTERS
VS BEN HARMODY

MILO AND HIS
MIGHTY HOOK
AGAINST THE
SPEED OF WINTERS

THE SCOTSMAN
DEFENDS HIS
TITLE AGAINST
THE POWER
OF HARMODY

SEATS
GALLERY $6.00
DRESS $10.00
CIRCLE
BOXES $15.00
RINGSIDE $20.00

SEATS
GALLERY $6.00
DRESS $10.00
CIRCLE
BOXES $15.00
RINGSIDE $20.00

METROPOLIS
HOTEL BALL ROOM
APRIL 5 7PM
BOOK EARLY TO AVOID DISAPPOINTMENT

METROPOLIS
HOTEL BALL ROOM
APRIL 5 9PM
BOOK EARLY TO AVOID DISAPPOINTMENT

ABOVE *A Belgian beer tavern in Sydney was dressed with fight posters and other boxing adornments to become the Ace O'Clubs. David James, June 2005.*

LEFT *Fight poster from the Ace O'Clubs bar. Nadia King and Suzanne Buljan, digital, May 2005.*

FAR LEFT *This concept illustration served as a guide for the filmmakers when transforming location footage of the Art Gallery of New South Wales into the Metropolis Museum of Natural History. Jeff Julian, digital, July 2005.*

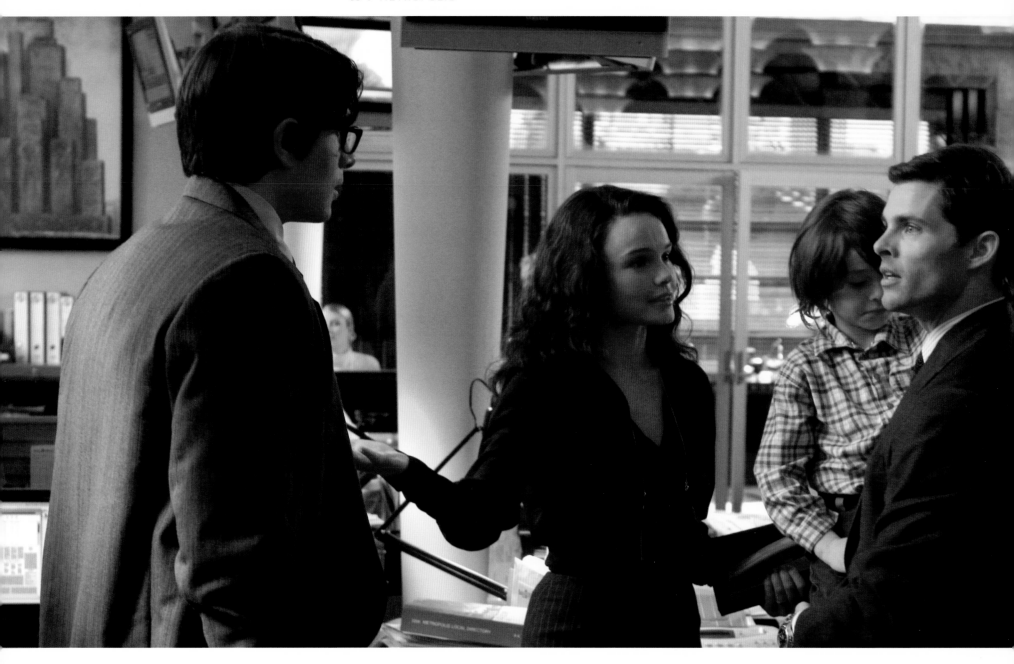

ABOVE *Clark, Lois, Jason, and Richard in the bull pen. David James, July 2005.*

OPPOSITE PAGE *Rejected by the costume department as "too sweet" for Lois Lane as portrayed by Kate Bosworth, this sketch was one of several explorations of 1950s-inspired fashion. E.J. Krizer, pencil, March 2005.*

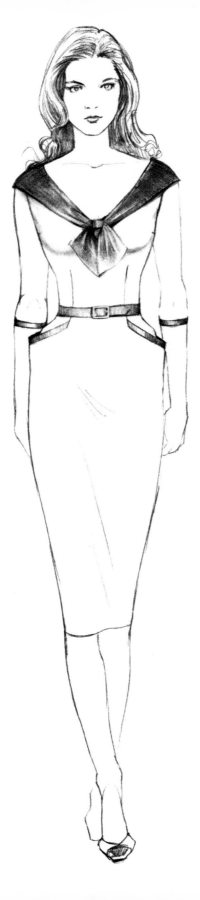

Lois Lane is an inseparable part of the Superman mythos, both as the hero's professional rival and as his love interest. As a fellow reporter at the *Daily Planet,* Lois has a quick wit and go-getting gusto that keep her several steps ahead of Clark Kent. Lois and Superman shared immediate sparks during their first meeting, and in the sequel to *Superman: The Movie* their mutual flirtation grew into a physical relationship. Now, half a decade after Superman vanished from the public eye, Lois has moved on to a new life with Richard White, whose uncle is *Daily Planet* editor Perry White. The two are raising a five-year-old son named Jason.

"Lois has moved on with her life," says screenwriter Dan Harris. "She's in love, she has a family, and she's not ready for Superman to be back in her life. By coming home to meet Lois's child, Clark/Superman has to deal with a whole variety of contemporary issues that have never been part of a Superman film before." Dougherty acknowledges that audiences "don't want to see Superman as a home wrecker." Adding to the character's dilemma is the fact that Richard is a likable individual and not a two-dimensional cad. "It gives [Superman] something very real to confront."

Kate Bosworth plays Lois Lane in *Superman Returns*. In the costume department are dozens of concepts for Lois that draw upon nearly every era of fashion. Costume designer Louise Mingenbach explains: "Superman's been influential since the '30s, so in terms of the day wear, we thought it would be nice to incorporate some from every decade." Her fingers tap specific costume sketches pinned to the wall. "References to the '30s, the '40s, the '50s, the '60s, the '70s . . . " She hesitates. "Well, not so much the '60s. We kind of skipped over the '60s."

"I showed Bryan these sketches as conceptual ideas," Mingenbach continues, "and he said yes, yes, yes, but it depended on who he casts." When Bosworth came on board, the costume department had a new focus. Bosworth would be 22 at the time of filming, and the script described a Lois who was presumably in her 30s. "Our challenge was to make [Bosworth] look older than she is," says Mingenbach. "Anything with bows went away." She pauses over one drawing of a short dress with a sailor-inspired neckline sash, then quickly dismisses it.

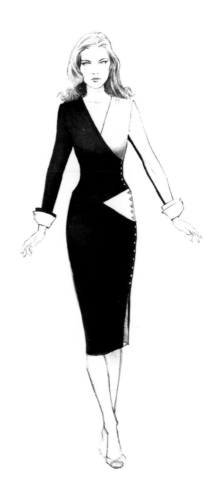

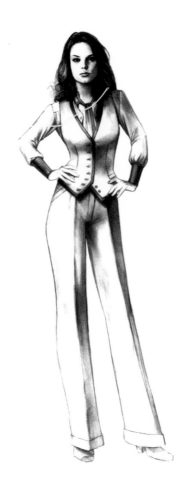

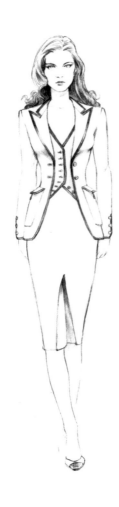

ABOVE LEFT *Lois Lane costume sketch, exploring 1940s design influences. E.J. Krizer, pencil and digital, March 2005.*

ABOVE MIDDLE AND RIGHT *Costume sketches of Lois Lane, inspired by the 1970s styles worn by Margot Kidder in* Superman: The Movie. *E.J. Krizer, pencil and digital, March 2005.*

OPPOSITE PAGE *Lois Lane's Pulitzer ceremony dress, overcoat, and shoes. The dress evokes a 1930s–1940s art deco feel. David James, 2005.*

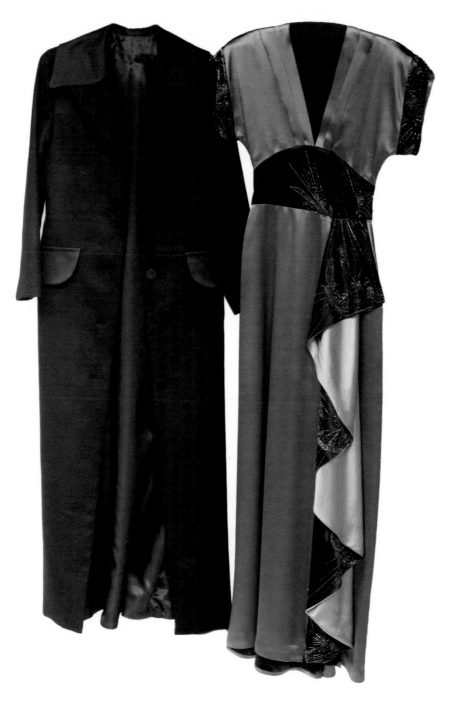

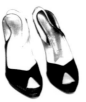

"Too sweet. The look ended up being a little more pantsuit, working woman. It was about keeping her in dark colors."

In the film, Lois wins the Pulitzer Prize for a story entitled "Why the World Doesn't Need Superman." Awkward as the moment might be in the midst of Superman's return, Lois isn't about to miss the ceremony. Lois's Pulitzer dress is art deco all the way, in the spirit of the 1940s. Approximately twenty of the dresses were made in the same design, including trouble-free stunt versions and wet and dry varieties for Lois's adventures aboard the yacht *Gertrude*. "This is extremely expensive to hand bead," explains Bronson, as his hands trace the sparkling loops of the dress's ornamentation, "so we used puff paint [to simulate hand-beading] on the stunt pieces to minimize the cost."

Metropolis is a teeming city, and its residents have been costumed with great care. The style guide for the Metropolitans incorporated elements from all eras, but nothing that audiences would subconsciously flag as having a time stamp. The forbidden list included all revealing modern items such as short shorts and halter tops (Mingenbach: "There's no Paris Hilton in this movie"), as well as any awkwardly retro touches such as fedora hats on men (thus robbing Clark Kent of one of his trademarks, though in truth his hat was already out of place in 1978). "It's subliminal pulses that we're putting out there," says Bronson. "We don't want it to look like a period film, but to have a timeless feel."

"It's really a cosmopolitan town," he continues. "It's a city where you see people in business wear, you see people dressed in suits, sport coats, separates—but they're *dressed*." In Mingenbach's eyes, the costume department's style guide helps create a world that is a distilled and purer version of our shared history. "Ultimately, when you look at this movie it looks classic," she says. "So you look at it [in the future] and don't know when it was made."

It's a sentiment echoed by Harris. "There won't be any reference to modern-day events or pop culture, because we don't want the film to date itself or get old in two or five or ten years. By using classical architecture, colors, and wardrobe from decades ago alongside new cars, phones, and televisions, Metropolis has taken on a sophisticated look of its own."

KRYPTON

The Ultimate Immigrant ◇ Red Sun ◇ The Fortress of Solitude
Pajamas for Space Travel ◇ King Arthur
A Giant Crystal Taproot ◇ New Krypton
Hubble Bubble Toil & Trouble

⌄

Although Superman is an adopted son of Earth, like many adoptive children he remains curious about his origins. Prior to the events of *Superman Returns,* this urge led him into space on a quest for Krypton, which is where we come in at the start of the movie.

"Superman himself is the ultimate immigrant," says screenwriter Dan Harris. "He leaves Earth believing that there is a chance that part of Krypton still exists. So he feels that he *must* leave to erase any doubt that he's the Last Son of Krypton."

There is, of course, no planet to return to. One of the key elements of the Superman myth is the destruction of his birth world. As recounted in 1978's *Superman: The Movie,* the people of Krypton built a civilization as flawless as the crystals that powered it, yet refused to heed the scientist Jor-El, who warned that Krypton was about to tear itself apart.

Jor-El and his wife, Lara, sent their infant son, Kal-El, to Earth. There, the rays of a yellow sun gave him powers far beyond those of mortal men. The ruddier hue of Krypton's star inspired the film's cover name, *Red Sun,* which appeared on all production materials during the making of *Superman Returns.*

The pod that rocketed Kal-El away from Krypton in the original film was a small, spherical structure bristling with jutting cones and crystalline spikes. This vehicle also makes a brief appearance in *Superman Returns,* and was one of the first Kryptonian artifacts tackled by the art department.

In his office, Guy Dyas lingers over a sketch labeled *Red Sun: Baby Superman Crystal Pod Conceptual 3-D Model, Crashed Cellar Version.* The sketch seems to capture the audience's collective memory of what Kryptonian things *should* look like, but the production designer feels obliged to point out a few differences.

"We want people to relate this to the original film," he says, "but if you actually go back and look at the John Barry design from 1978, it's not the same. The difference between their design and ours is, their Krypton had mechanical things on it. Large cylinders with slots in them. The baby pod had triangular metal spikes; it was sort of a weird nonorganic structure. Our version is a lot more organic." The sketch captures the silhouette of the original pod but reinterprets it to fit with the emphasis in *Superman Returns* on pure crystal technology.

The baby pod provided inspiration for the full-size spaceship that brings the adult Superman back to Krypton. Dyas's first sketches attempted to imbue the original craft with the essence of a phosphorescent marine creature from the ocean depths. "Think about deep-sea fish, the way they have this internal luminosity," says Dyas. The full-size spaceship, he points out, "isn't like the baby pod, which was spinning crazily through space. This ship has a pilot, so it needs a front and a back." The journey to Krypton and back again will take nearly five years. The ship that Dyas and his crew eventually designed was over 250 feet long.

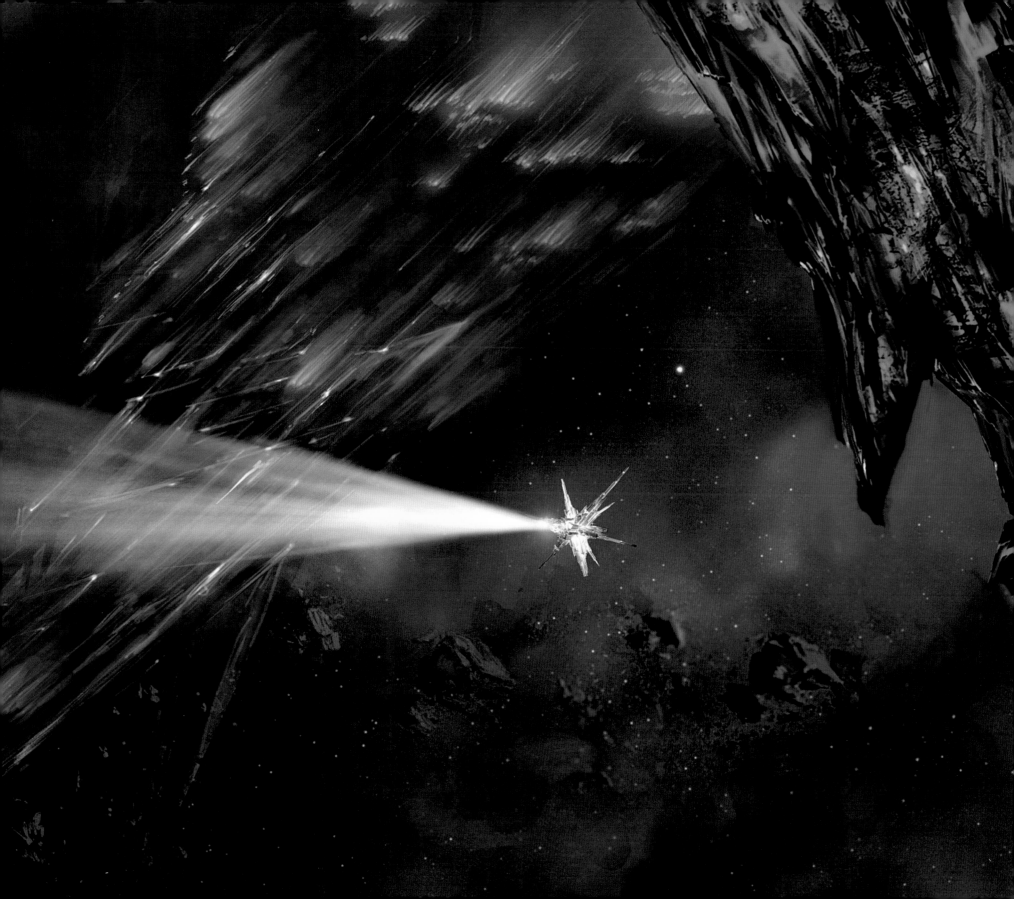

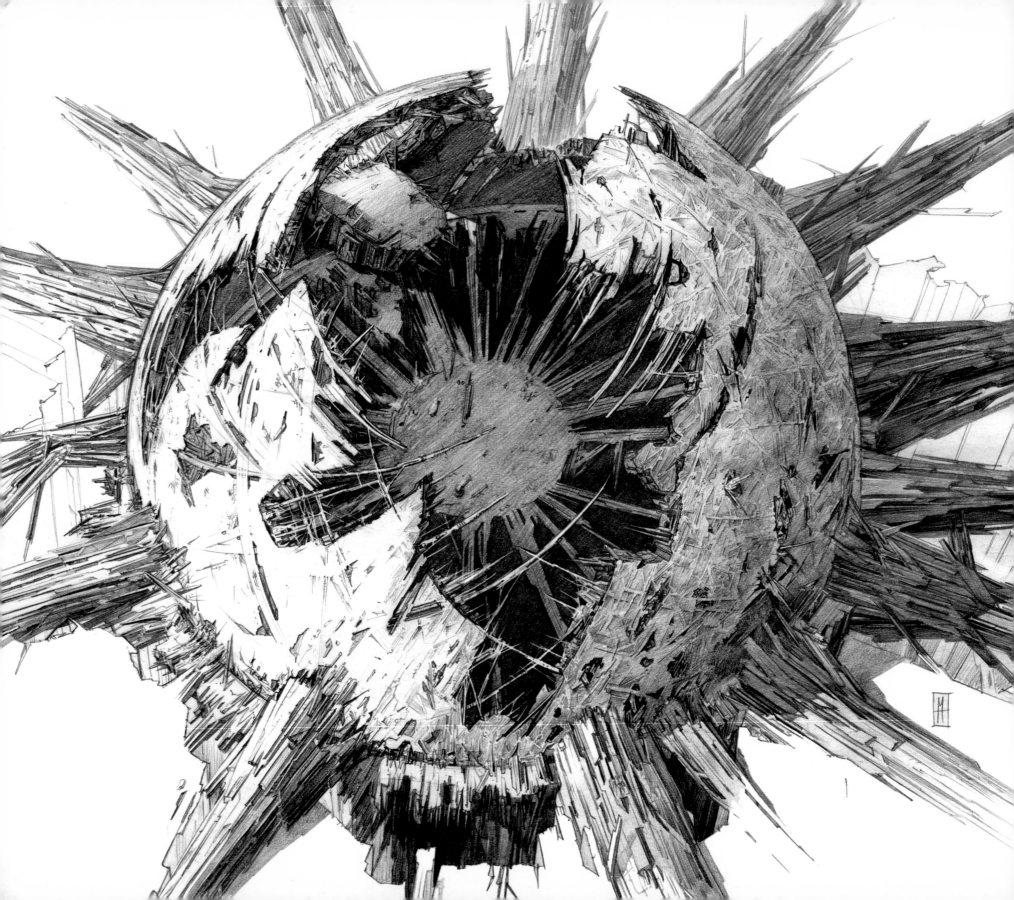

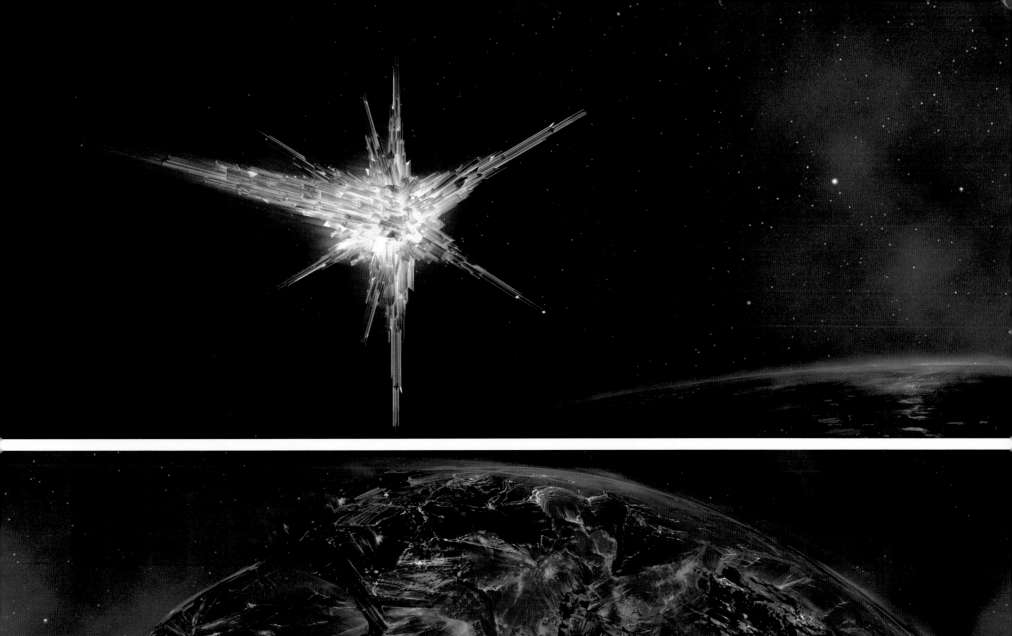
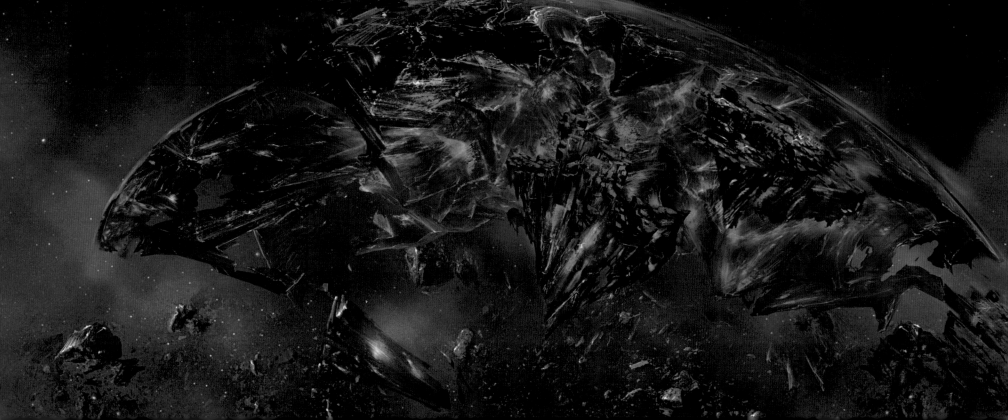

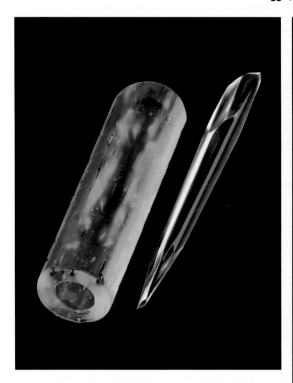

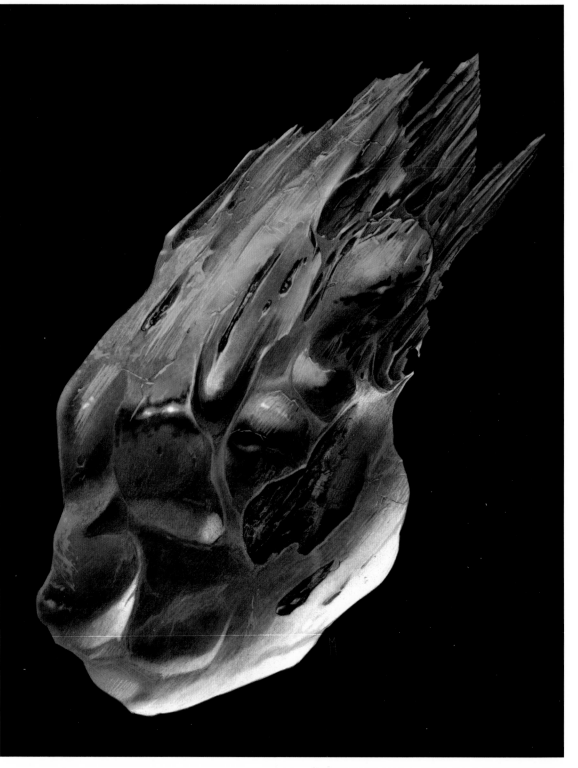

ABOVE *Painting of Kryptonian crystal and kryptonite sheath. Matt Hatton, digital, April 2005.*

RIGHT *Kryptonite meteor, its glassy skin fused from the heat of atmospheric reentry. Matt Hatton, digital, April 2005.*

OPPOSITE PAGE *Cutaway of Kryptonian meteor showing its internal crystalline structure. Matt Hatton, digital, April 2005.*

PAGE 93 *A spotlight pans over the graveyard that is Krypton, illuminating the ruins of a dead civilization. Ben Procter, digital, February 2005.*

PAGE 94 *This Kryptonian structure plays an important role in the 1978 film. Here, the dome lies in ruins and clings to a drifting chunk of a shattered planet. Matt Hatton, pencil, February 2005.*

PAGE 95 TOP *Superman's spaceship approaches the remains of Krypton. Ben Procter, digital, February 2005.*

PAGE 95 BOTTOM *Krypton's curvature is still apparent in this wide view of a fragment. Ben Procter, digital, February 2005.*

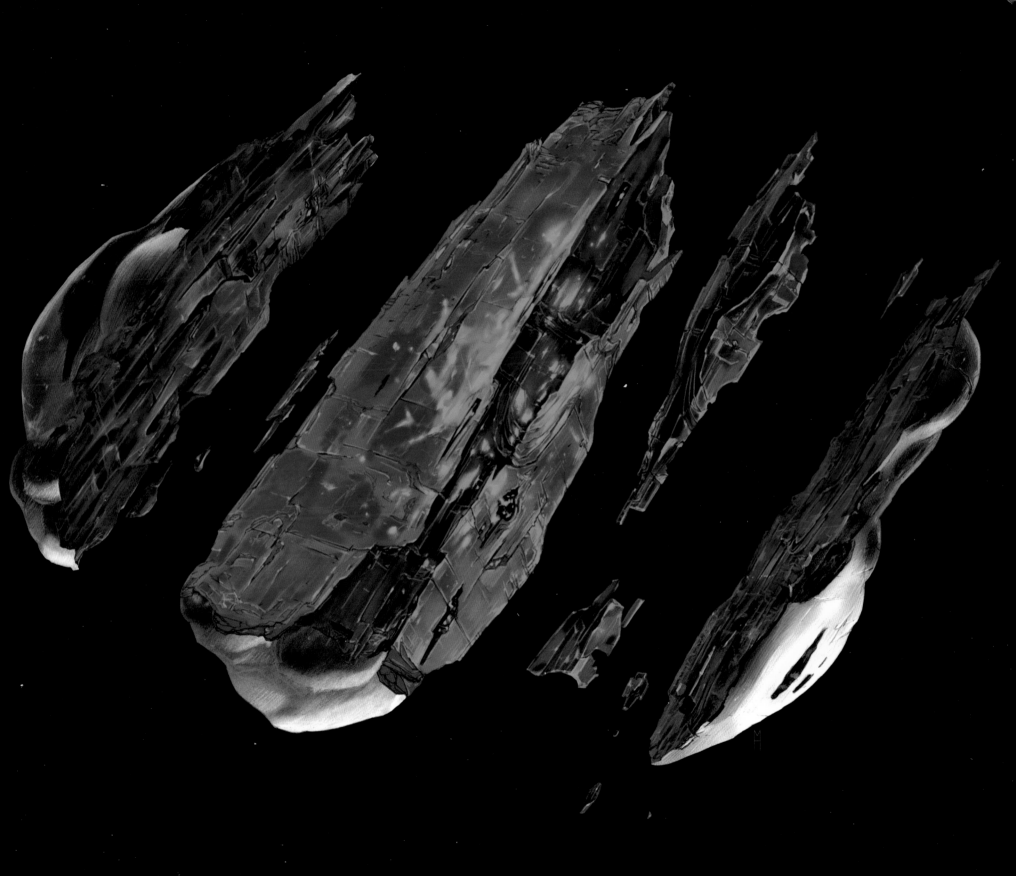

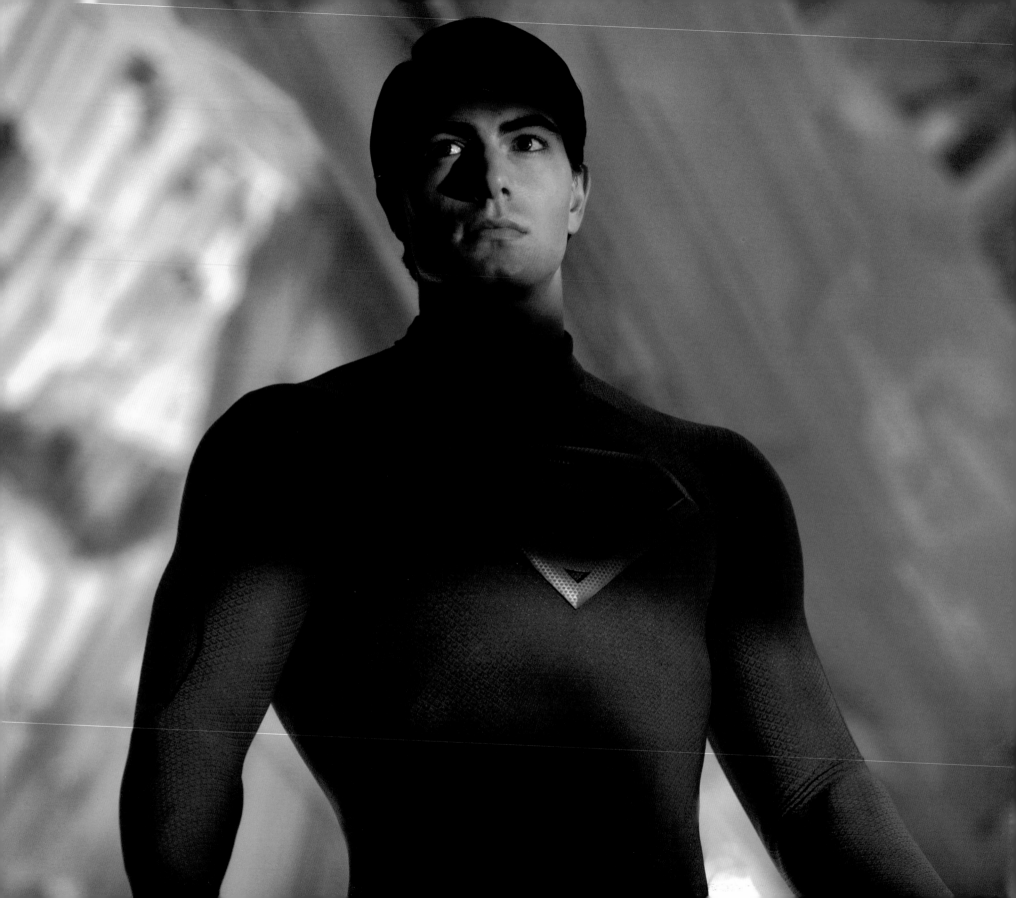

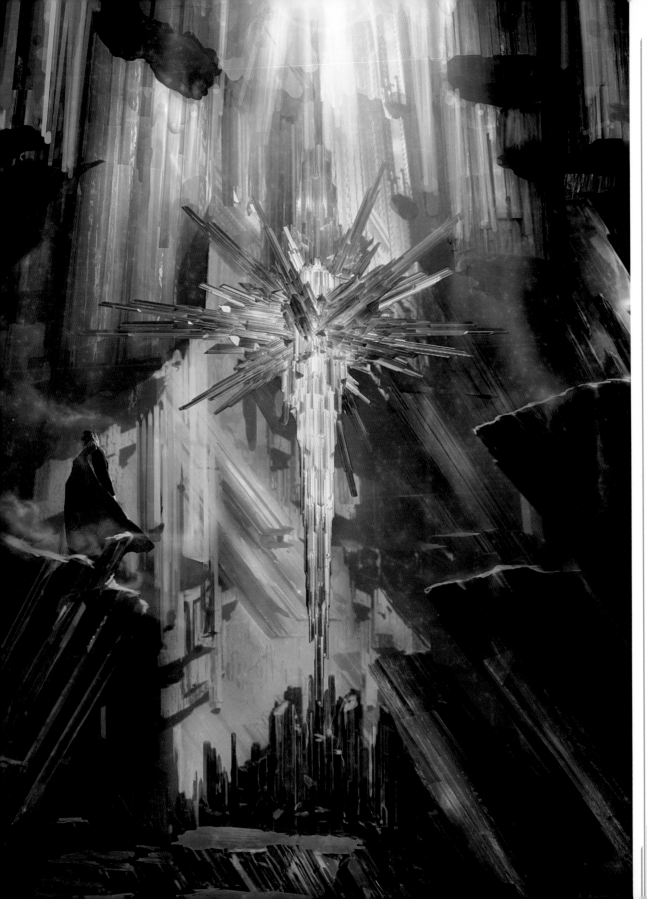

"We're suggesting that Superman actually grew this in his fortress." Dyas points to a conceptual painting tacked to a bulletin board, depicting Superman inside the Fortress of Solitude watching his starship take form. This scene does not appear in *Superman Returns,* nor was it ever intended to be filmed. "A lot of the artwork we do is for story development," says Dyas. "A lot of questions were asked: 'Now wait a minute. Where does the ship come from? How does he grow the ship?' So to produce an illustration like this, you're helping out a director or writers to say, '*That's* how it works.' It's as much a part of our job in the art department to inspire them as it is to do anything else."

Five years is a long time, so Superman needed something comfortable to wear during his galactic voyage. In the film, he eschews his traditional blue-red-and-yellow costume for what costume supervisor Dan Bronson calls "pajamas for space travel." The pod suit is a one-piece outfit with attached boots. Bronson and Louise Mingenbach intended it to echo some of the highlights of Superman's costume, including a muted S shield. "It's the same print," says Bronson, "but it's a different color and there's no waistline. It's platinum."

For inspiration on the color, the costume department first looked to the outfits worn by Marlon Brando and other Kryptonian elders in the 1978 film, which were made of a reflective material and almost blindingly white. Bronson recalls the trial-and-error process that resulted in the pod suit: "We did lots of experiments. We did lights, and light-up fabric. But it started to look like a stick-and-paste doll." The final design of the pod suit is meant to blend in subtly and organically with its surroundings. "When it's all lit, he looks like he's a part of the spaceship," he says. "Bryan wanted it to look as if he's a crystal shard himself."

LEFT *Superman admiring his spaceship.*
Ben Procter and Jeff Julian, digital, May 2005.

OPPOSITE PAGE *Brandon Routh wearing the pod suit.*
David James, July 2005.

It certainly *looks* like a comfortable suit, but Mingenbach knows it's made from the same highly tensioned material that covers Brandon Routh's muscular body in Superman's regular costume. She nods with a smile. "A nice *tight* comfortable suit."

Once the art department had fixed on a starship design, they produced the craft in three distinct forms: on a soundstage for interior shots, as a virtual CGI model for effects shots, and as a full-size version for crash-site filming in Tamworth at the Kent family farm.

Within the soundstage that holds the spaceship interior, tree trunk–size crystals are stacked atop one another in a structure that resembles a translucent log cabin. Closer examination reveals that the assemblage is a gargantuan mobile, suspended from the ceiling by hundreds of cables. "We like to create depth, and the best way to create it is to hang the pieces different depths away," says Dyas, explaining that ceiling suspension is the only way to achieve this delicate crystalline illusion. "This set is . . . transparent, so when you light it, you would see metal support structures behind. If we had them."

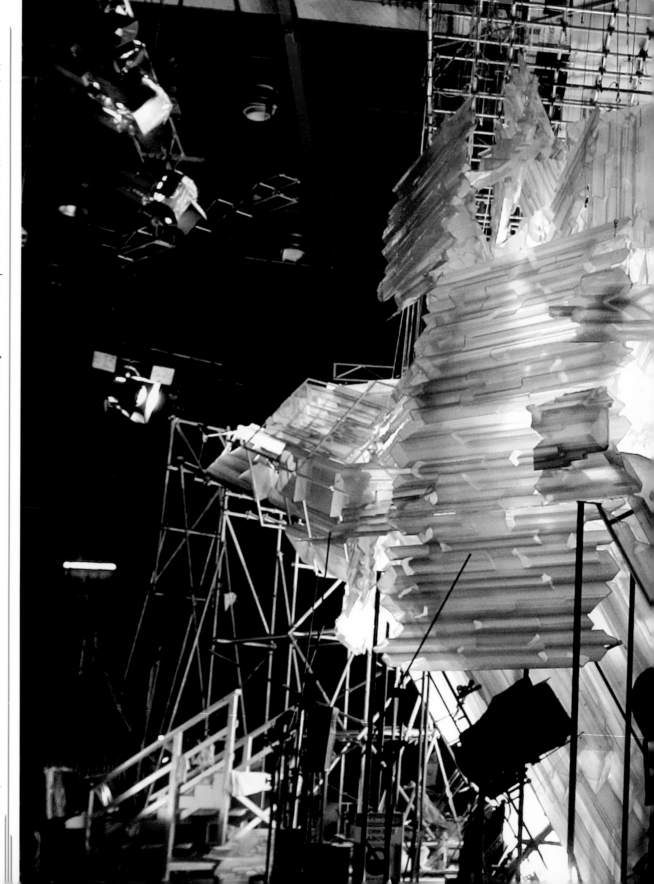

RIGHT *Brandon Routh inside the Kryptonian starship set during filming. To achieve the illusion of an airy, crystalline architecture, crew members suspended set pieces from an overhead rig. David James, July 2005.*

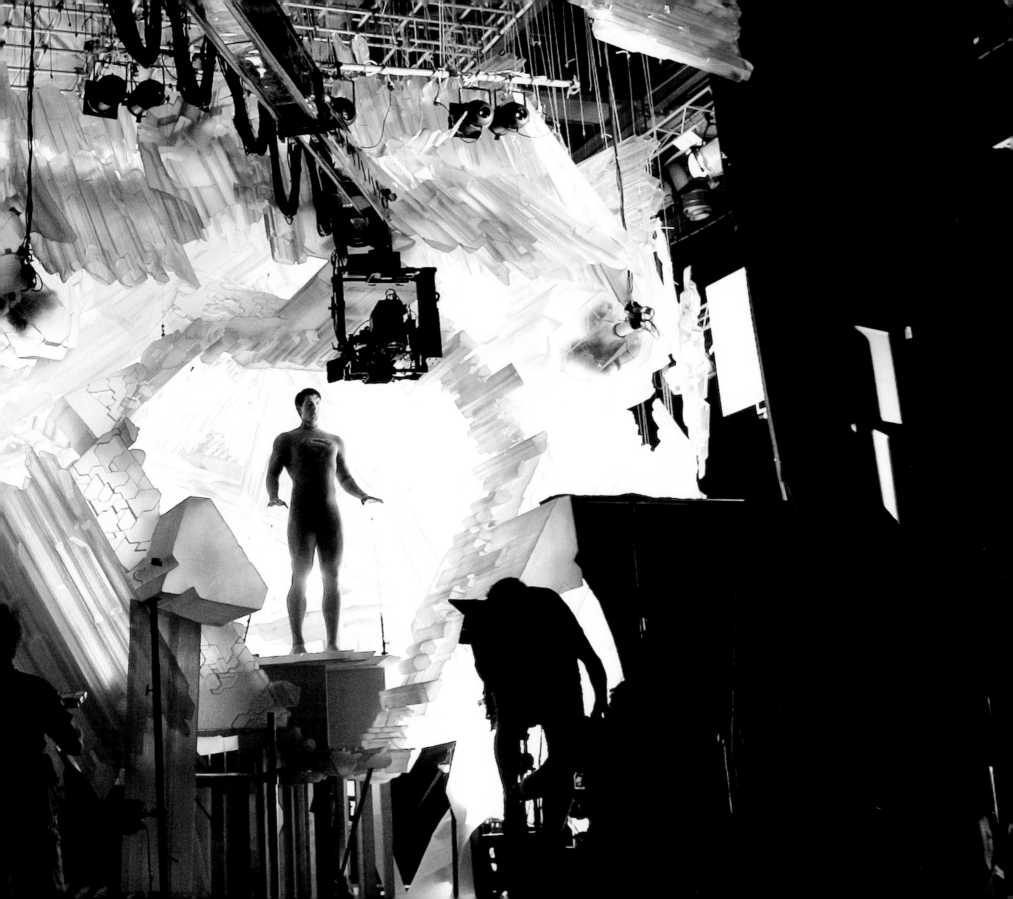

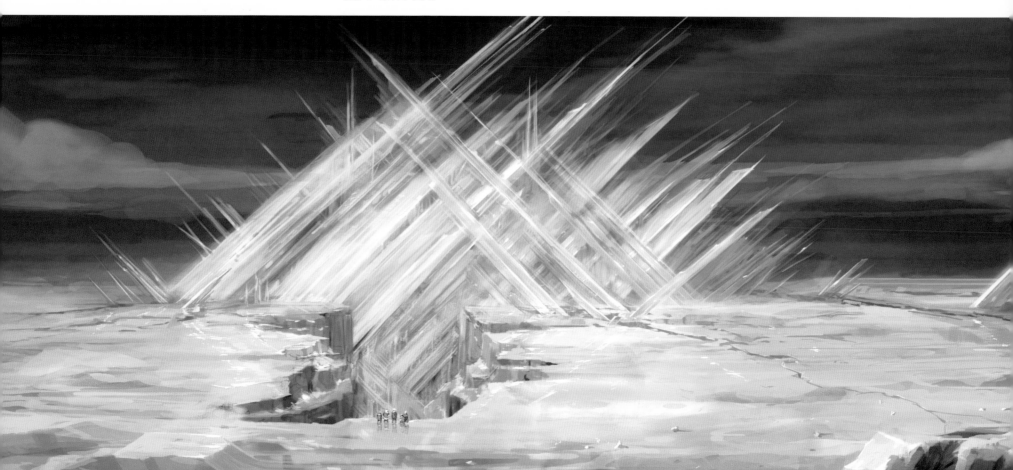

ABOVE *The illuminated symmetry of the Fortress of Solitude stands in contrast to the bleak glacier top. Tani Kunitake, digital, April 2005.*

OPPOSITE PAGE *The crystal pillars that make up the Fortress of Solitude cut into the surrounding glaciers, some jutting out far from the structure itself. Matt Hatton, pencil, April 2005.*

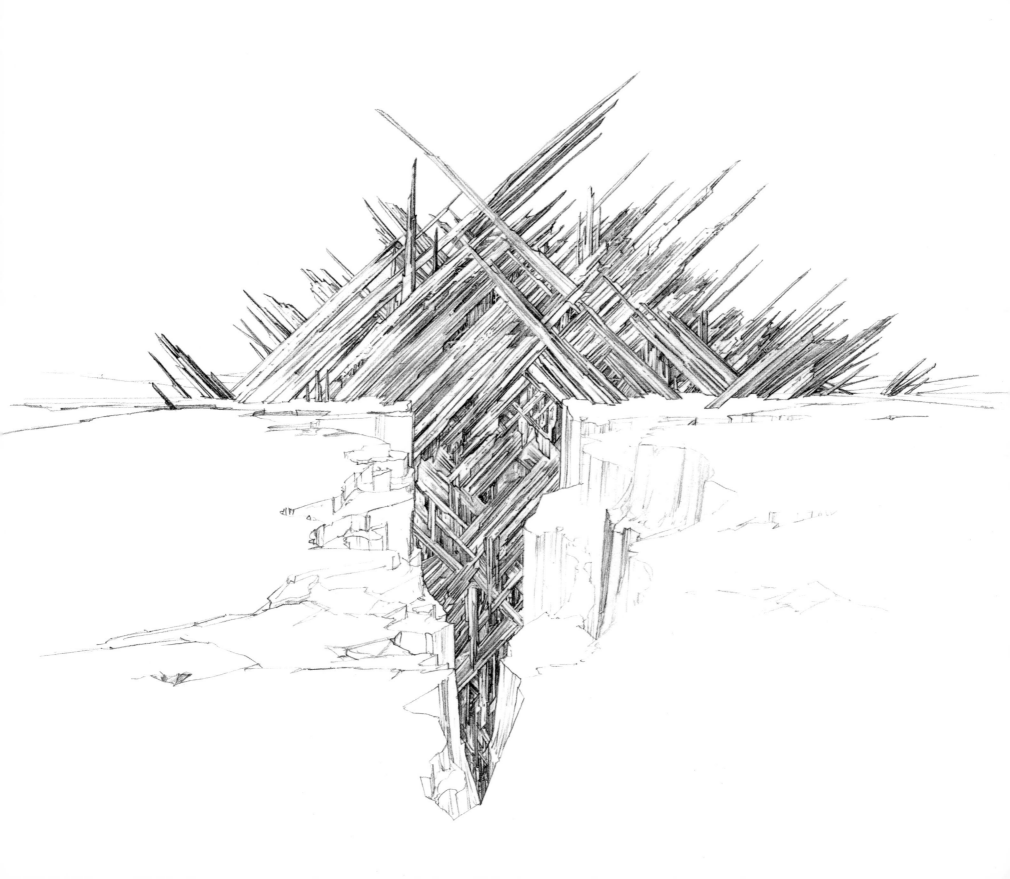

The Fortress of Solitude is a little piece of Krypton in a remote corner of the Arctic. In the 1978 film, it built itself in a frenzy of crystal replication after Clark provided a crystal taken from his baby pod as a self-propagating seed. Inside the Fortress, recordings of his father made Clark realize his true identity as Kal-El.

"I draw an analogy to King Arthur and his years of study with Merlin," says Bryan Singer. "Superman has two educations. He has the humble education of growing up on this bucolic farm in Kansas, and he has the Kryptonian education that came from the Fortress of Solitude—which would be like Arthur's education as a page, and as a subject of Merlin. It's very much an Arthurian legend. Arthur had a greater destiny, but it took years to find that destiny, to find Excalibur. And in Superman's case, to find his identity."

Next to the stage hosting Superman's spaceship is a different building containing some familiar crystalline columns. At the moment, the set for the Fortress of Solitude is a simple structure that will reach its full potential in postproduction. The huge fiberglass pillars are dim and dusky. (During filming they will glow with interior light varying between pure white and a warm amber-white.) The columns are also brusquely chopped off at the edges of the set, but visual effects will make this pocket of crystal architecture stretch in every direction when seen onscreen. "All this development of the Fortress of Solitude is very close to the original film," says Dyas. "The Fortress of Solitude is such a strong graphic image. It's absolutely tattooed in my head. To totally redesign it would be an error."

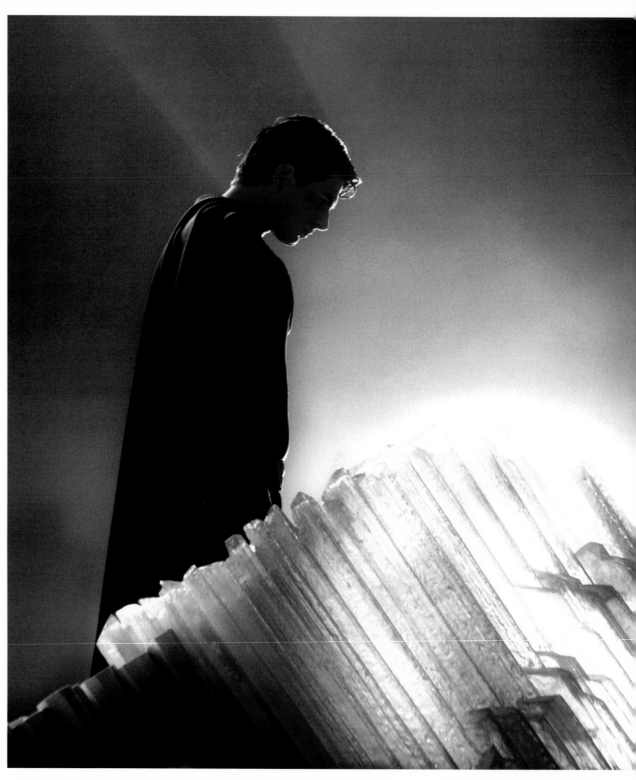

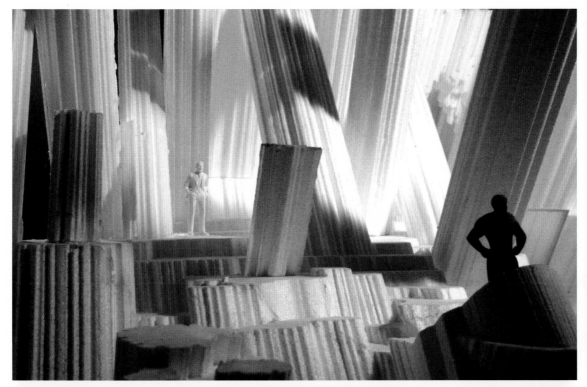

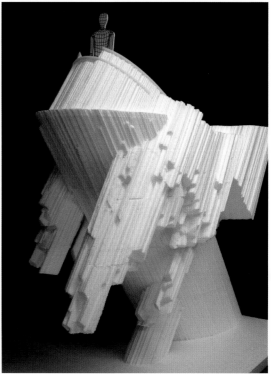

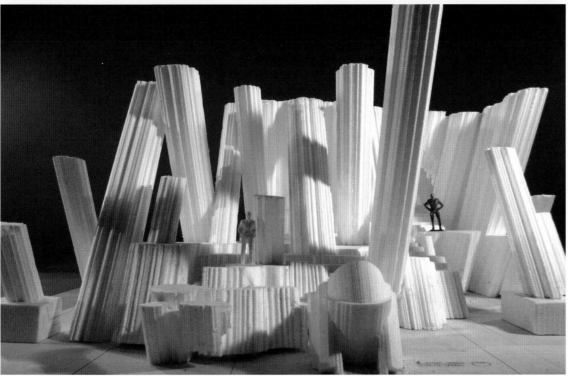

ABOVE *Model of a control console from the Fortress of Solitude. Lewis Morley, Brad Burnet, and Shari Finn; styrofoam and plaster; April 2005.*

LEFT TOP AND BOTTOM *Model of the Fortress of Solitude interior. Lewis Morley, Brad Burnet, and Shari Finn; styrofoam and plaster; April 2005.*

OPPOSITE PAGE *Brandon Routh as Superman in front of a Kryptonian control board. David James, July 2005.*

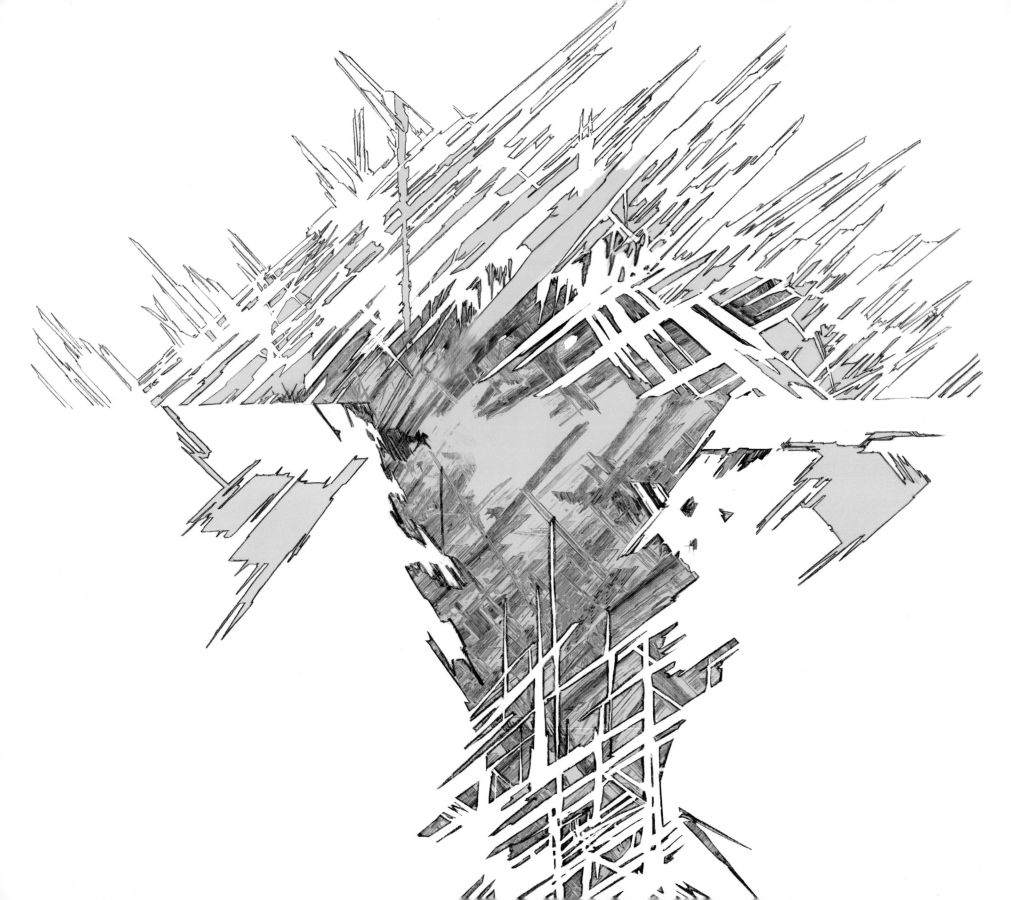

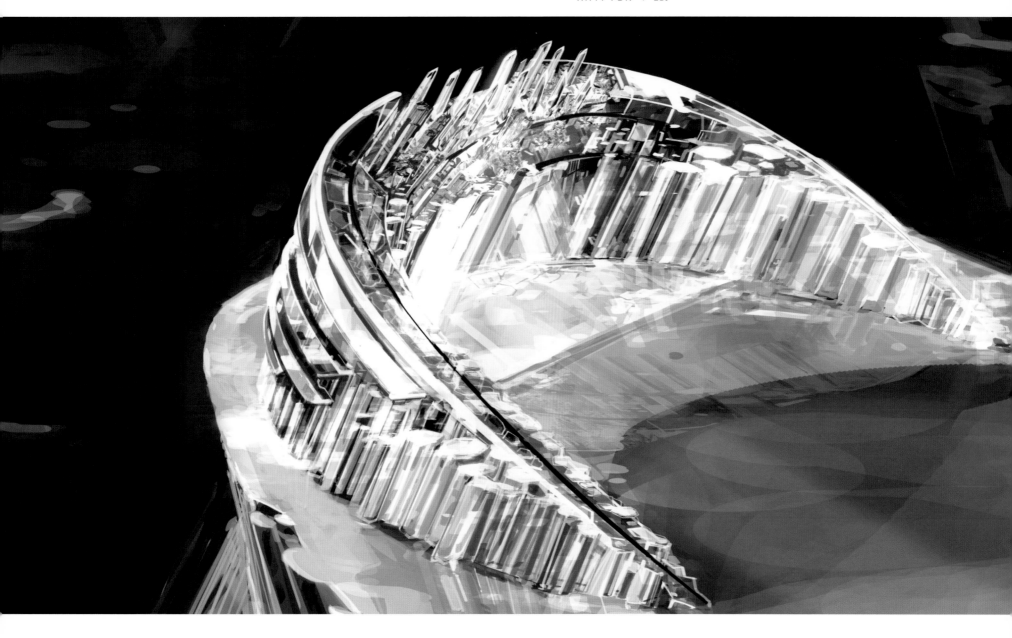

ABOVE *A control console made entirely of crystals sits inside the Fortress of Solitude. Tani Kunitake, digital, April 2005.*

OPPOSITE PAGE *Like an iceberg, only a fraction of the Fortress of Solitude is visible above the arctic surface. Matt Hatton, pencil and digital, April 2005.*

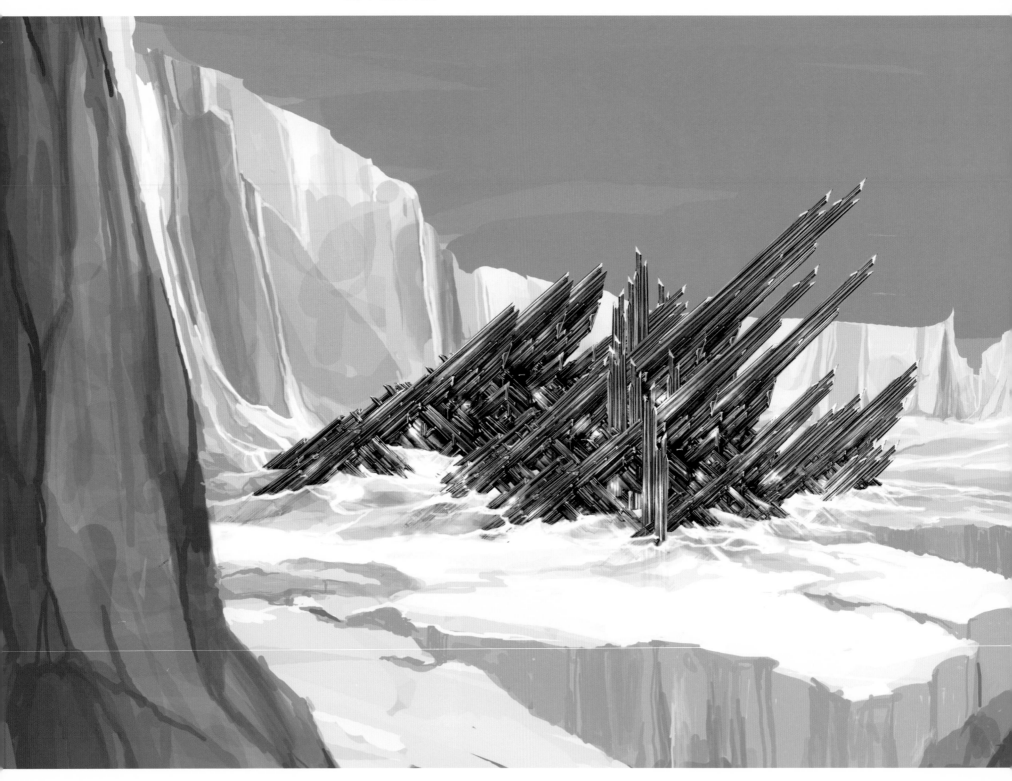

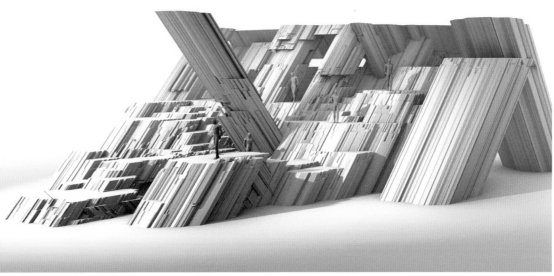

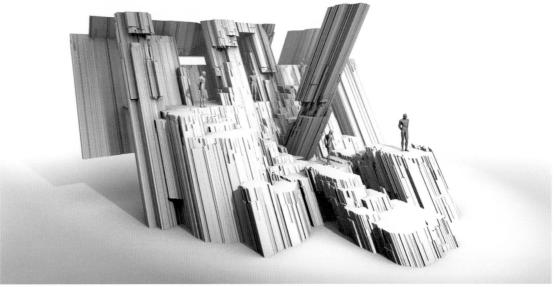

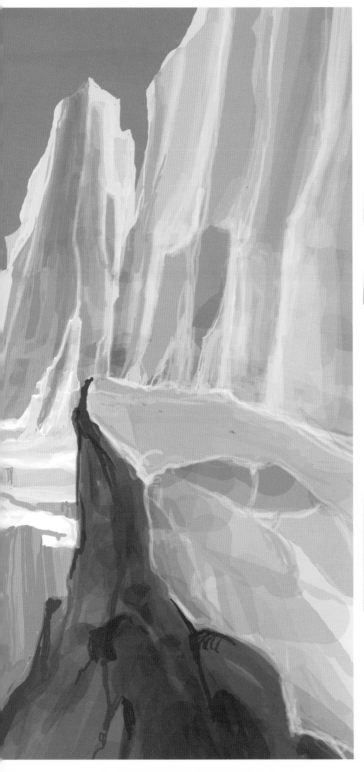

TOP AND ABOVE *Conceptual renderings of the interior of Superman's Fortress of Solitude. James Oxford, digital, April 2005.*

LEFT *The Fortress of Solitude lies sheltered within an arctic valley in this conceptual sketch. Ben Procter, digital, April 2005.*

That being said, there are limits to how much can be restored after a gap of nearly thirty years. In researching the topic, Dyas learned that the Fortress in the original film had been rebuilt multiple times to accommodate different shooting dates for director Richard Donner. "This is not a religious re-creation of the original film," Dyas explains. "It's an interpretation, based on what ended up being, I think, about four different sets in the Donner film."

But designing the Fortress of Solitude for *Superman Returns* meant sketching out areas that had never even been thought of before. Dyas found himself wondering just what was going on beneath the ice. "Imagine a giant crystal taproot," he says. "We imagined the Fortress of Solitude grows down as deep as it does up." And if it grows down, the chances are good that some of the offshoot crystals have stretched for miles through the arctic ice and broken the surface by accident. It is one of these root crystals that Lex Luthor discovers in the film as he and his crew make their approach to the Fortress.

It's not long before Luthor's criminal mind unlocks the secrets of Kryptonian crystal formation. His megalomania inspires him to sink the continents of the Earth and build a new landmass, which he dubs New Krypton. The unwelcome island is made from the same stuff as the Fortress of Solitude, but exponentially huger. "What we tried to do is build up a language of crystals that play on the fact that we can actually grow them," says Dyas, pointing out that the swift expansion of New Krypton would have been impossible to achieve on the scale seen in *Superman Returns* before the age of digital effects.

"Back in 1978 they had the crystal technology—Superman had the Fortress of Solitude—but we never saw anything grow," he says. "[The filmmakers] kind of hinted at it when Clark throws the crystal and we kind of see some 'hubble bubble toil & trouble.' Now we have the technology to make things grow." While this is good for the artists of *Superman Returns,* it's bad news for the people of Metropolis.

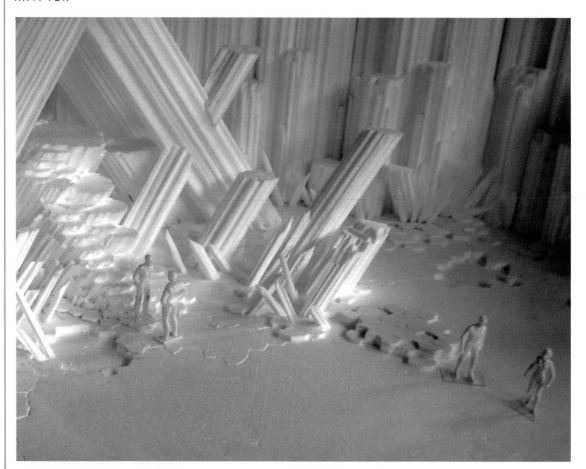

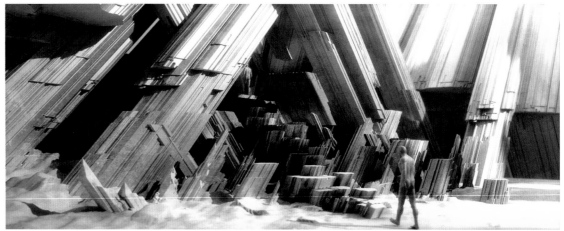

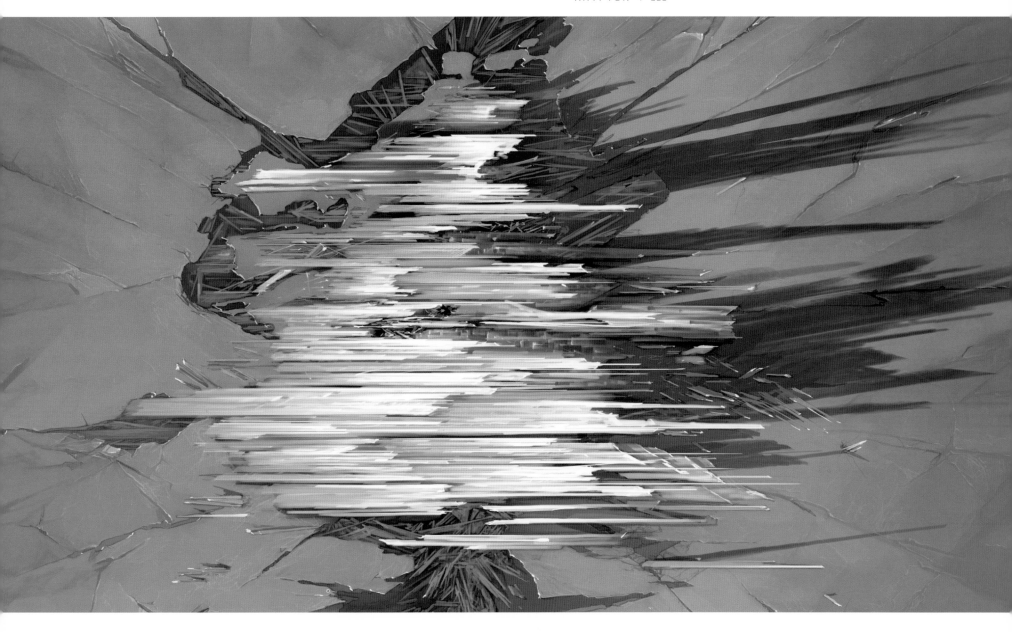

ABOVE *This delicate crystal latticework is indicative of the detail found throughout the Fortress of Solitude. Matt Hatton, digital, 2005.*

OPPOSITE PAGE TOP *Model of New Krypton. Lewis Morley, Shari Finn, Brad Burnet; styrofoam and plaster; May 2005.*

OPPOSITE PAGE BOTTOM *Illustration of New Krypton. Ben Procter, digital, May 2005.*

Although Kryptonian design looks and feels alien, it bears some surprising similarities to the visual aesthetic of Metropolis. "The Krypton language of architecture and that of art deco are not really that far apart when you get down to it," says Dyas, back in his office. "They're both built up of a series of straight lines that are put together in an interesting way." He pulls down from the wall a photograph of an art deco window above the revolving doors that lead into the Planet Building's lobby. "If you analyze this sort of stepping notion in this," he says, "and you look very carefully at the way we've constructed some of these Kryptonian spires, it's the same thing. A series of steps."

Krypton and Metropolis also play important roles in the movie's overall color scheme. Krypton is sterile white, while Metropolis is suffused with earthen brick tones. Both provide monotone back-drops so that other colors will pop off the screen. Green screams danger, being the sickly sign of radioactive kryptonite. The primary colors of blue, yellow, and red serve as a trumpet blast announcing the heroic arrival of the Man of Steel.

RIGHT *Accompanied by his thugs, Lex Luthor unlocks the secrets of the Fortress of Solitude. Ben Procter and Jeff Julian, digital, May 2005.*

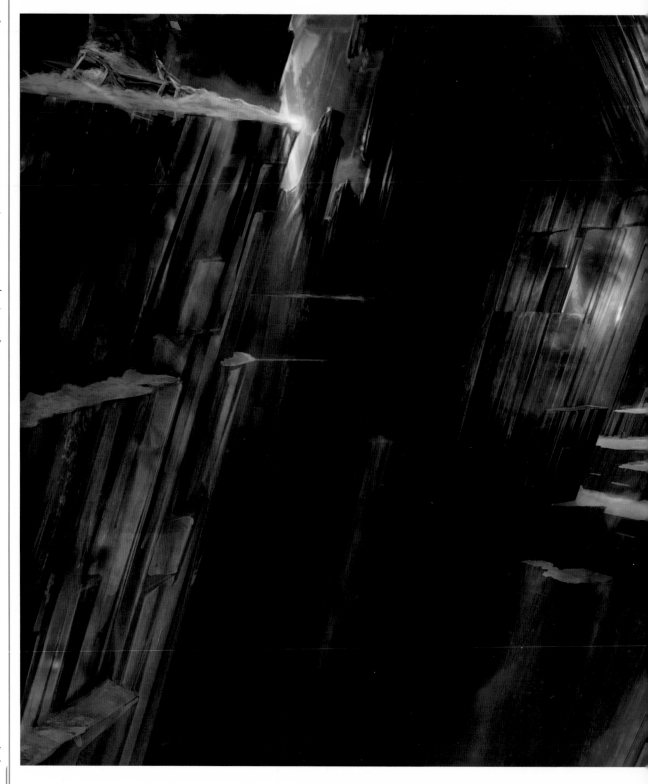

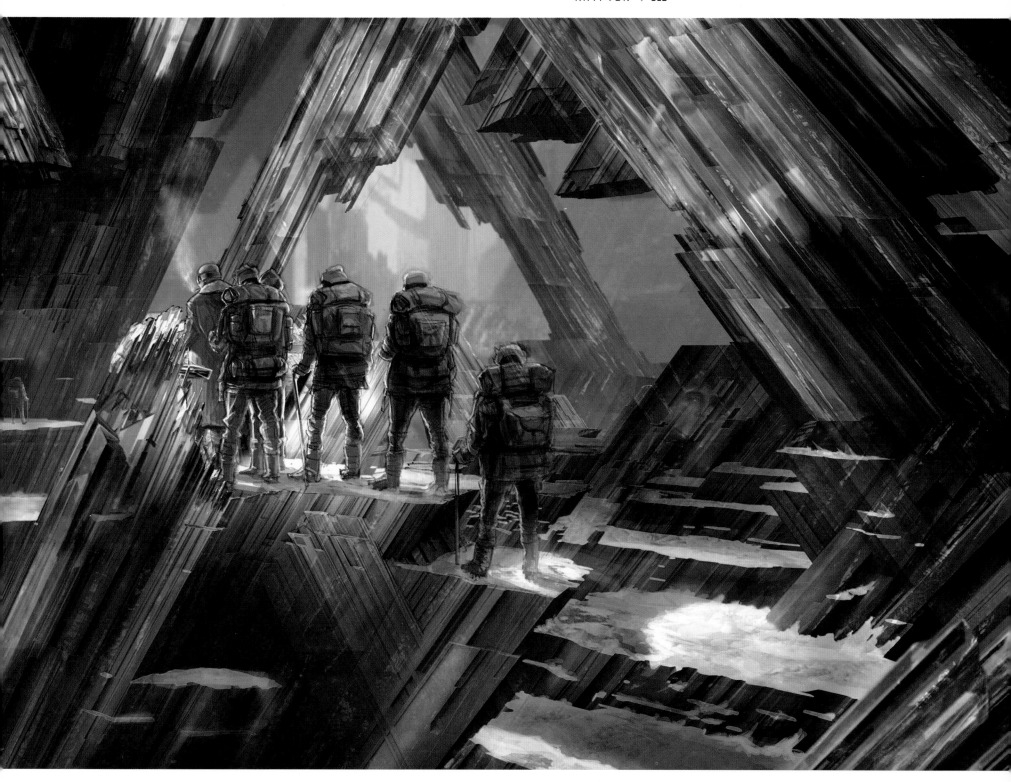

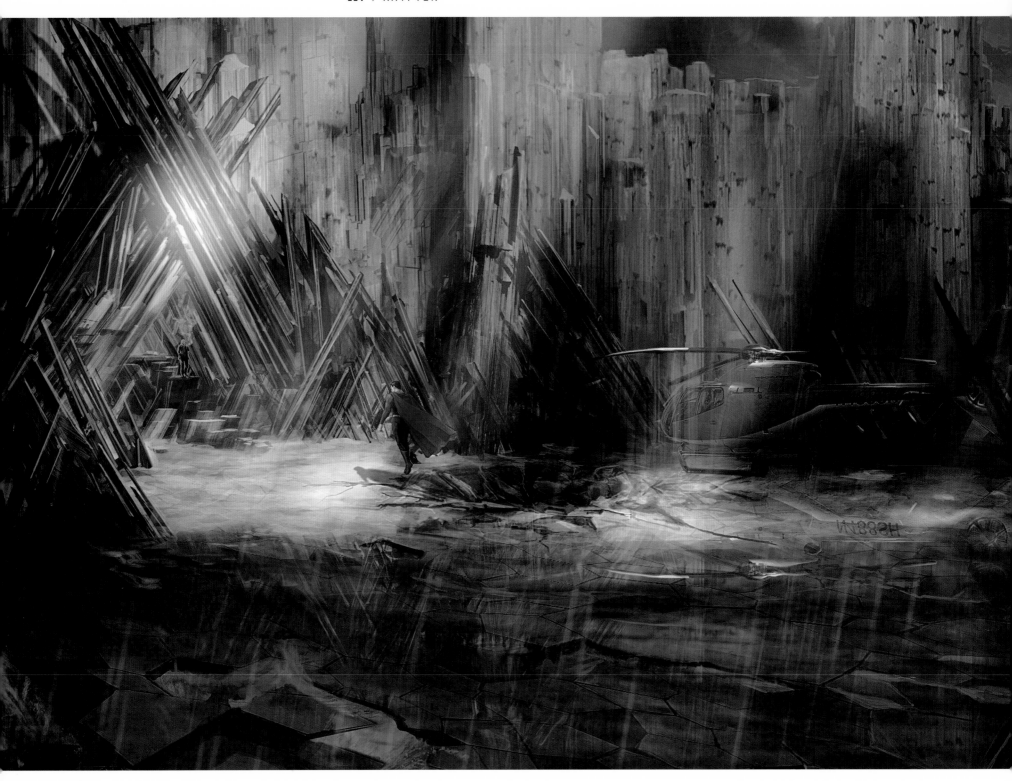

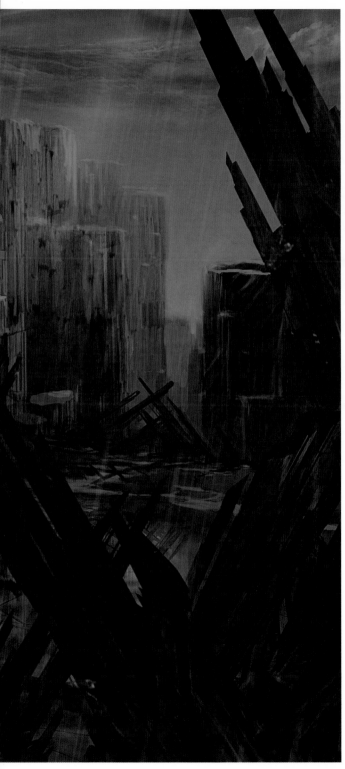

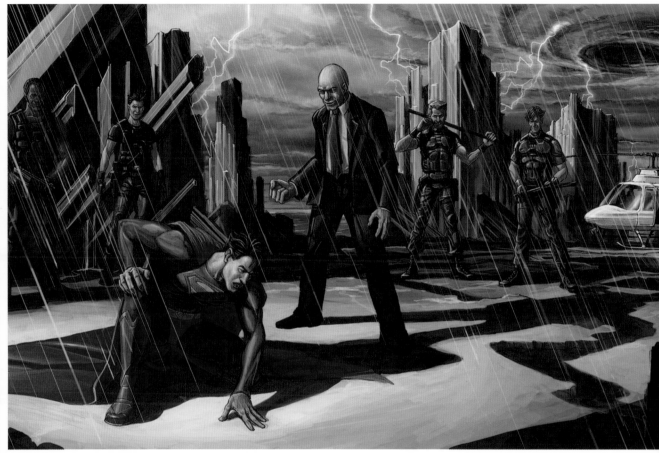

ABOVE *Superman suffers at the hands of Lex Luthor in this early illustration. James Oxford; pencil, marker, and digital; April 2005.*

LEFT *Lex's helicopter and the Man of Steel are the sole oases of color against the monotone background of New Krypton. Jeff Julian, digital, May 2005.*

PAGES 116-117 *The designers photographed volcanic rock formations and applied nature's contours in their illustrations of New Krypton Island. Philip Holliday and Matt Hatton, pencil, April 2005.*

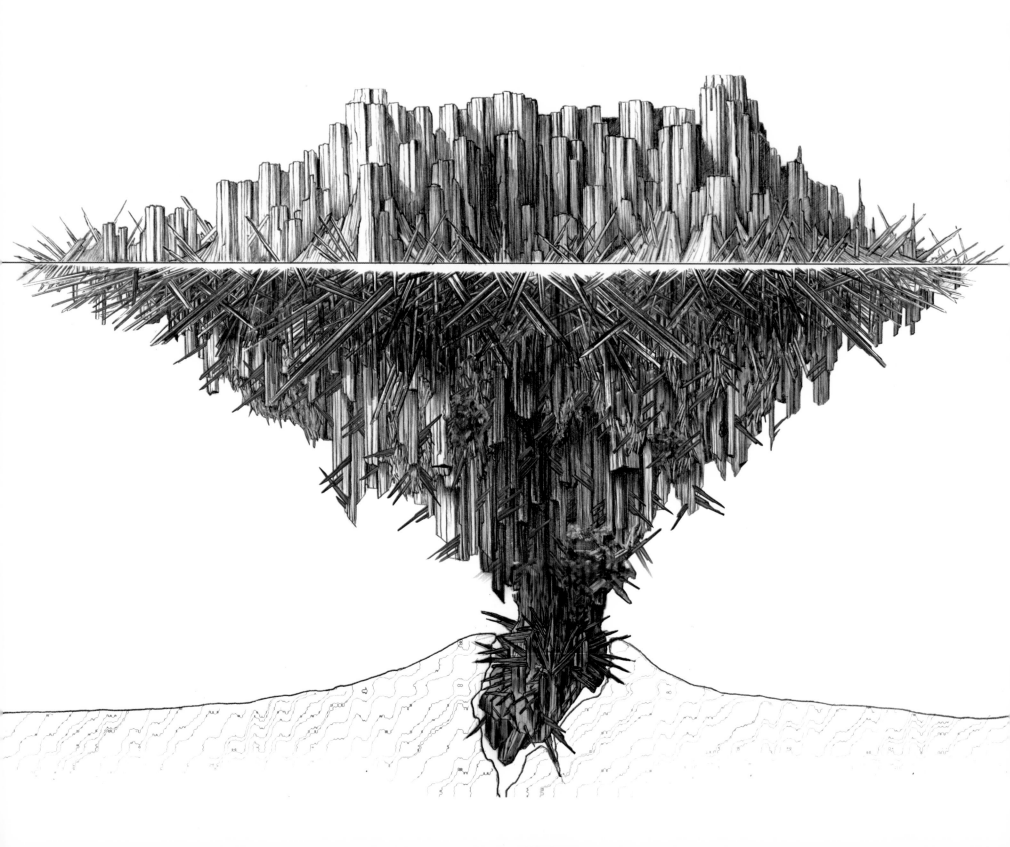

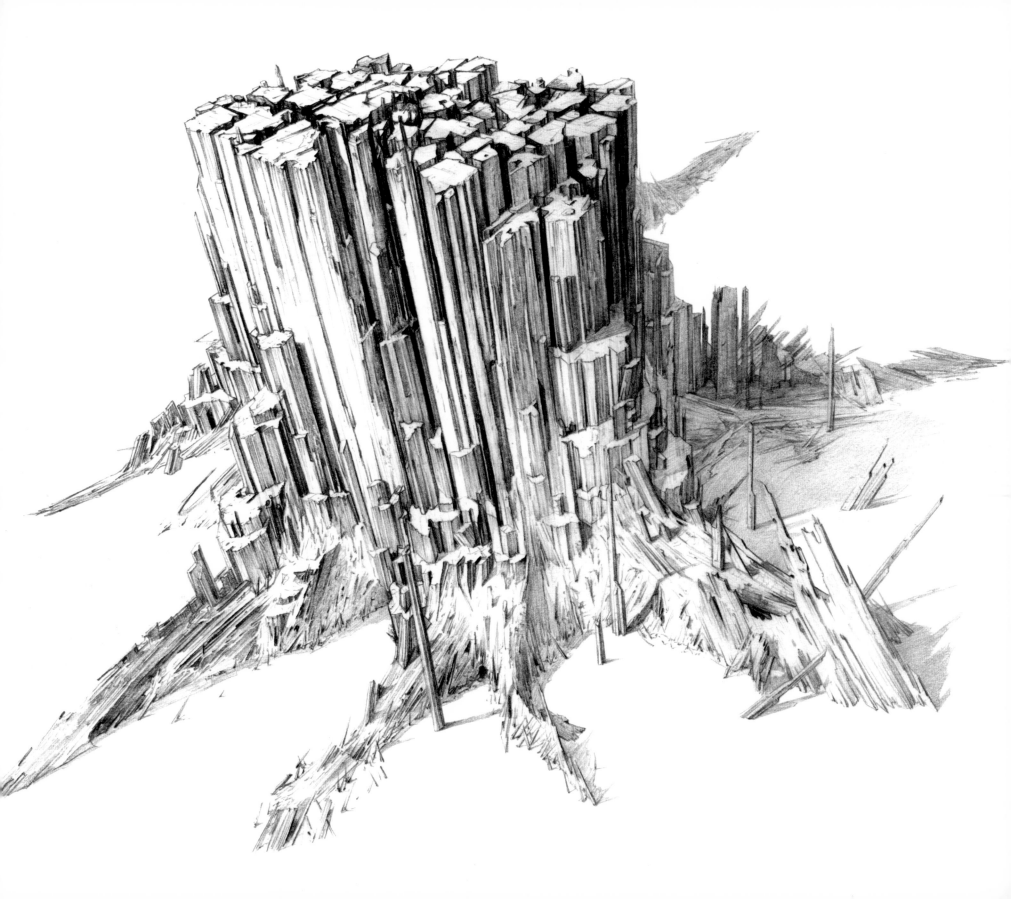

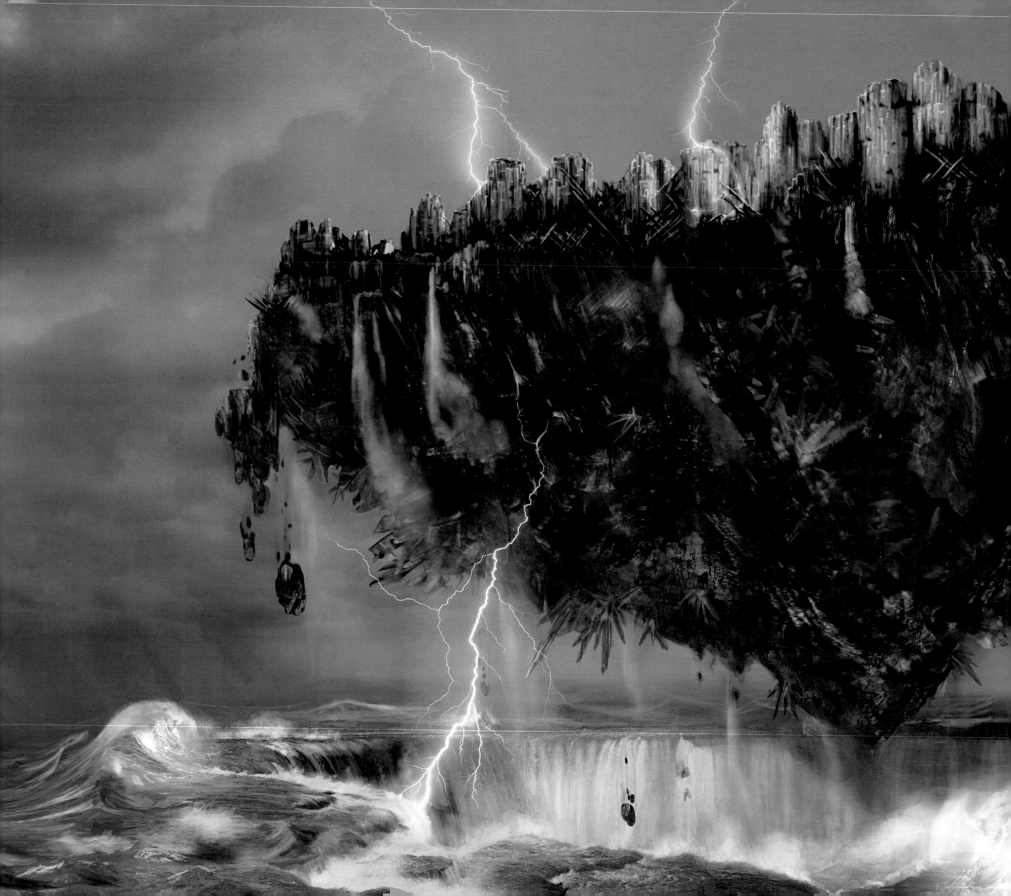

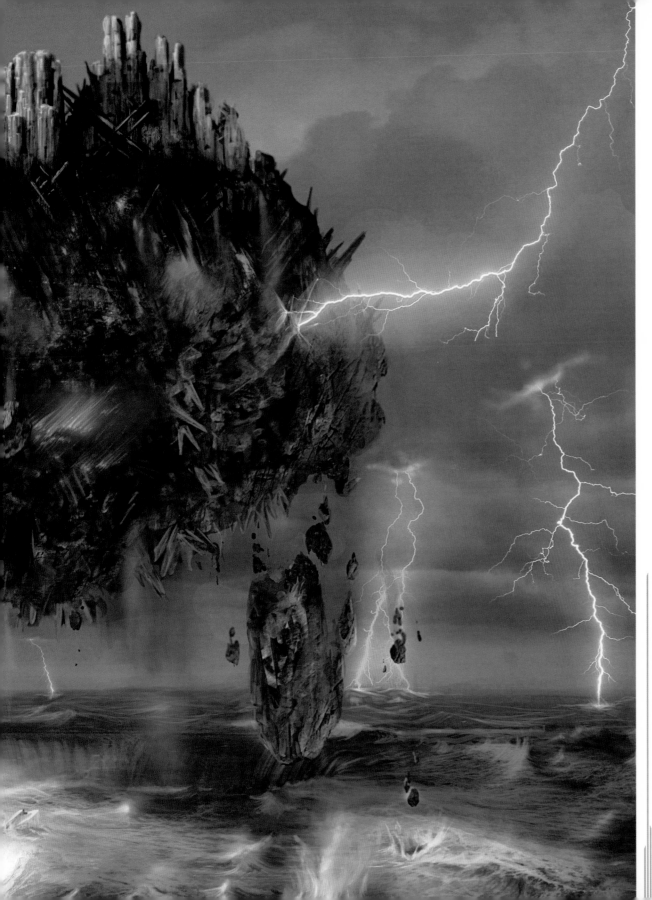

LEFT *Superman removes the cancerous threat to the planet represented by New Krypton Island in one of his greatest feats of strength. Jeff Julian, digital, May 2005.*

PAGE 120 LEFT *New Krytpon Island extends crystalline roots that anchor it to the seabed. Matt Hatton, pencil, April 2005.*

PAGES 120-121 RIGHT *Chunks of New Krypton Island break off and splash back into the ocean. Philip Holliday, pencil, May 2005.*

PAGE 122 TOP AND BOTTOM *New Krypton Island rises from the sea under a gloomy sky. Jeff Julian, digital, May 2005.*

PAGE 123 *Lex's helicopter touches down in the alien environment of New Krypton. Jeff Julian, digital, May 2005.*

PAGES 124-125 *A map of Earth featuring the newest continent, if Lex gets his way. Matt Hatton and Beth Garswood, digital, June 2005.*

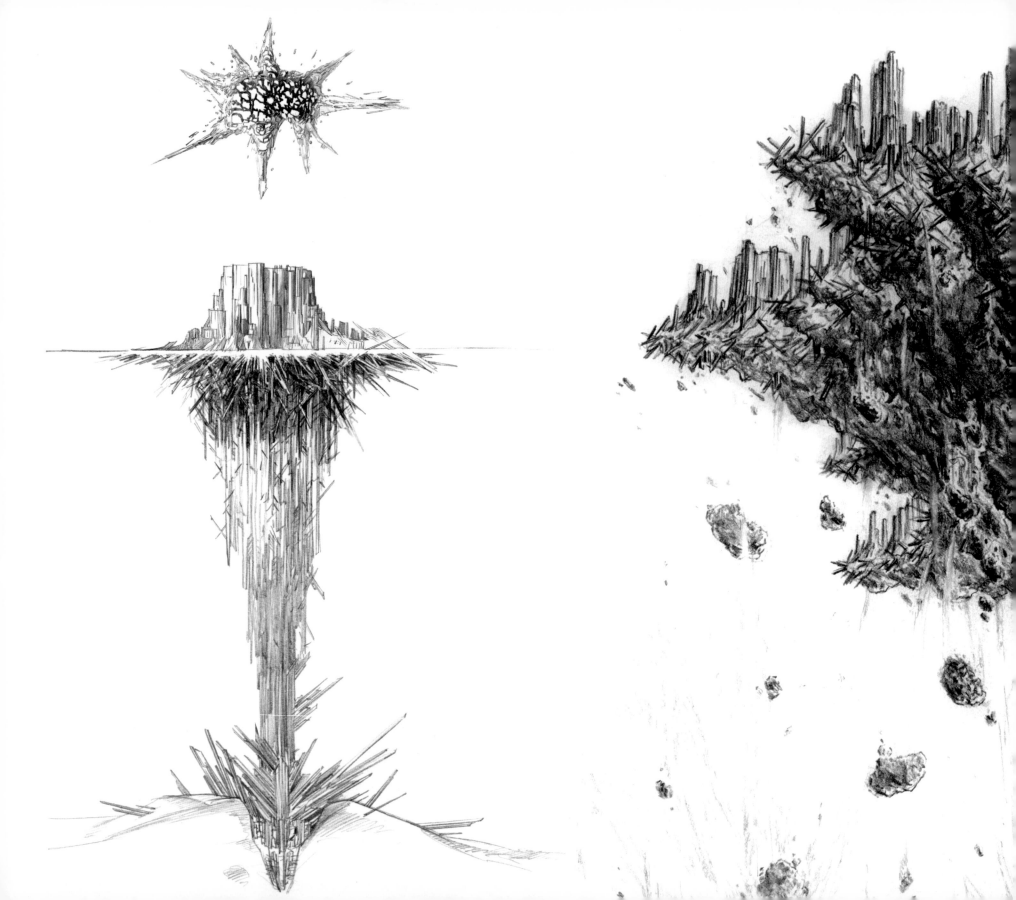

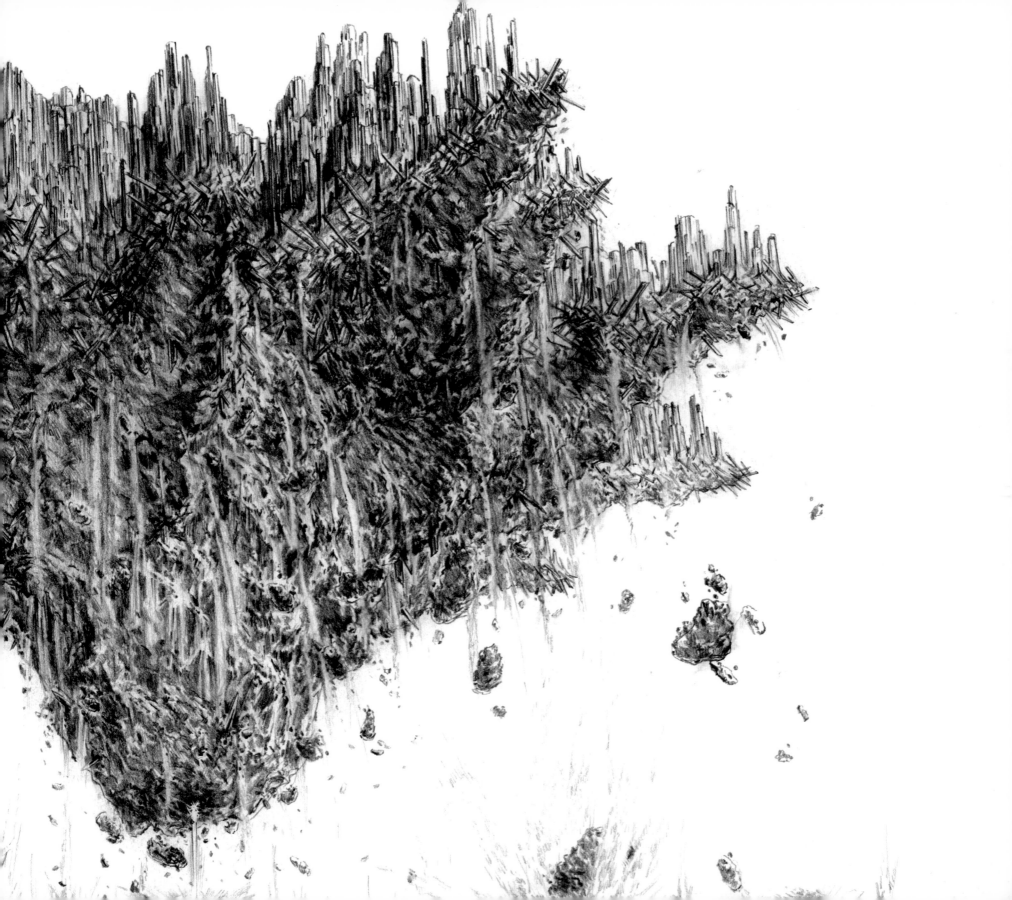

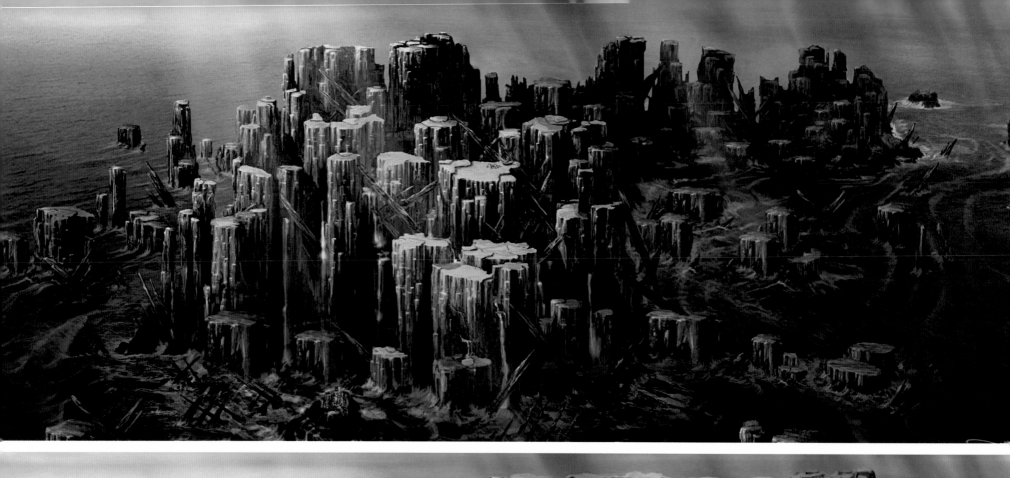
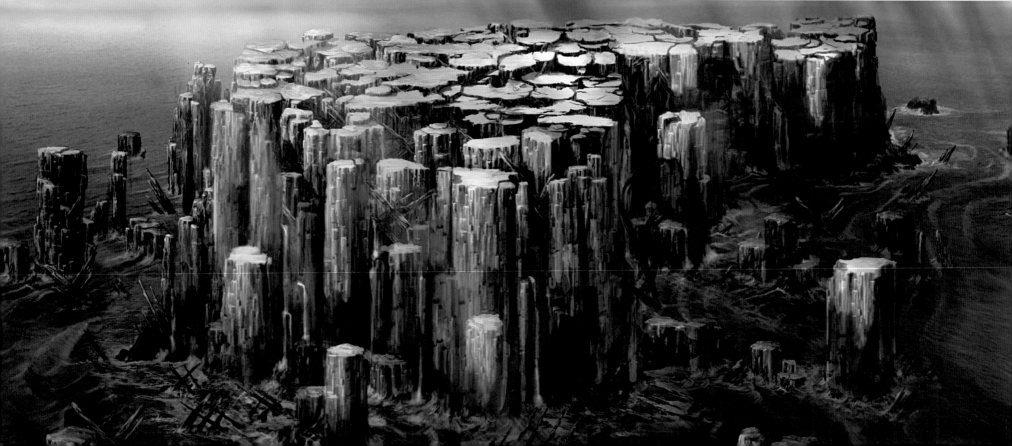

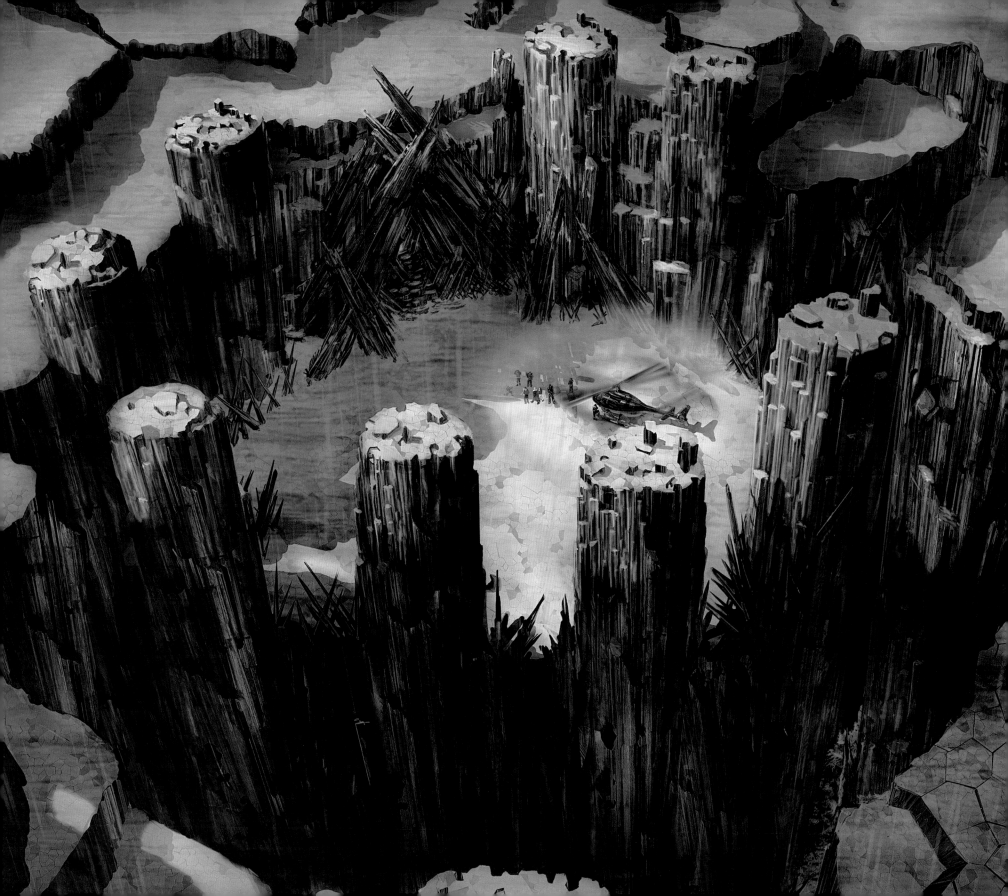

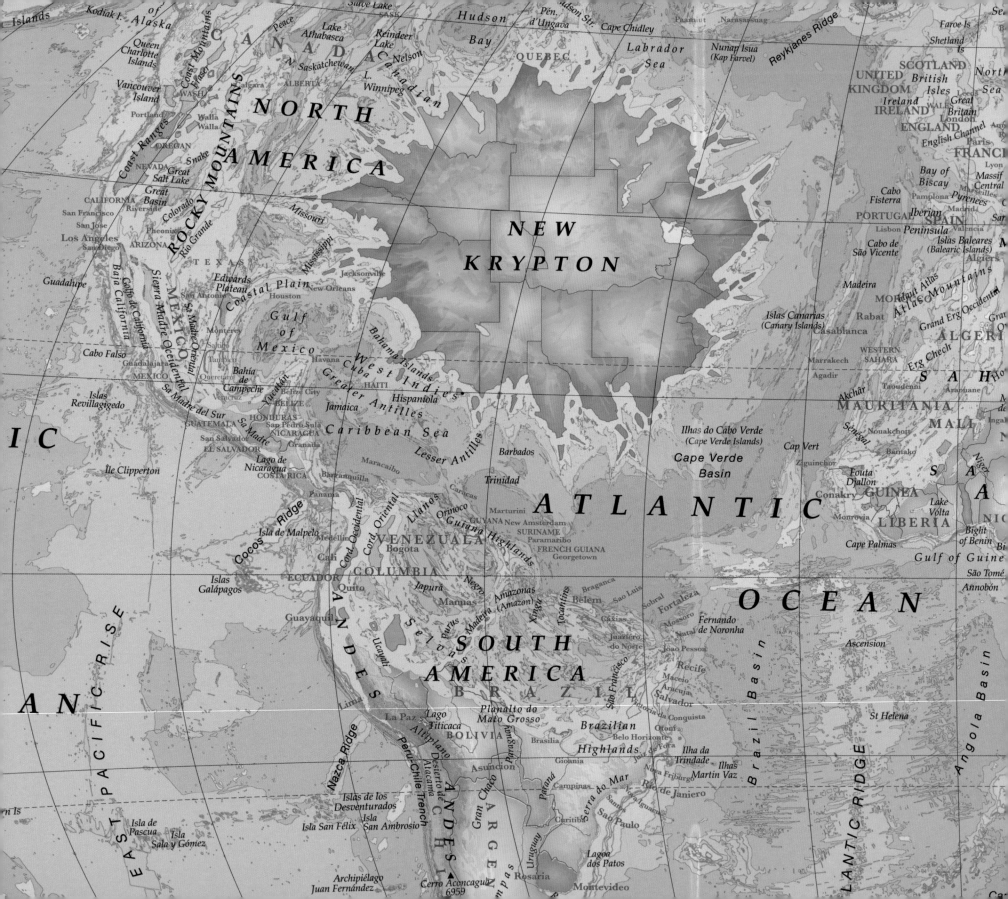

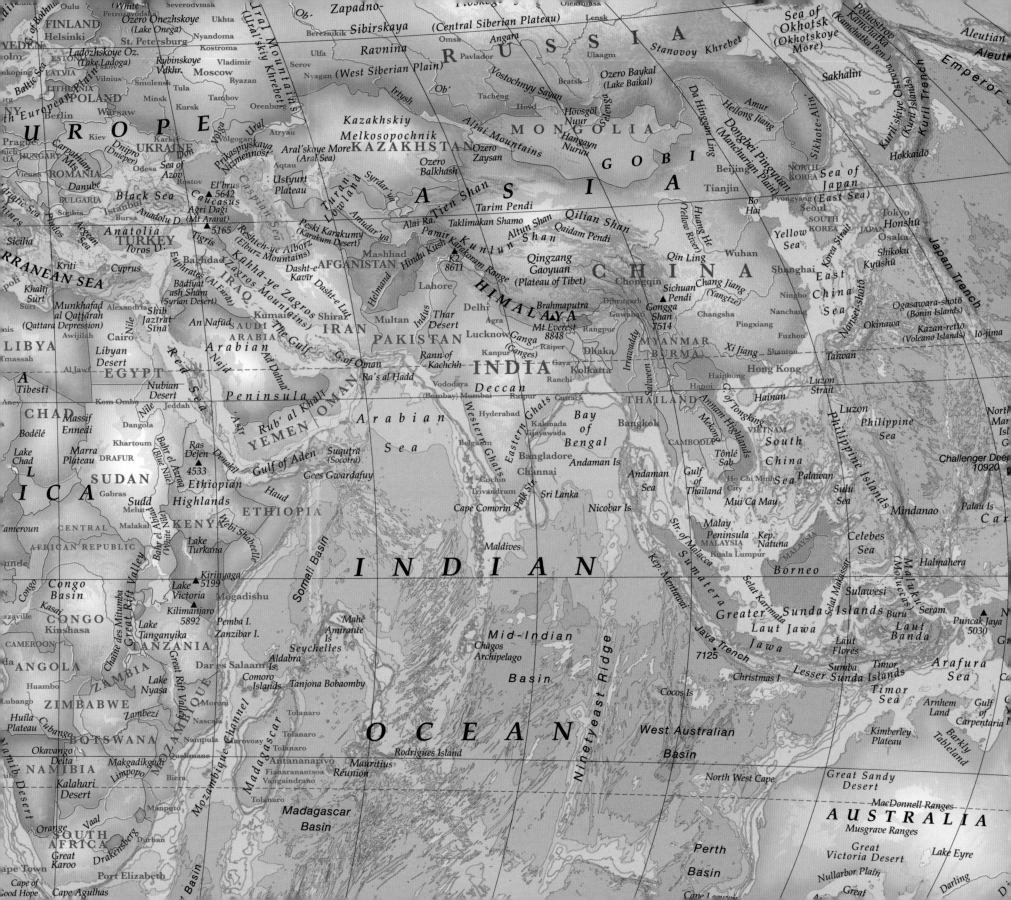

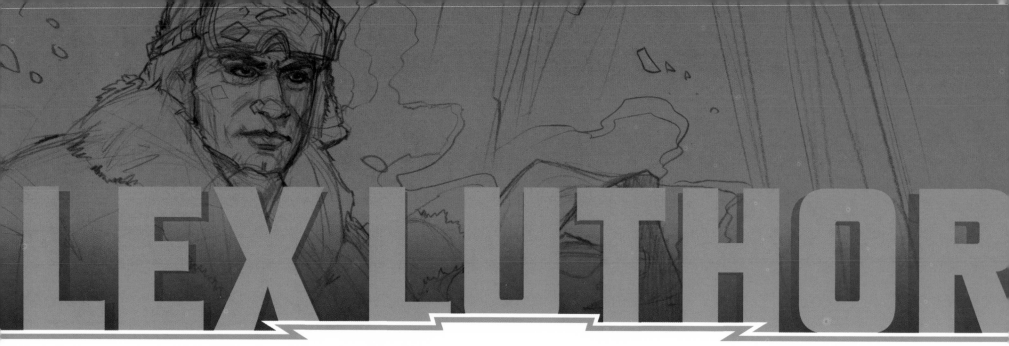

LEX LUTHOR

That Sinister Nature ◇ The Widow Vanderworth ◇ Gertrude
A Trip Very, Very Far North ◇ Santa's Grotto
Jacques Cousteau ◇ Wigs and Wounded Vanity
The Four Selves of Superman

It wouldn't be a Superman movie without Lex Luthor. Superman, who can bend steel with his bare hands, has a raw physicality that practically begs for a cerebral counterpoint. Lex's intellect evens the scales.

First appearing in a 1940 issue of *Action Comics,* Lex evolved over the decades from a super-scientist to a ruthless business tycoon but has always been the smartest person in the room. As an early comic book put it, "He could have been a mighty force for good in the world, yet he chose to direct his great scientific brain into criminal channels."

In *Superman: The Movie,* Gene Hackman took on the role of Luthor, who cracked the San Andreas Fault in an effort to sink California and create miles of priceless beachfront property.

Superman Returns gives the role to Kevin Spacey, who played the cunning Roger "Verbal" Kint in Bryan Singer's first major feature, *The Usual Suspects.* "Having worked with him in the past, and knowing his range in areas of both humor and darkness, he just seemed absolutely ideal," says Singer. "In this picture there will be humor, but Spacey also has that sinister nature that very few people can do as well as he can." Although the California scheme may not have worked the last time around, in *Superman Returns* Luthor's interest in real estate crops up again with his New Krypton plan.

Lex isn't behind bars when *Superman Returns* begins. Scheming to better his station, Lex has designs on the Vanderworth shipping fortune, and the widow Vanderworth is all that stands between him and a billion-dollar inheritance. For the rest of the film, Lex will be associated with icons of obscene affluence.

The Vanderworth mansion is a magnificent waterfront structure. Its decor, on the other hand, might charitably be called "style impaired." Guy Dyas and his production crew, painting in broad strokes, have created an aesthetic that would suit well-heeled bluebloods wearing monocles and sneers.

"The Vanderworths are extremely wealthy," says Dyas, referring to the gilded adornments that stand everywhere on the mansion grounds. "It's very eclectic. It's a collection of Victorian, baroque, and deco things that the Vanderworths acquired over the years. They're people of immense wealth and somewhat limited taste."

Just outside Dyas's office, two tiny pieces of furniture rest atop a bookshelf. Conspicuous among the sketches and storyboards, these meticulously detailed items, a four-poster bed and a fireplace, look like misplaced parts from a million-dollar dollhouse. These are conceptual models, built for internal use to sell the director on the full-size versions.

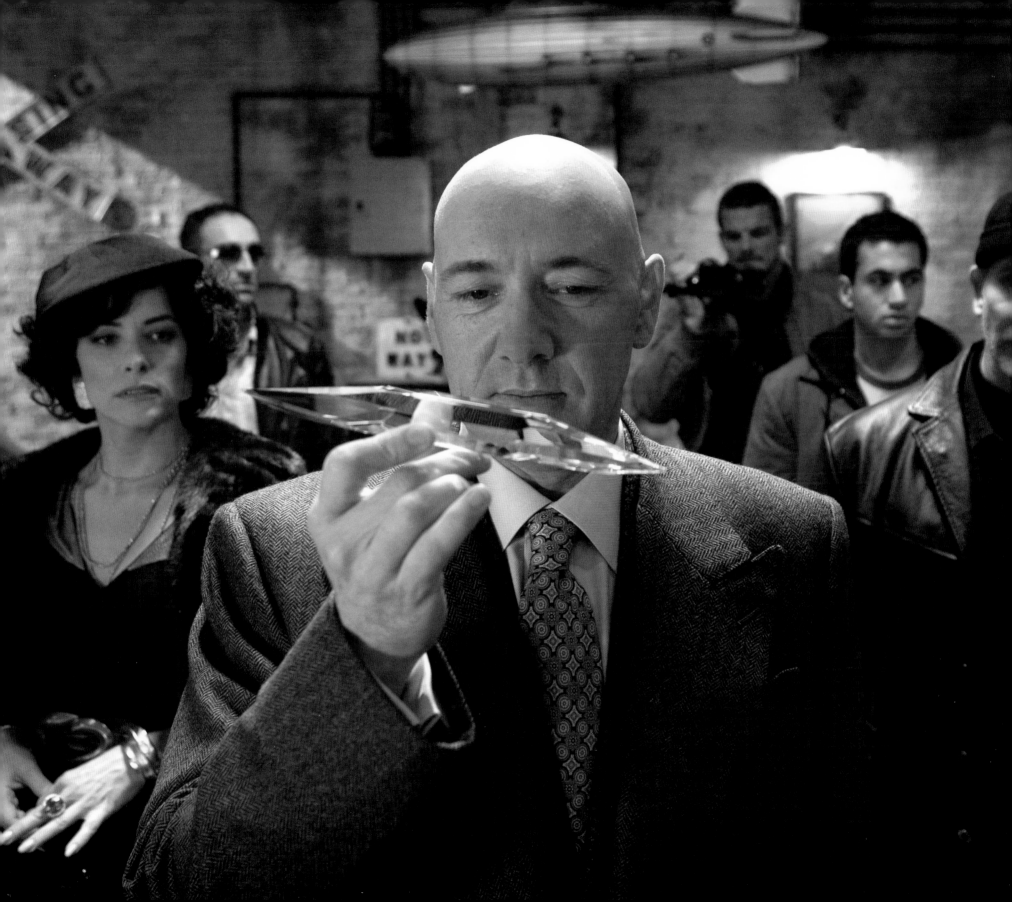

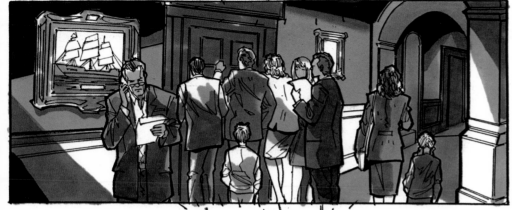

KNOCK KNOCK!!

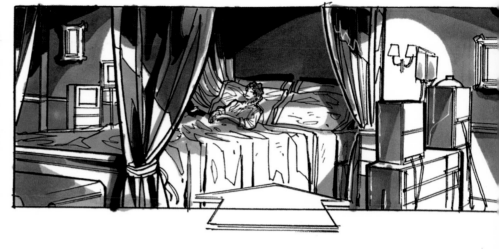

KNOCK KNOCK!!

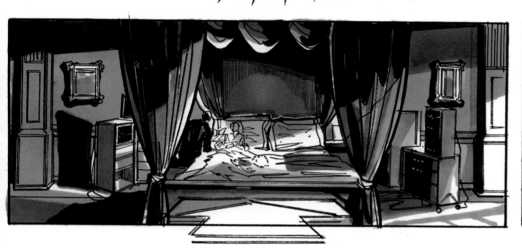

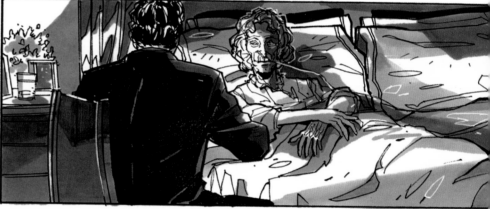

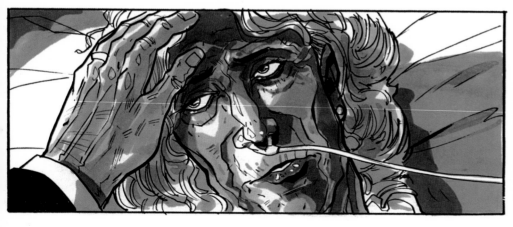

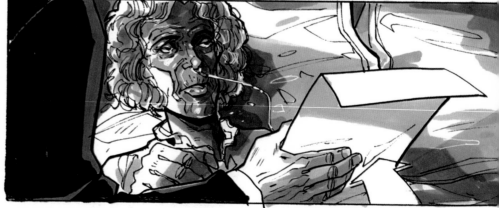

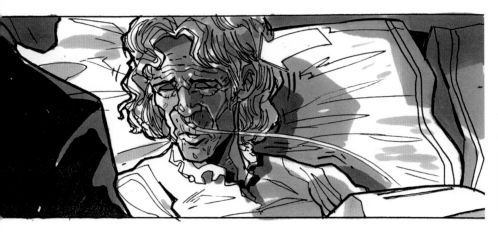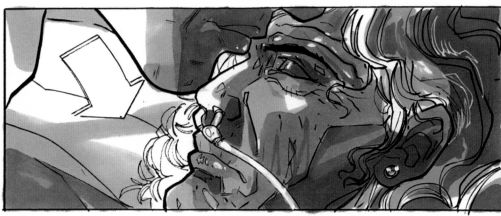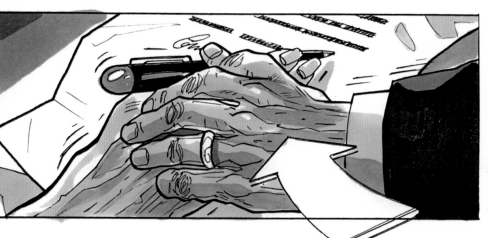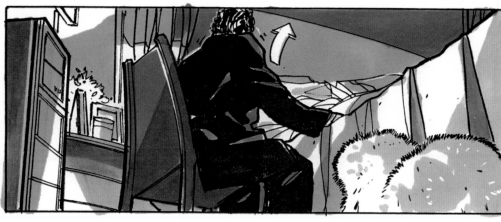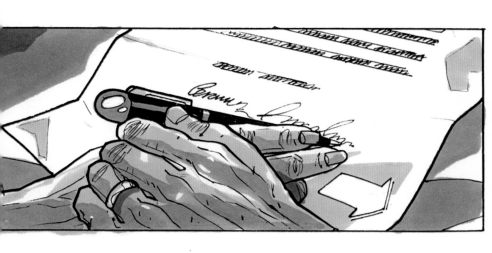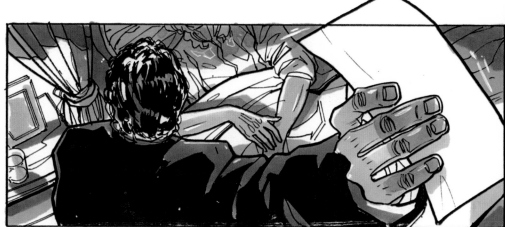

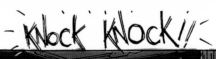
KNOCK KNOCK!!

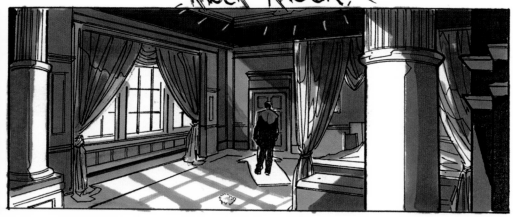

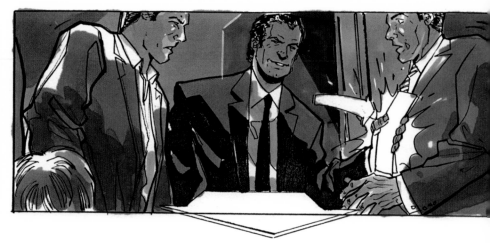

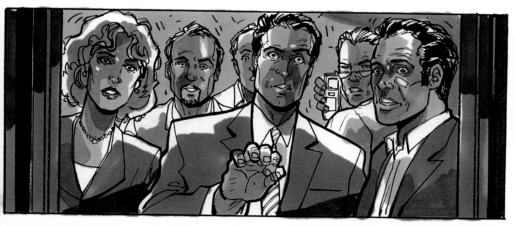

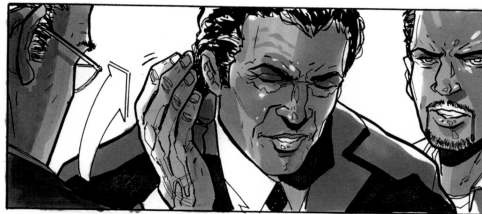

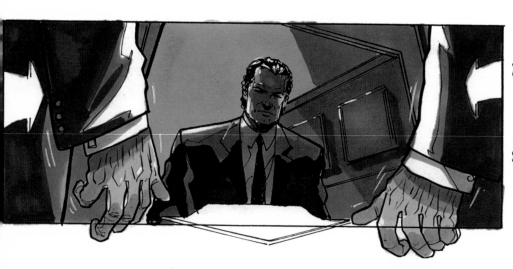

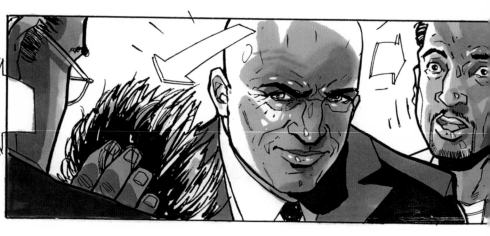

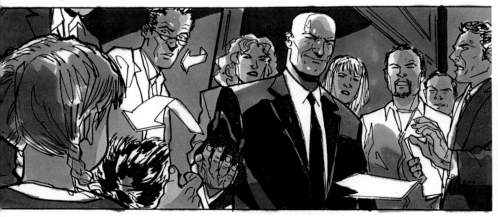

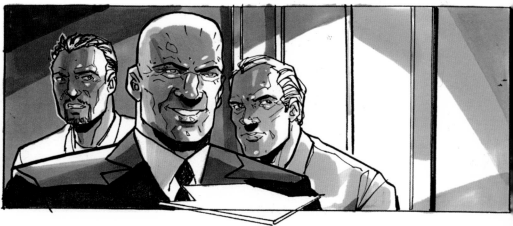

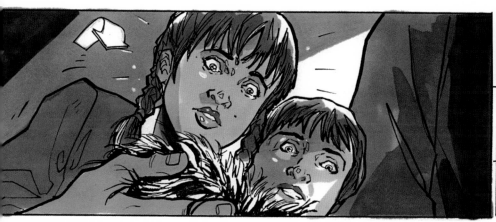

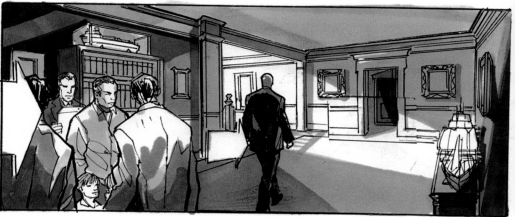

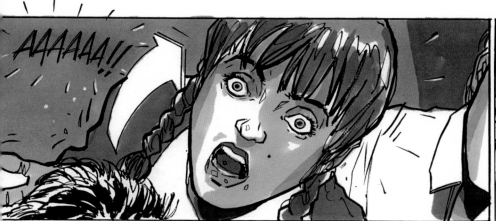

AAAAAA!!

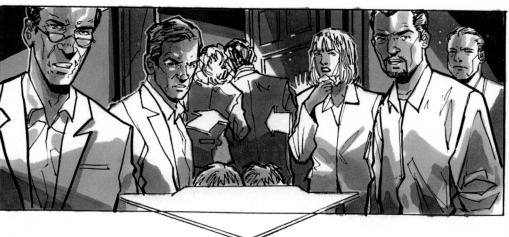

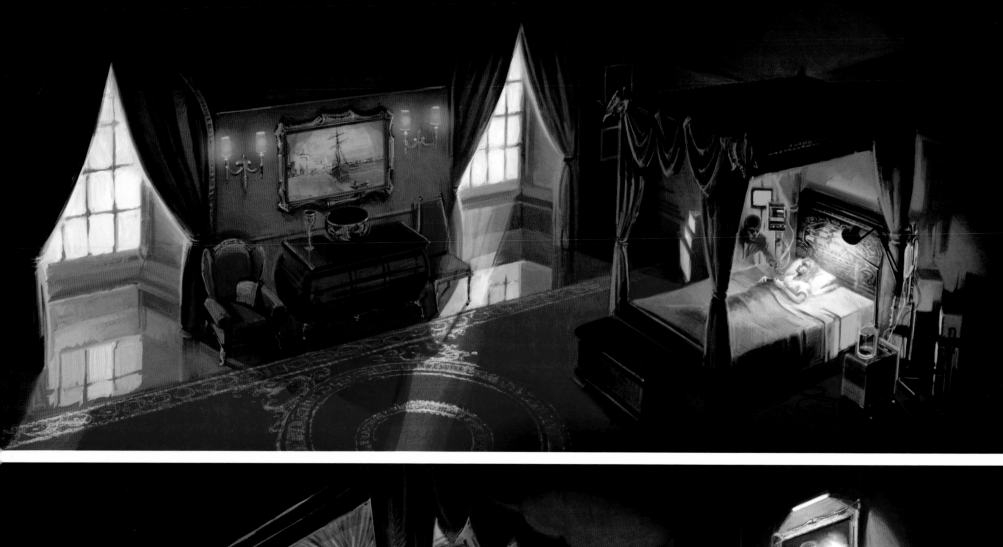
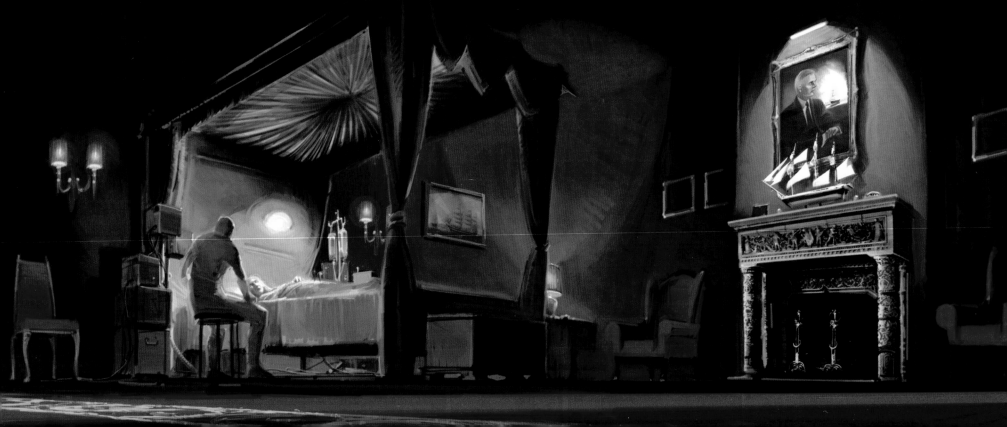

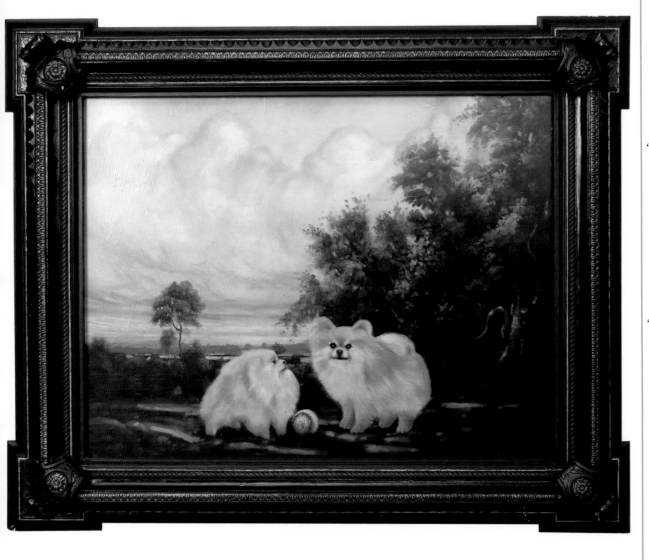

Dyas pulls one of his art binders from the bookshelf and opens it. A fluffy pooch gazes back from the page, its black eyes framed by a puffball of white. "We've made a lot of the artwork around the Vanderworth property these dogs, in different classical poses," says Dyas, explaining that Mrs. Vanderworth's syrupy sentimentality for her canines led her to commission a run of tacky oil portraits. "We took Constable-type paintings [after nineteenth-century British artist John Constable] and put these dogs in them."

The most important room in the Vanderworth mansion is the basement. Dyas points out a model made from cardboard and paper that could fit inside a shoebox. It's a rough miniature layout of the basement set, which in *Superman Returns* will become the site for an impromptu demonstration of Kryptonian technology. "We build these models to make sure we're happy with the design," says Dyas. "It's a great way to quantify and show a construction crew. A lot is involved in putting a set together."

The actual basement set looks like the fever dream of the world's most obsessed model-railroad enthusiast. Railroad tracks run everywhere in the room, traversing miniature landscapes that simulate the Swiss Alps, the American West, the Black Forest of Germany, and even downtown Metropolis.

OPPOSITE PAGE, TOP AND BOTTOM *Lex holds vigil at Gertrude Vanderworth's bedside. The fireplace and Gertrude's bed were also constructed as miniature models. Rick Buoen, digital, January 2005.*

LEFT *Mrs. Vanderworth's beloved dogs are captured in oil paintings seen throughout the Vanderworth Mansion. Steve Sallybanks, oil paint, May 2005.*

PAGE 127 *Kitty Kowalski looks on as Lex Luthor gloats over his latest acquisition. Lex's quartet of thugs are visible in the background. David James, August 2005.*

PAGES 128-131 *In this storyboard, titled "Lex Gets Funded," Lex Luthor schemes his way into billions. Colin Grant; pencil, pen, and marker; January 2005.*

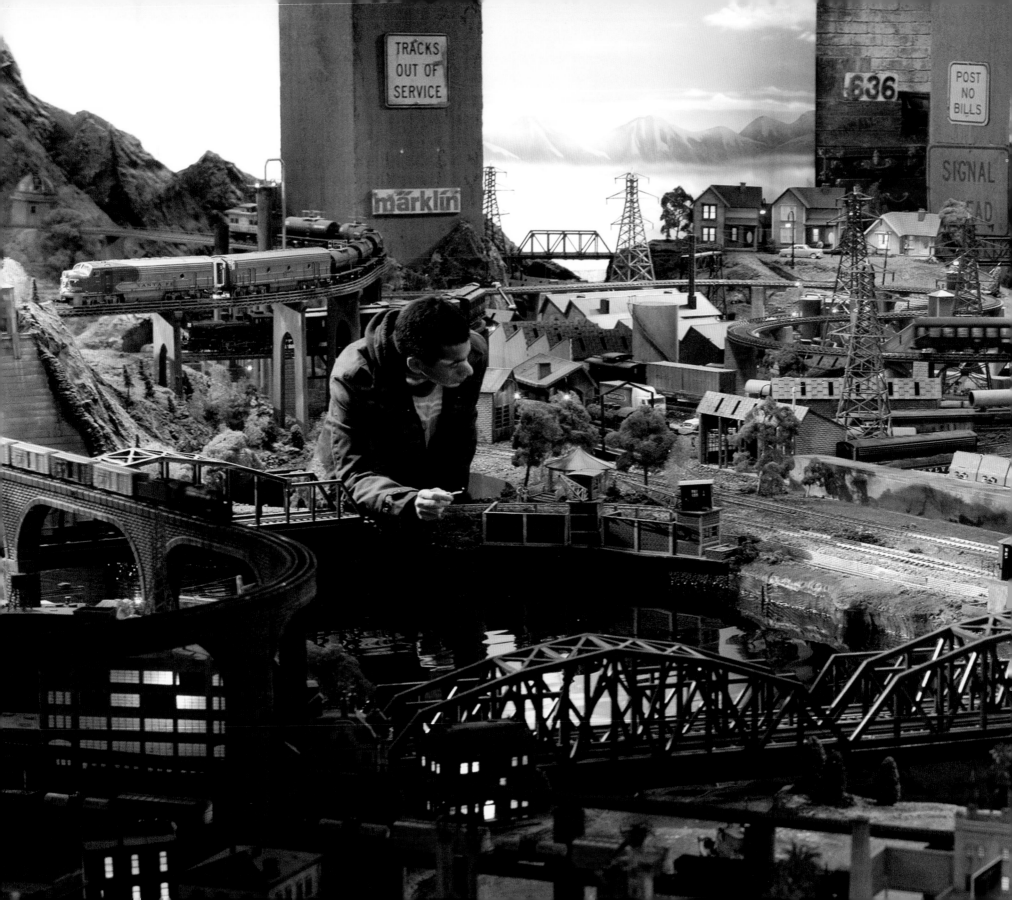

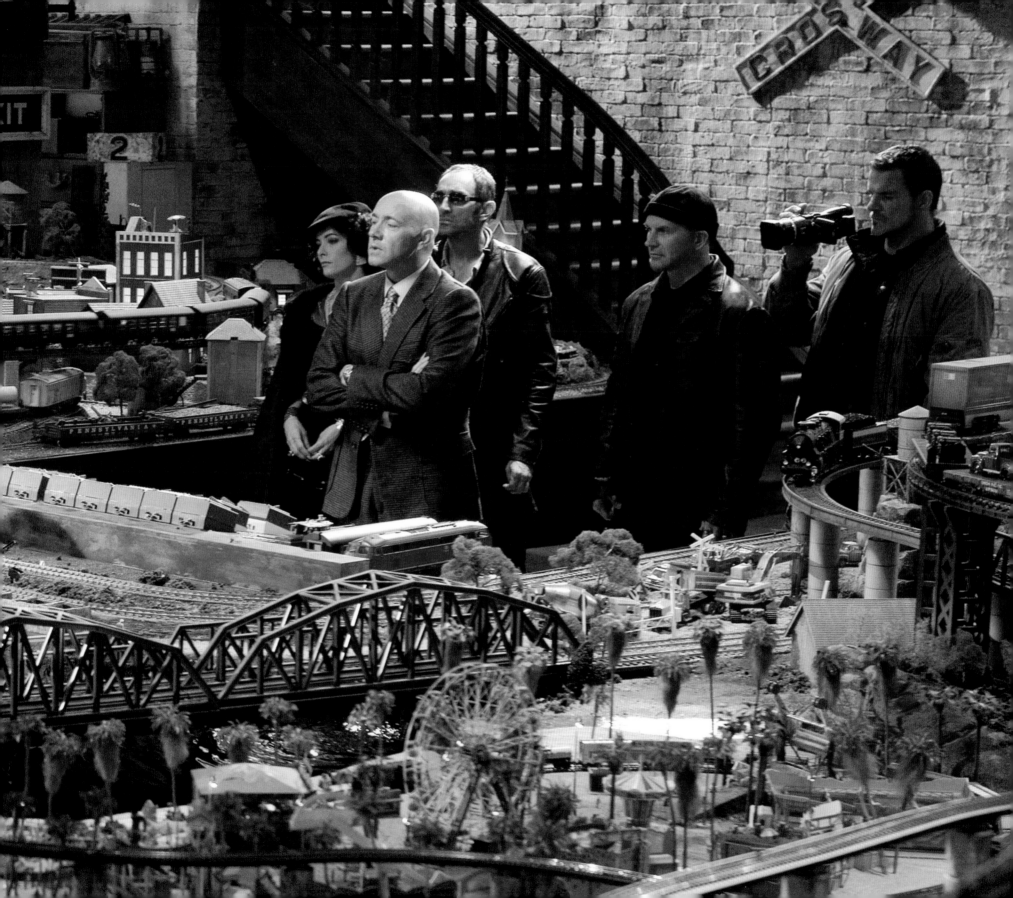

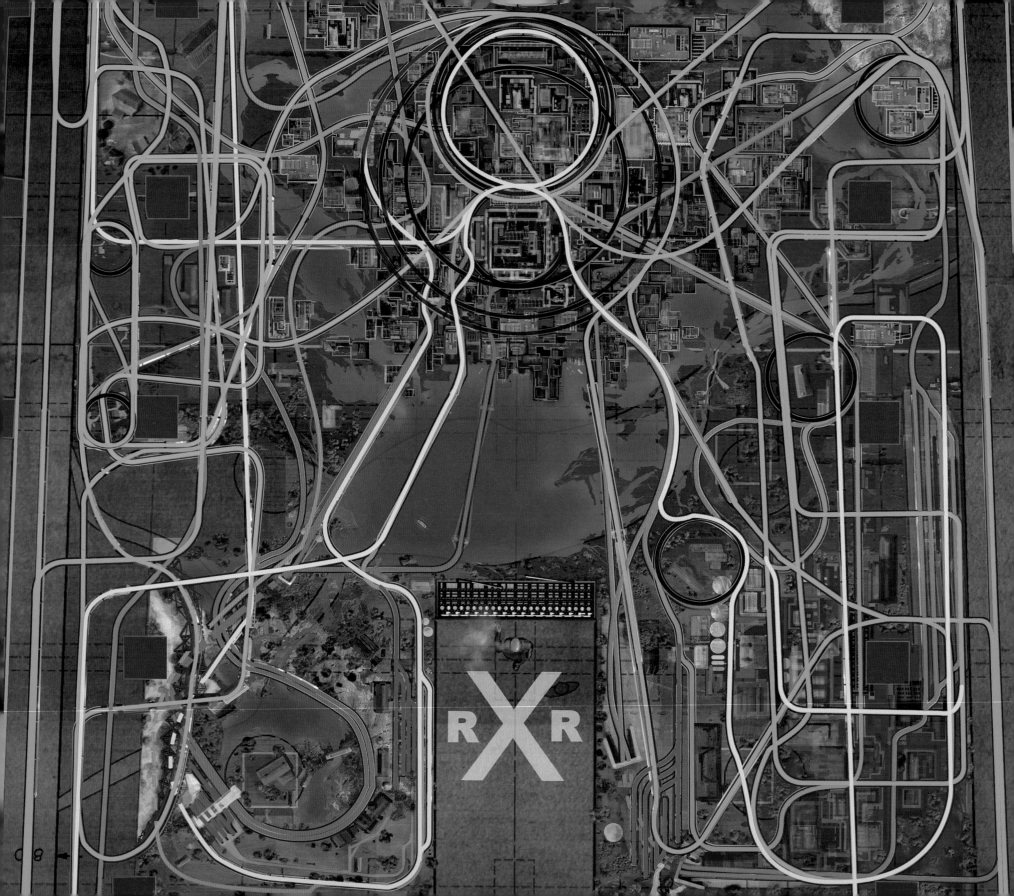

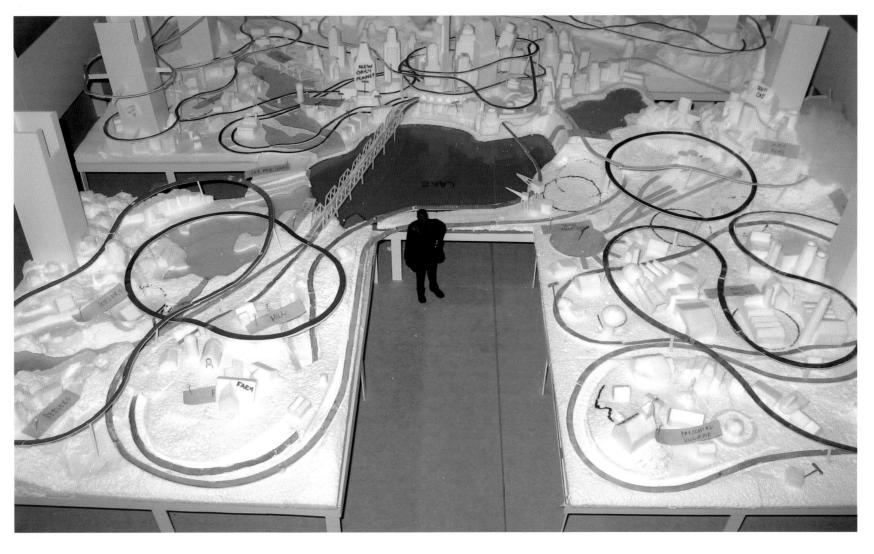

ABOVE *Simplified model of the train set, which served as a guide for eventual set construction. Shari Finn, Lewis Morley, and Brad Burnet; card, paper, and styrofoam; May 2005.*

OPPOSITE PAGE *Overhead layout of the train set. Color coding delineates the distinct track loops. Jeff Julian, digital, May 2005.*

PAGES 134–135 *Lex and his crew visit the Vanderworth basement. David James, August 2005.*

"So imagine that the late husband had built this," shouts Dyas over the noise of the workers who are sawing support boards, laying fresh track, and setting tiny plastic trees. Overhead, a rotating bar awaits a 1:100-scale zeppelin that will soon hang from its span. "He was a very eccentric hobbyist. Hence the set dressing, which is a little bit odd and weird." In an effort to cram as much into the basement as possible, the crew has employed an old-school visual effects trick. Large-gauge model trains are prominent at the front of the set, smaller-gauge trains seen only in the back. The crew has produced what is surely among the finest model train sets ever built, and it is one of the heartbreaks of moviemaking that filming for the crystal-growing scene will make it necessary to destroy this set in only a few weeks.

Although most of the Vanderworth mansion is shot on location at the Rivendell School outside of Sydney, the crew is assembling the set dressings at the studio. Outside a soundstage, crew members paint Greek-inspired statues with a coating of white to simulate marble. "These are over-the-top," says Dyas apologetically. "In a comic book world, rich people would have these."

RIGHT *Dozens of small details were tucked away in the landscape of the train set, including a miniature church. Katrina Adams, September 2005.*

OPPOSITE PAGE *Kitty Kowalski admires the church's tiny wedding party. David James, August 2005.*

PAGES 140–141 *Lex Luthor surveys the elaborate model railroad set left behind by the late Mister Vanderworth in his mansion's basement. Jeff Julian, digital, June 2005.*

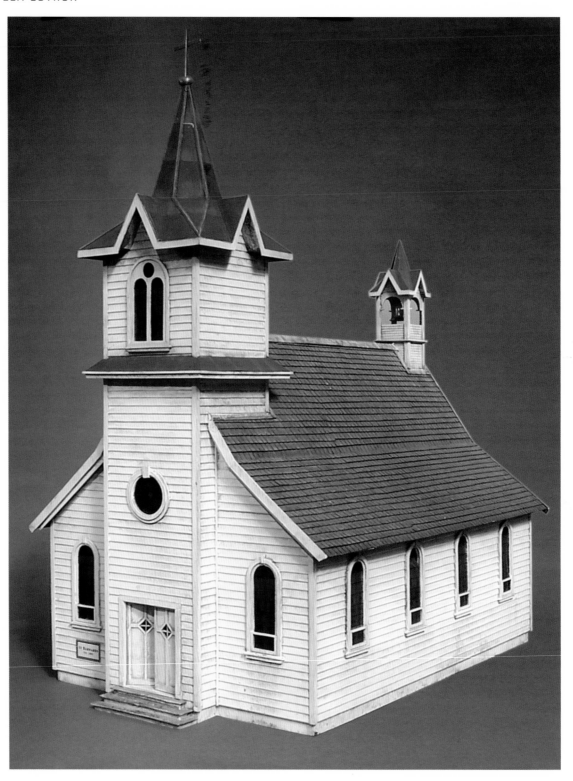

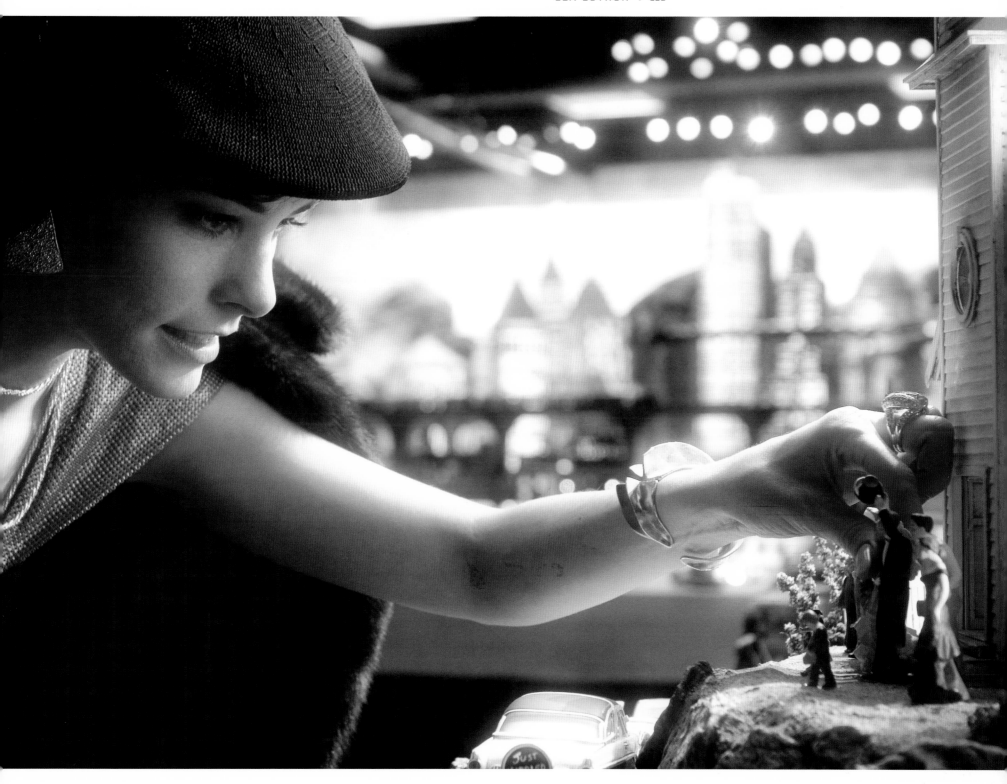

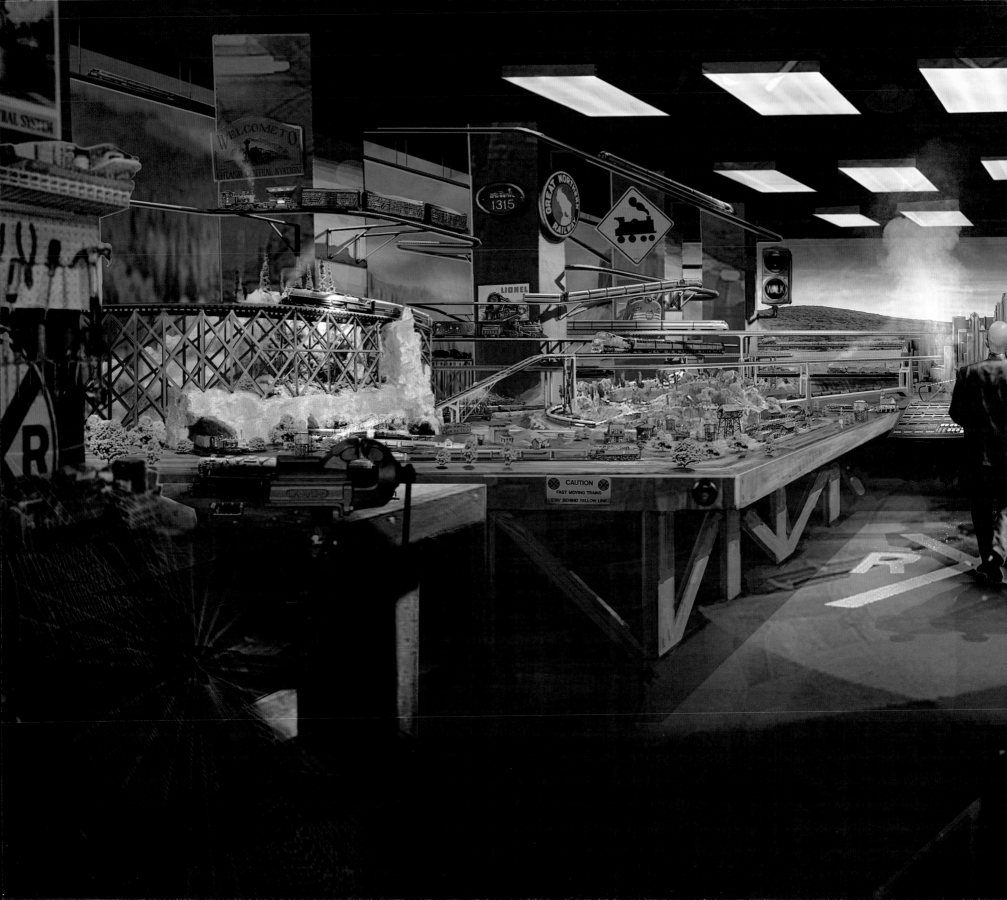

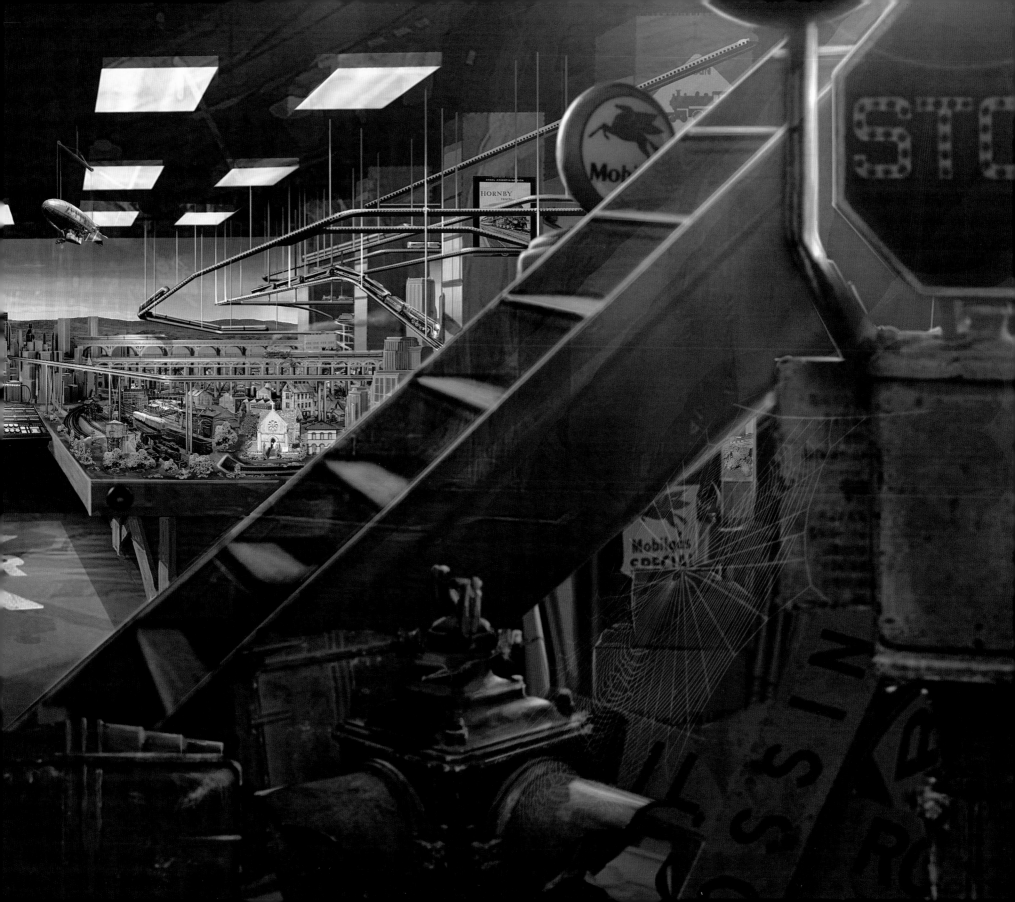

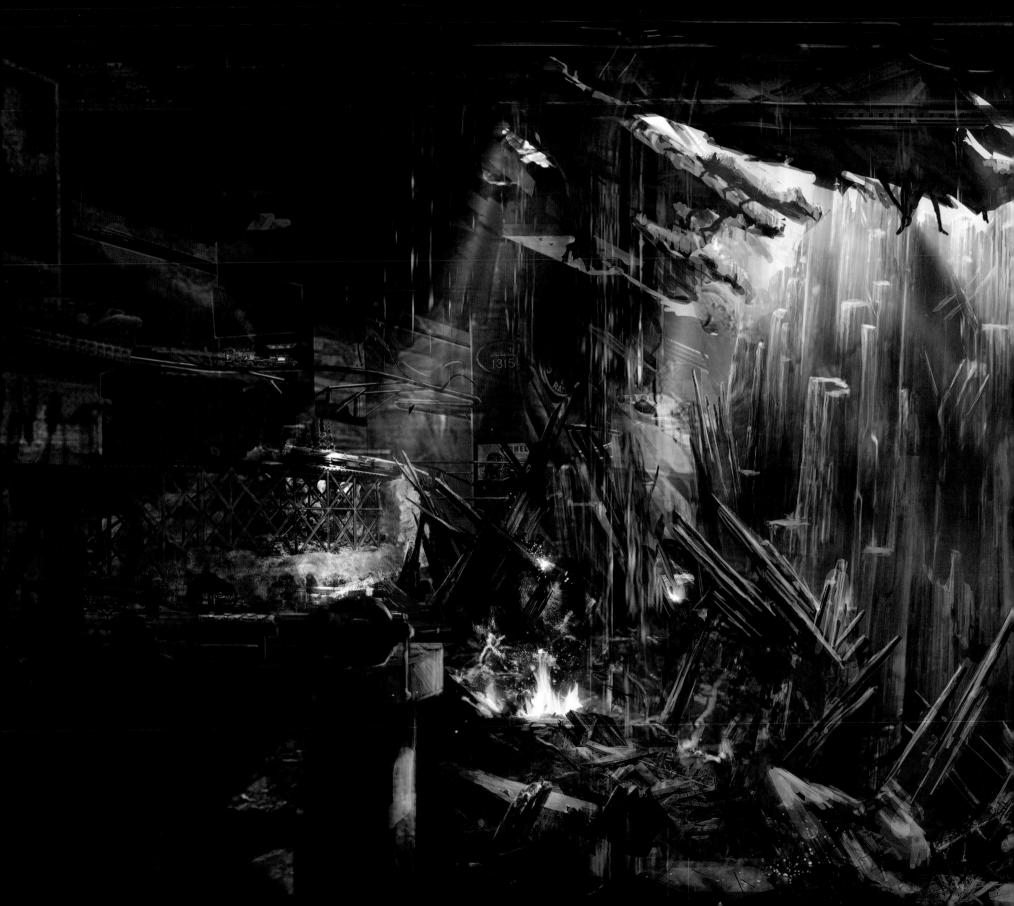

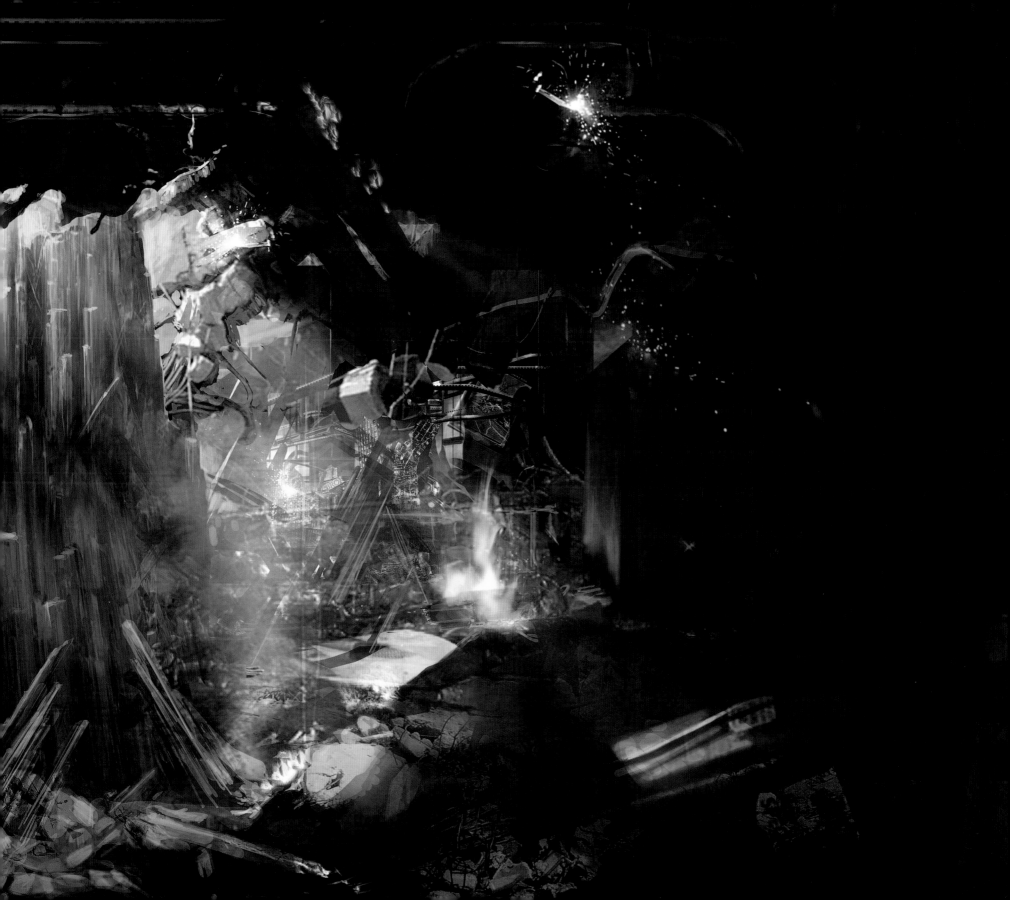

The most important Vanderworth asset exploited by Lex is the yacht *Gertrude,* named after Mrs. Vanderworth herself (and, in the real world, screenwriter Dan Harris's grandmother). The ship is breathtaking, boasting polished wood and brass accents in a style favored by boat club millionaires. Dyas admits that the *Gertrude* is in a different class than the garish excess that characterizes the mansion. "Yachts generally look beautiful," he shrugs. "No matter how hard the Vanderworths could try to make this look bad, it's going to look nice. They would've had someone actually design it *for* them."

Many art pieces were designed for installation aboard the *Gertrude,* including a large amber frieze depicting mermaids that appears to glow as if made from hand-cut glass. As is typical for a film of this magnitude, the art department did a great deal of work on the yacht that ultimately went unused. "There were a lot of rooms we'll never see," says Dyas, noting the *Gertrude*'s deck plans and detailed illustrations of the utility room and engine room. "They were created and shown to Bryan, and he either rejected them or decided to change the storyline."

Once Lex is in possession of the *Gertrude,* he takes it on a trip very, very far north. Dyas, in fact, reveals that the yacht was originally conceived as an industrial icebreaker, the better to facilitate its journey into frozen waters. After making landfall somewhere inside the Arctic Circle, Lex and his hangers-on seek the site that holds the secrets of the universe.

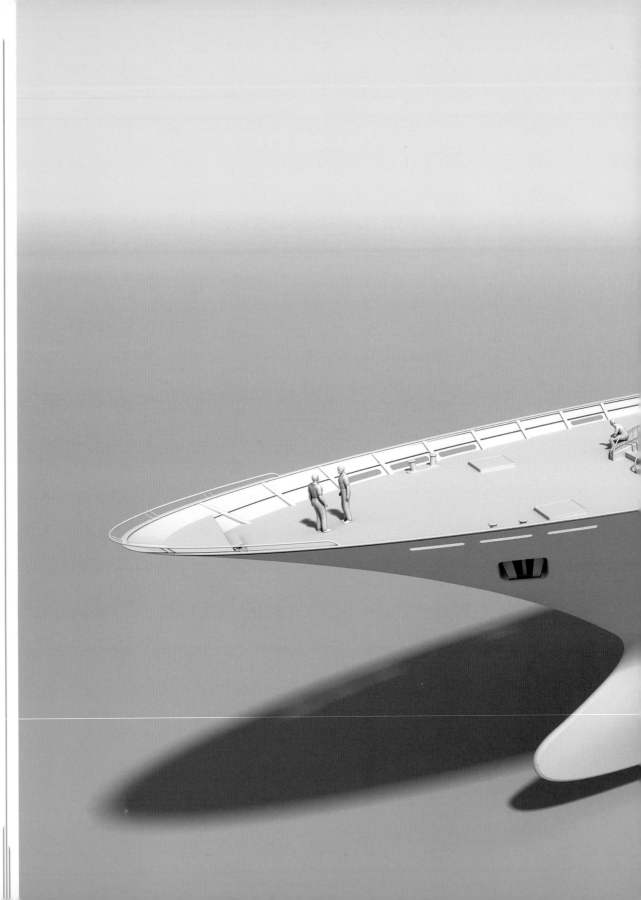

RIGHT *Rendering of the* Gertrude *yacht. Paul Ozzimo, digital, May 2005.*

PAGES 142-143 *Little remains of the model railroad set after Lex's impromptu experiment with a Kryptonian crystal shard. Jeff Julian, digital, June 2005.*

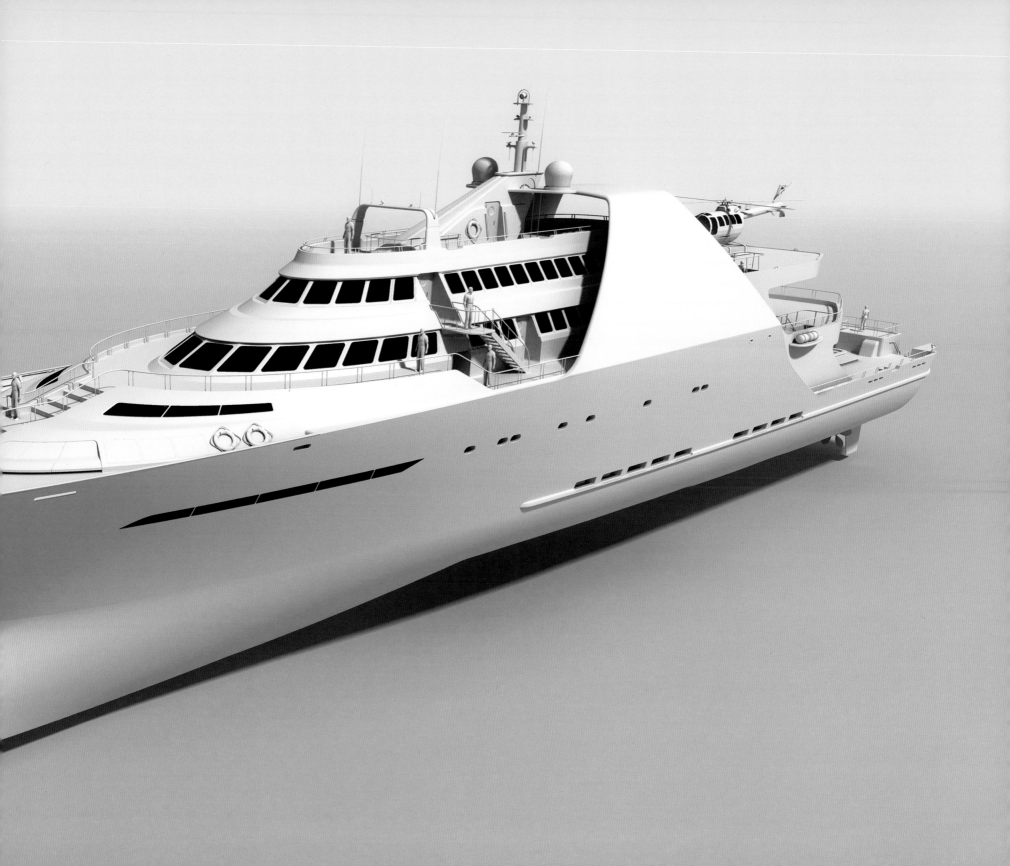

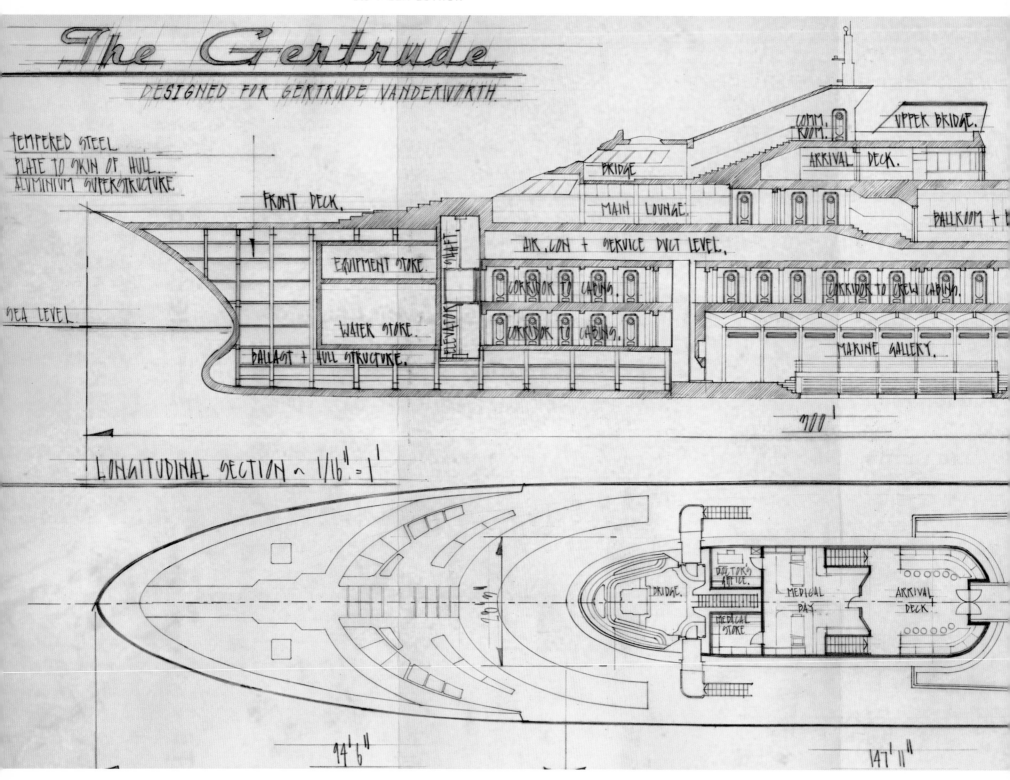

The Gertrude

DESIGNED FOR GERTRUDE VANDERWORTH.

TEMPERED STEEL
PLATE TO SKIN OF HULL.
ALUMINIUM SUPERSTRUCTURE

FRONT DECK.

COMM. ROOM.

UPPER BRIDGE.

BRIDGE

ARRIVAL DECK.

MAIN LOUNGE.

BALLROOM +

AIR CON + SERVICE DUCT LEVEL.

EQUIPMENT STORE.

ELEVATOR SHAFT.

CORRIDOR TO CABINS.

CORRIDOR TO CREW CABINS.

CORRIDOR TO CABINS.

SEA LEVEL

WATER STORE.

MARINE GALLERY.

BALLAST + HULL STRUCTURE.

LONGITUDINAL SECTION ~ 1/16" = 1'

DOCTOR'S OFFICE.

BRIDGE.

MEDICAL BAY

ARRIVAL DECK

MEDICAL STORE.

94'6"

147'11"

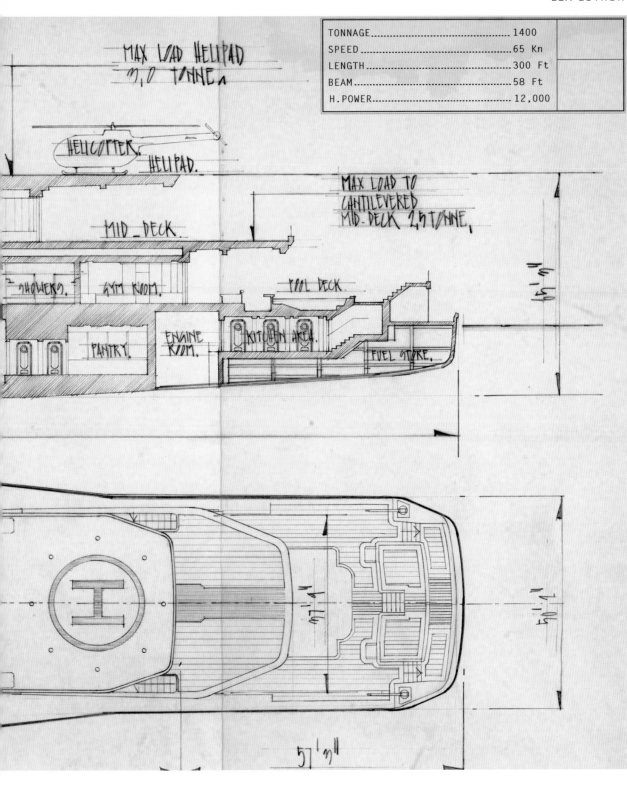

MAX LOAD HELIPAD
~,0 TONNE~

TONNAGE	1400
SPEED	65 Kn
LENGTH	300 Ft
BEAM	58 Ft
H. POWER	12,000

HELICOPTER. HELIPAD.

MAX LOAD TO
CANTILEVERED
MID-DECK 2.5 TONNE.

MID-DECK.

SHOWERS. GYM ROOM. POOL DECK.

PANTRY. ENGINE ROOM. KITCHEN AREA. FUEL STORE.

57' 3"

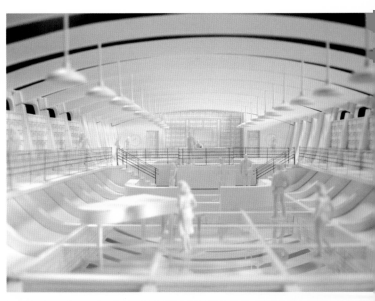

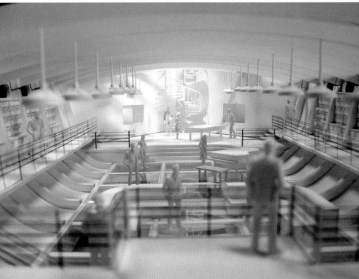

ABOVE *Models of the Gertrude's interior, showcasing the yacht's glass-bottom floor. Brett Philips and Scott Lukowski, card and paper, April 2005.*

LEFT *Blueprints of Lex Luthor's yacht, Gertrude. Amanda Clarke and Beth Garswood, pencil on trace paper, May 2005.*

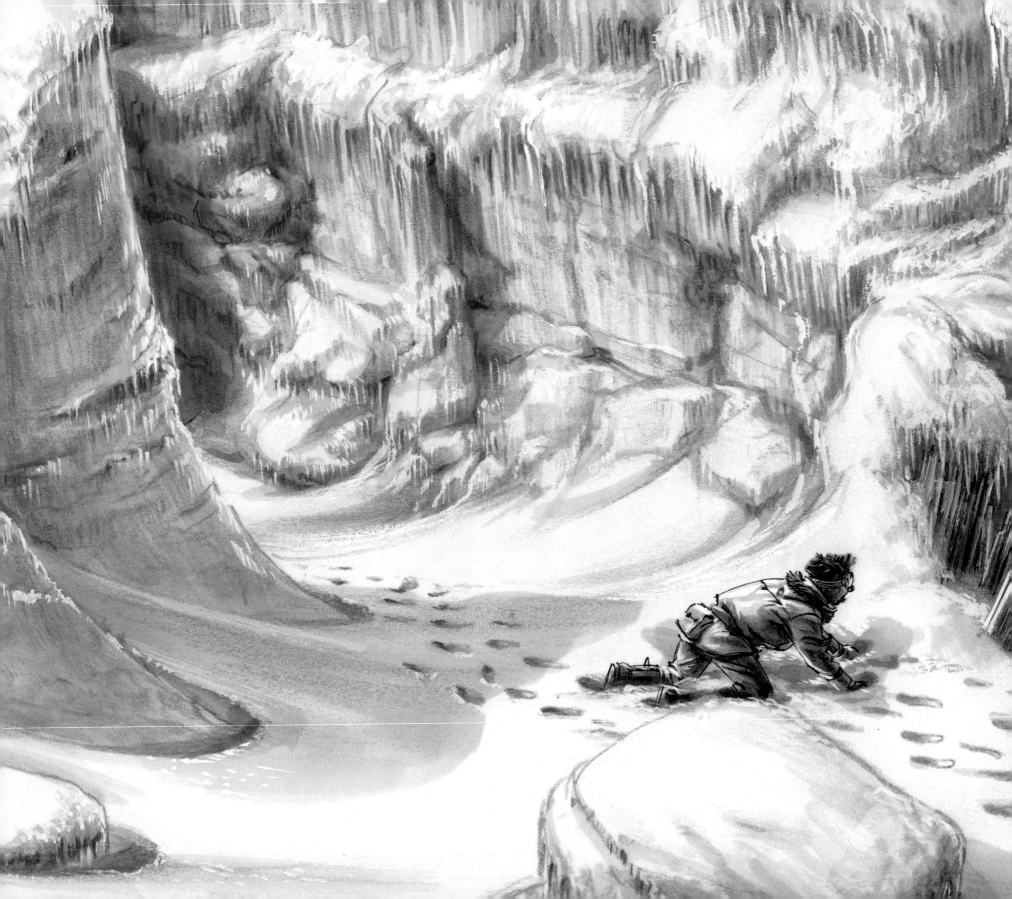

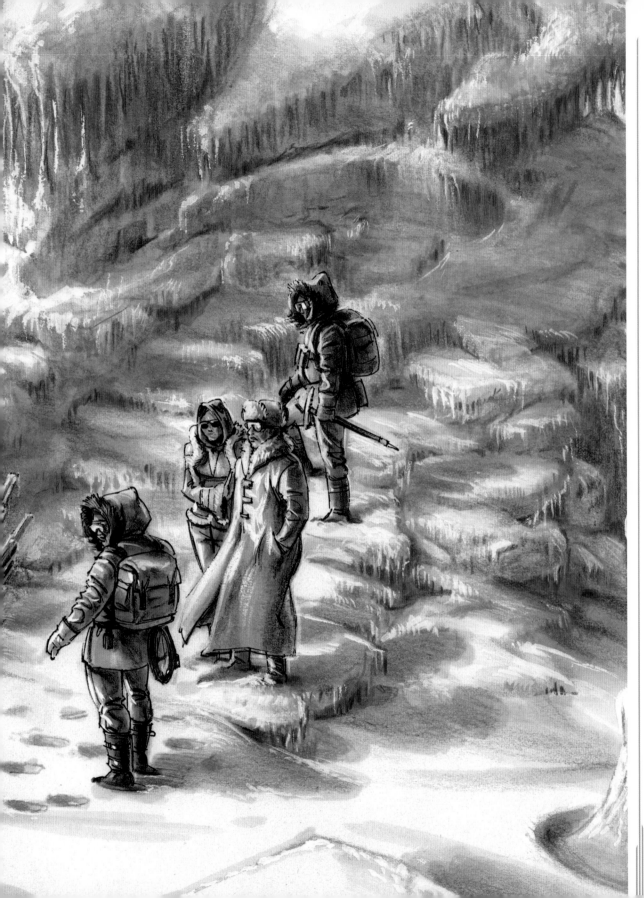

The approach to the Fortress of Solitude is a wonderland of glittering white snow and blue polar ice, fissures and crevasses in the hard bulk of the glacier beneath. The journeyers' path loops around in a tight curlicue, with various sections of the switchback representing different locations in the Arctic. Forced to fit a large set into a small plot, Dyas hit on the space-saving solution of designing a twisty path and filming it multiple times.

From inside the set, what looks like a subzero ice crevasse is revealed as a trench of expanding foam and white industrial insulation. Tiny flakes of shredded paper simulate fallen snow. The illusion holds power—despite the Sydney heat, it's *cold* in here. Dyas agrees, noting that crew members working on this stage often unaccountably ask for sweaters. "Bryan loves this set," says Dyas, nodding to the ersatz icicles that drape from the overhangs of crusted snow. "He calls it Santa's grotto."

In the film, Lex possesses other items not necessarily associated with the Vanderworth fortune. He owns a helicopter, and after his thugs steal a precious item from the Metropolis Museum of Natural History, he obtains a missile launcher. After reading this scene in the script, Dyas's crew sketched out ideas for an exotic, high-tech launcher, but Singer decided it would be more in character for Lex to steal a rocket launcher than to build his own.

LEFT *One of Lex's thugs has a difficult time keeping pace in this illustration of Lex's arctic approach. Philip Holliday; pencil, ink, and markers; May 2005.*

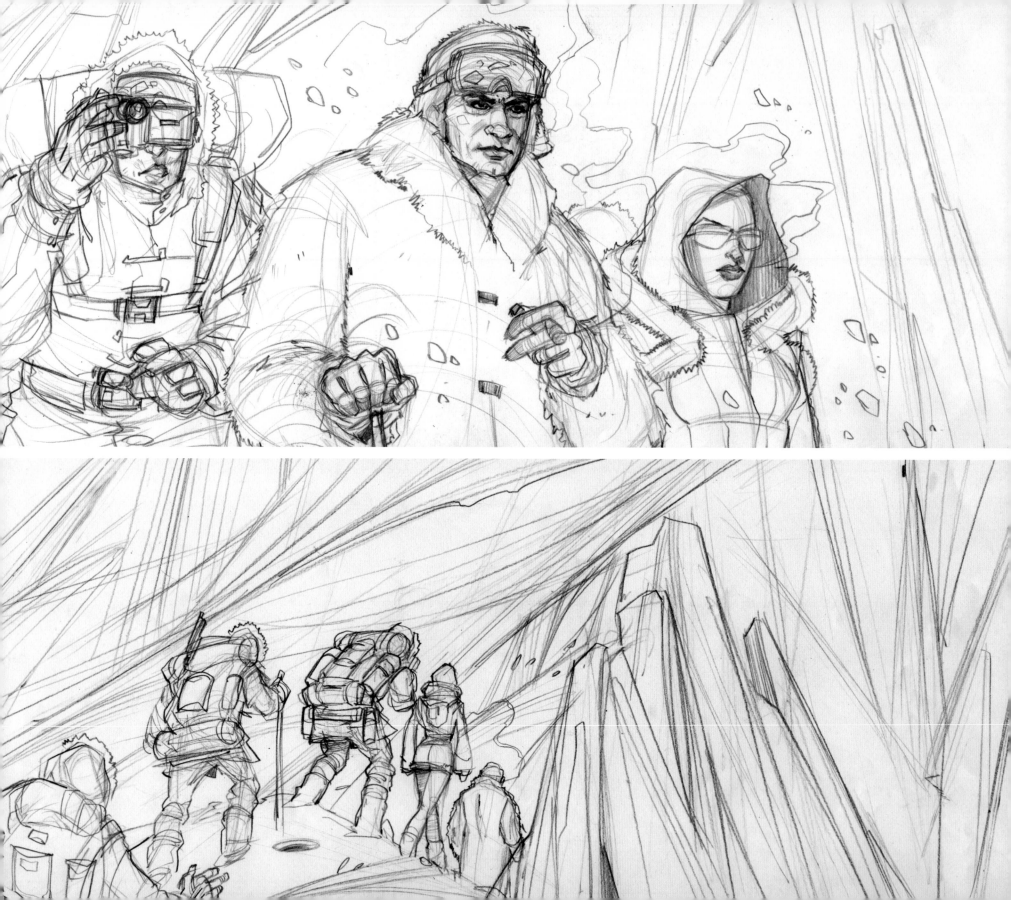

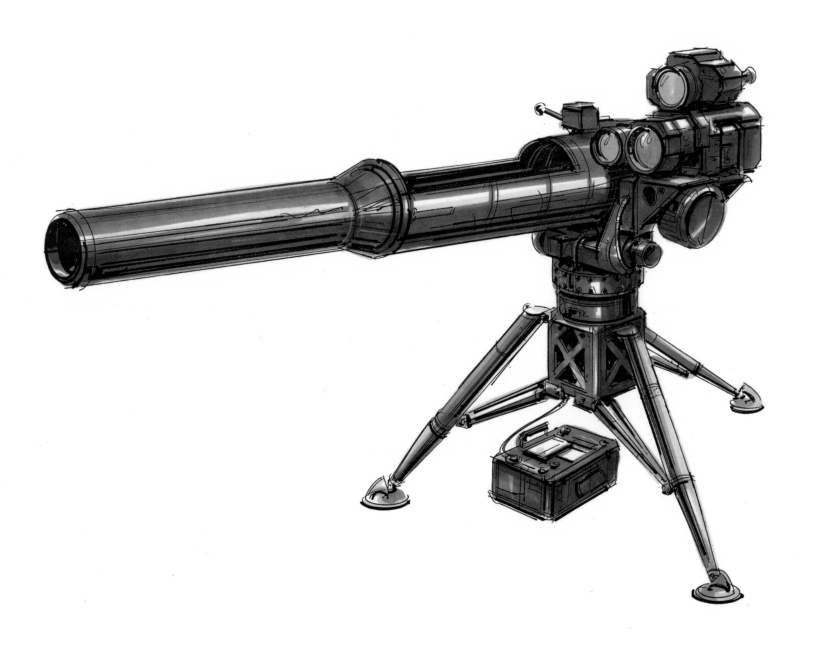

ABOVE *Military-style rocket launcher used to fire the crystal fragment that kick-starts New Krypton Island. Bryan Singer envisioned that Lex had stolen the launcher during a previous escapade. Ed Natividad, pencil and marker, June 2005.*

OPPOSITE PAGE, TOP AND BOTTOM *Lex, his henchmen, and Kitty Kowalski approach and descend into the Fortress of Solitude. Colin Grant, pencil, May 2005.*

A visit to the costume department reveals the sartorial styles favored by Lex Luthor and his followers. Of all the characters from the 1978 film, Lex was the one in the greatest need of an upgrade. "Bryan was certain that he didn't want Lex to be as jokey as he had been," says Louise Mingenbach, referring to Gene Hackman and his disco-era wardrobe, which went heavy on wide lapels and cravats. "He felt it had gotten a little loud."

Lex's costumes had to possess sufficient range to encompass both the opulence of the Vanderworth mansion and the biting cold of the Arctic. "It ended up being Savile Row suits and beautifully cut cashmere jackets with mink trim," the costume designer continues. "Lex also thinks of himself as an explorer, so we incorporated a bit of Jacques Cousteau." The urge for high fashion manages to find a way around restrictions. "Bryan said absolutely no to the big fur coat, but we're going to sneak in some fur collars."

But no matter what costumes Mingenbach and her crew dreamed up, they couldn't obscure Lex Luthor's most distinguishing feature. The original film played up his baldness as a source of insecurity, with Lex wearing different wigs as a salve for his wounded vanity. Lex has changed little by the time of *Superman Returns,* but this time the costume department chose subtle hairpieces for the film. From scene to scene, "you might not even notice that it's a different wig," Mingenbach allows.

Everything worn by the main characters in *Superman Returns* is made from scratch, including Clark's business suits and Lex's polar parka. This luxury extends to all characters who have as much screen time as Lex's dazzling partner in crime, Kitty Kowalski. Kitty's costumes include a variety of slinky dresses that aid in her schemes to entrap the Man of Steel.

Lex's goons, Brutus, Stanford, Riley, and Grant, mark a cutoff point in the costuming hierarchy. From their level down, all players wear a combination of created material and off-the-rack items purchased from clothing stores. Lex believes that in order to make his own light shine brightly, he needs to surround himself with dim bulbs.

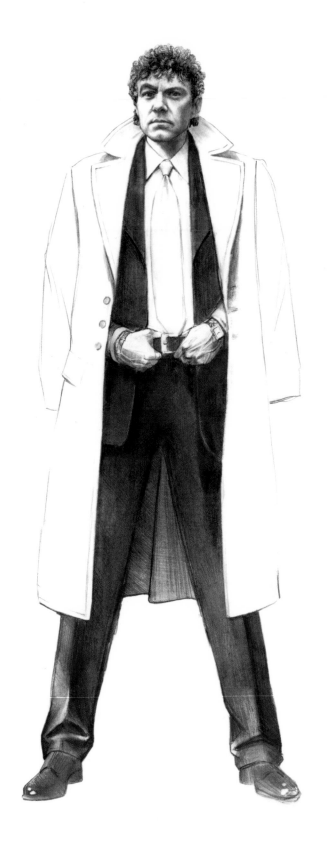

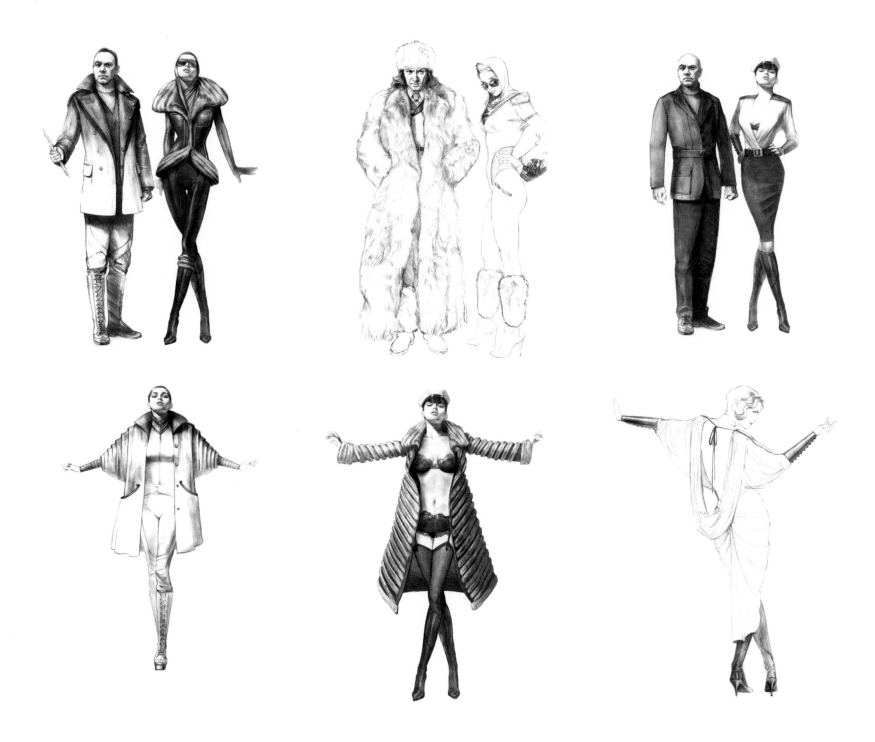

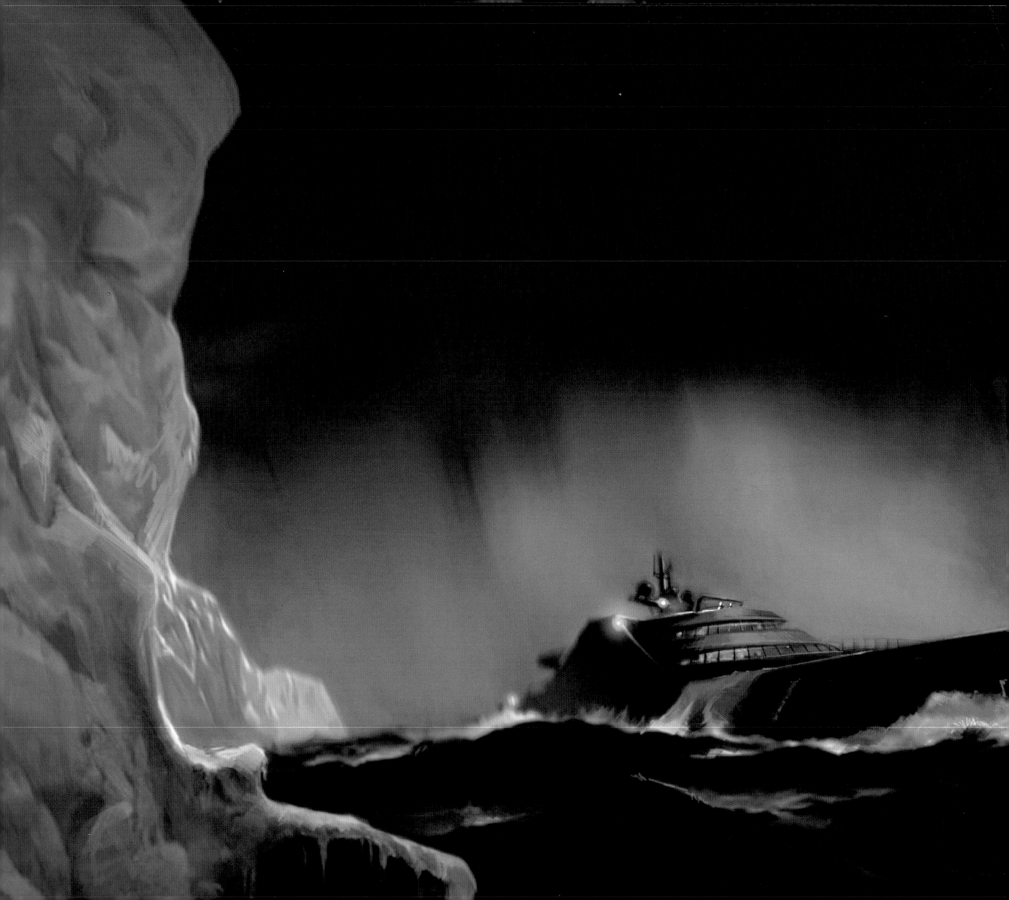

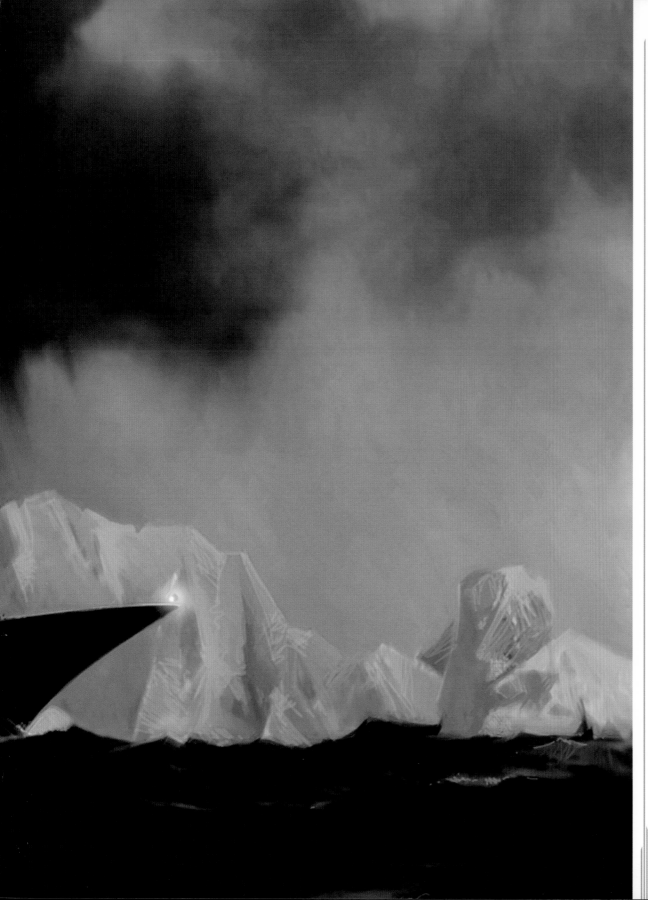

In storytelling and art, *Superman Returns* can be viewed as an exploration of the four selves of Superman: the costumed persona, the Kryptonian heir, the genuine Smallville Clark, and the "bumbling Clark" disguise worn in Metropolis to divert attention from his secret identity. Each contributes its own tenor to the film, with unique architectures and color schemes. Lex Luthor provides the fifth tone, set in opposition to everything the Man of Steel represents.

Looking back at the transformation from script to film, Dan Harris is struck by how well Guy Dyas and the crew captured his words as images. "Most of the time it's exactly what I was picturing, and when it's not, it's ten times better. In the end, the world of *Superman Returns* is visually an ideal place to be, where every texture on every wall speaks of decades of history."

The end of the film witnesses Superman finding his place in the world. So where does he go from here?

Says Bryan Singer, "There's a lot of possibilities out there."

LEFT *A dark, moody conceptual painting titled "Gertrude's Journey North." Rick Buoen, digital, March 2005.*

PAGE 152 *Curly toupee concept for Lex Luthor. Many hairpiece variations were considered, though the final selections proved to be subtler. E.J. Krizer, pencil and digital, April 2005.*

PAGE 153 *Lex bears what the costume department termed a "Jacques Cousteau influence" in these sketches. Parker Posey conceived of Kitty Kowalski as someone fascinated by vintage movie starlets, an inspiration carried over into this costume design. E.J. Krizer, pencil and digital, April 2005.*

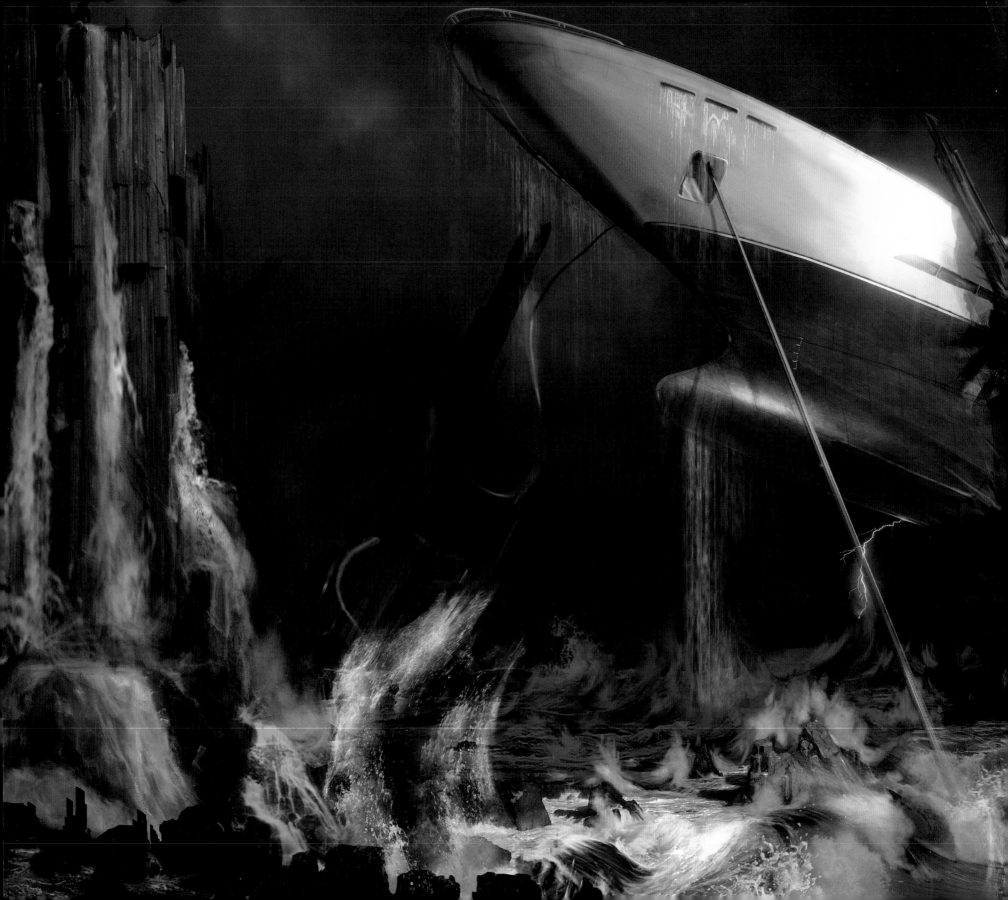

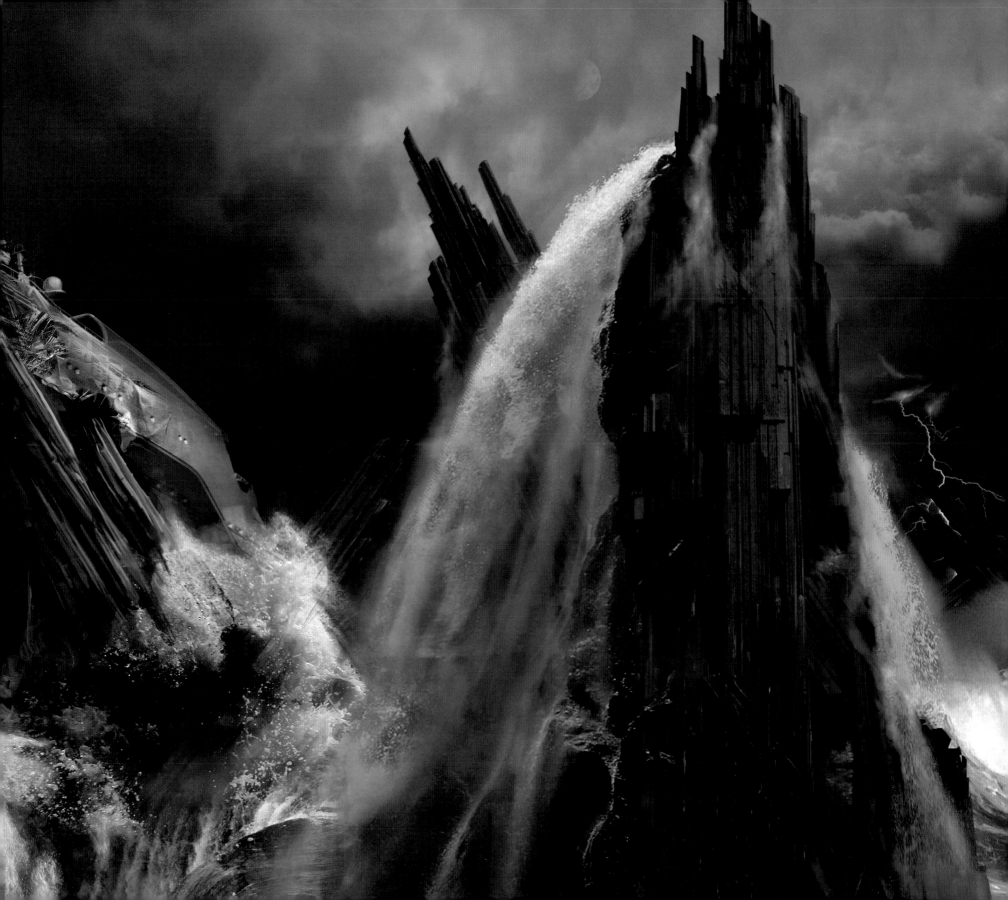

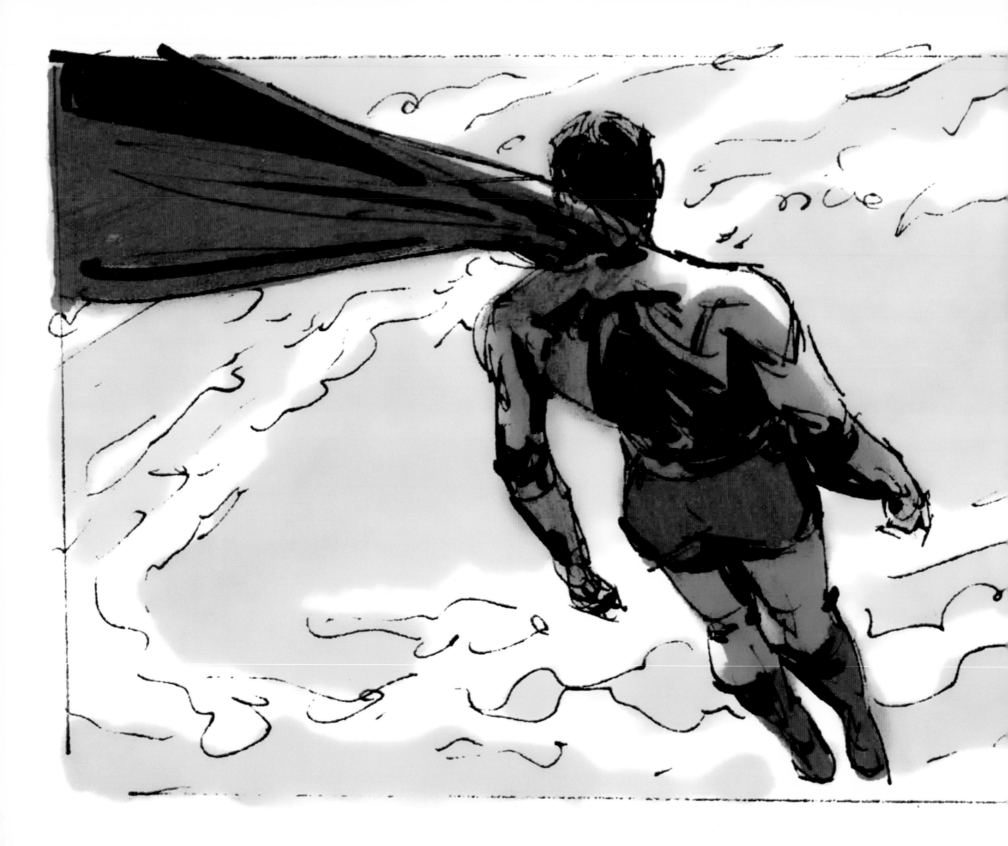

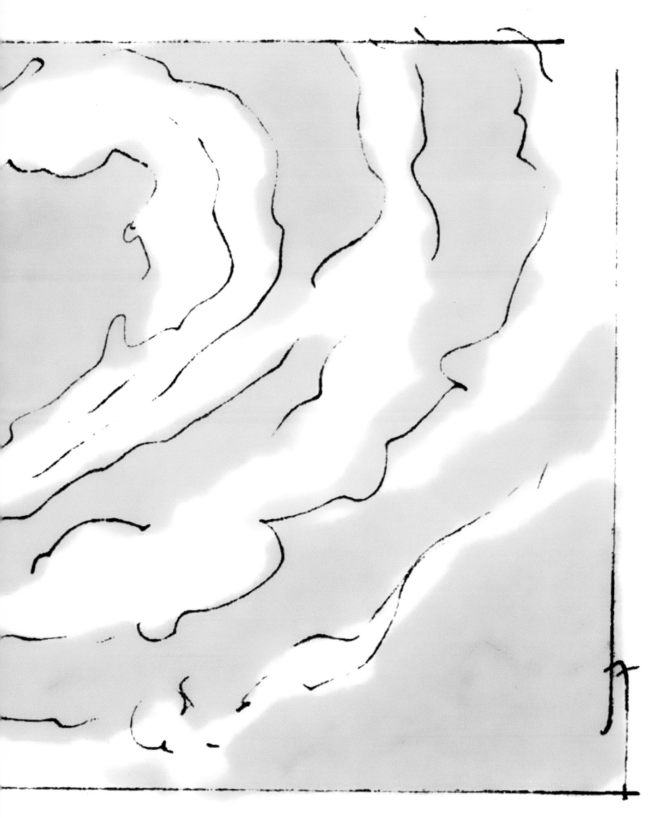

ACKNOWLEDGMENTS

The author would like to thank the following people for their invaluable help in putting this book together: Bryan Singer, Guy Dyas, Dominique Arcadio, Louise Mingenbach, Dan Bronson, Michael Dougherty, Dan Harris, David James, and Mike Essl; as well as Sandy Yi, Emma Rodgers, and Maureen Squillace at Warner Bros.; Steve Korté, Chris Cerasi, and Georg Brewer at DC Comics; and Sarah Malarkey and Matt Robinson at Chronicle Books.

LEFT *From his "listening post" high above the stratosphere, Superman keeps alert for trouble from any corner of the globe. Ed Natividad, pencil and marker, December 2004.*

PAGES 156–157 *The Gertrude's anchor chain strains to steady the ship as New Krypton Island erupts underneath. Jeff Julian and Paul Ozzimo, digital, July 2005.*

PAGE 160 *Director Bryan Singer makes his allegiances known. David James, 2005.*

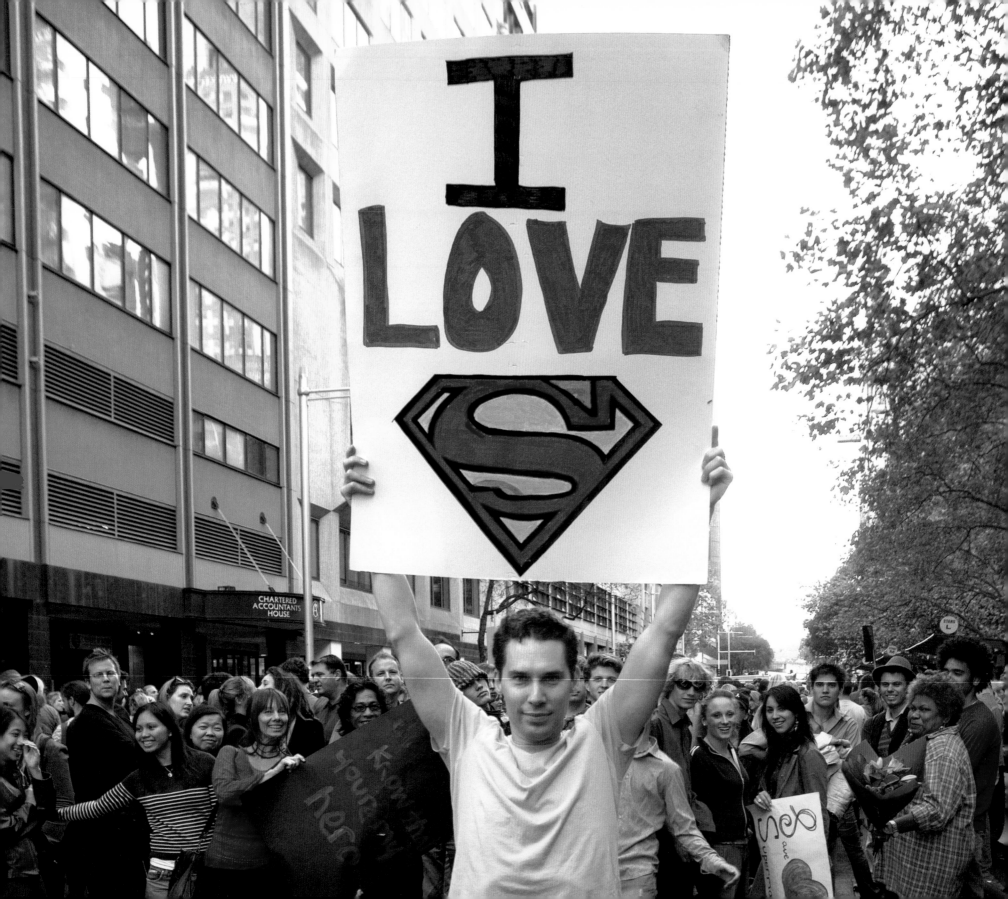